MW01629025

MANGA FEMALES CLIP ART

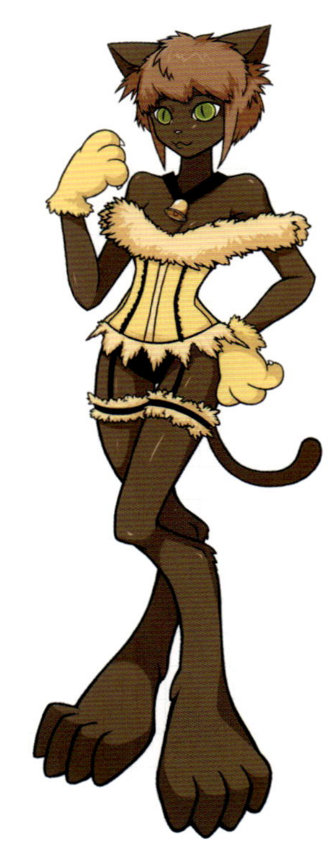

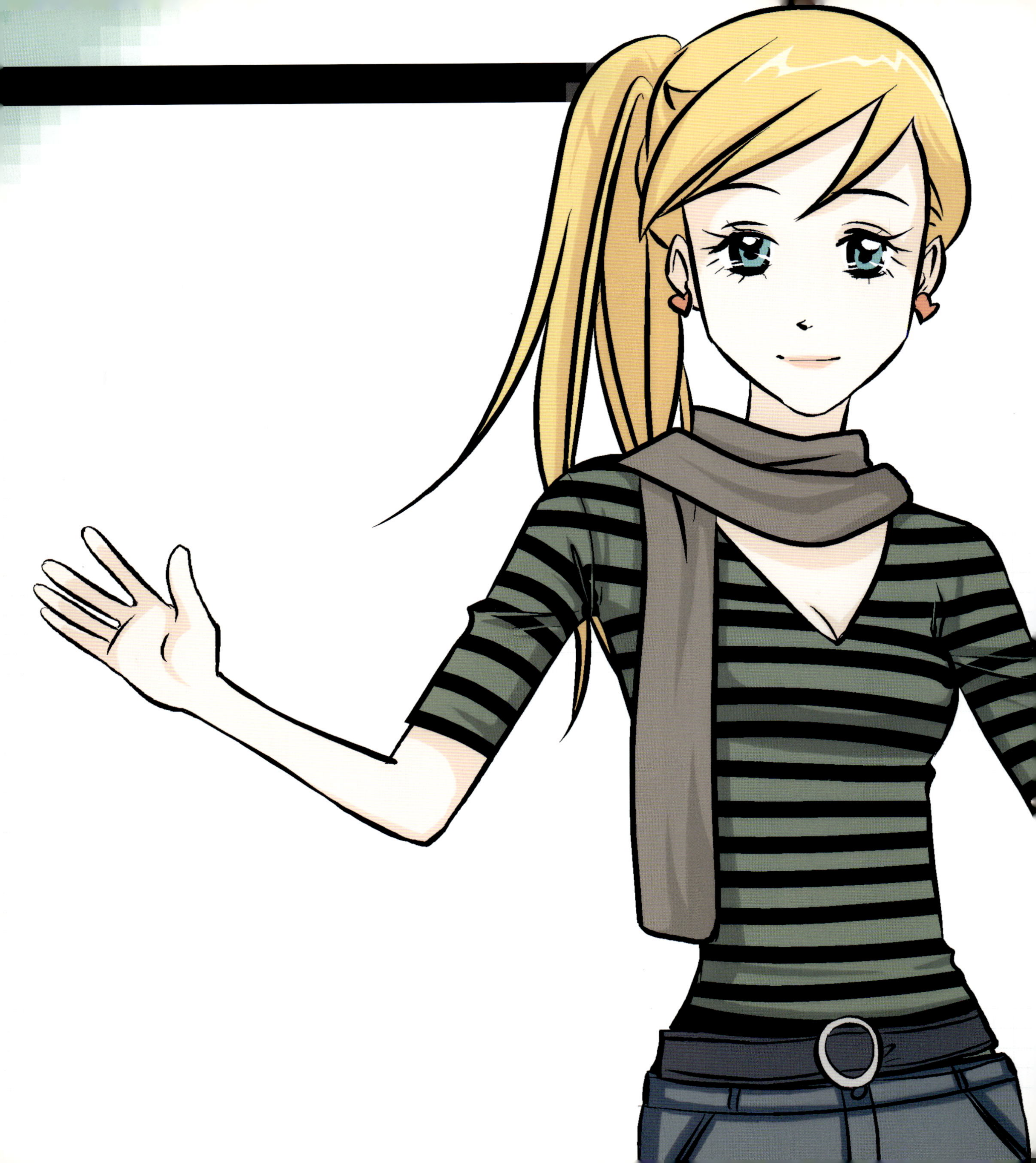

MANGA FEMALES CLIP ART

Everything you need to create your own professional-looking manga artwork

Yishan Studio

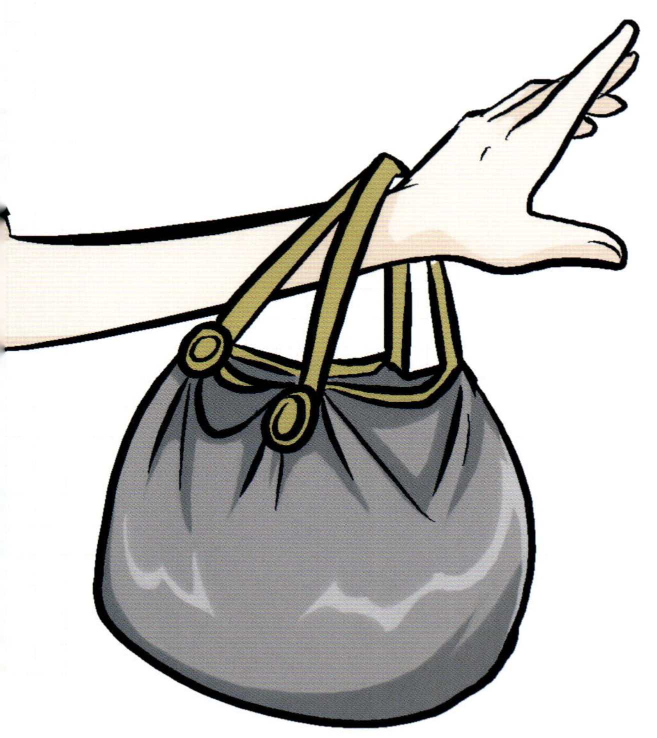

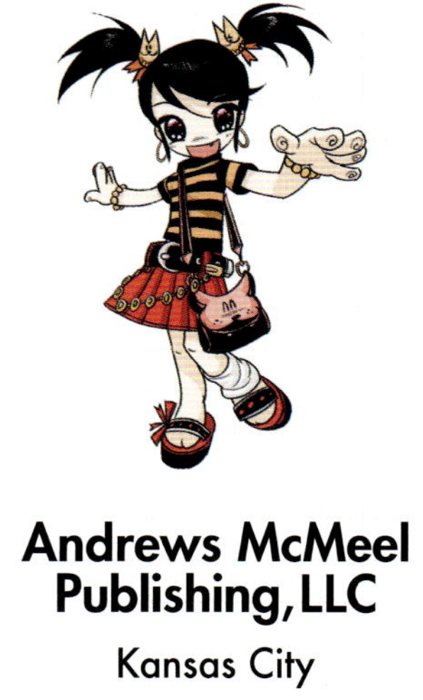

Andrews McMeel Publishing, LLC

Kansas City

CONTENTS

For information, write to:
Andrews McMeel Publishing, LLC,
an Andrews McMeel Universal company,
1130 Walnut Street,
Kansas City,
Missouri 64106

09 10 11 12 13 CTP 10 9 8 7 6 5 4 3 2 1

ISBN-13: 978-0-7407-7934-3
ISBN-10: 0-7407-7934-6
Library of Congress Control Number: 2008935739
www.andrewsmcmeel.com

This book was conceived, designed, and produced by
THE ILEX PRESS LIMITED
ILEX Editorial, Lewes:
Publisher: Alastair Campbell
Creative Director: Peter Bridgewater
Managing Editor: Nick Jones
Editor: Ellie Wilson
Art Director: Julie Weir
Designer: Chris and Jane Lanaway
Design Assistant: Emily Harbison

ILEX Research, Cambridge:
Development Art Director: Graham Davis
Technical Art Director: Nicholas Rowland

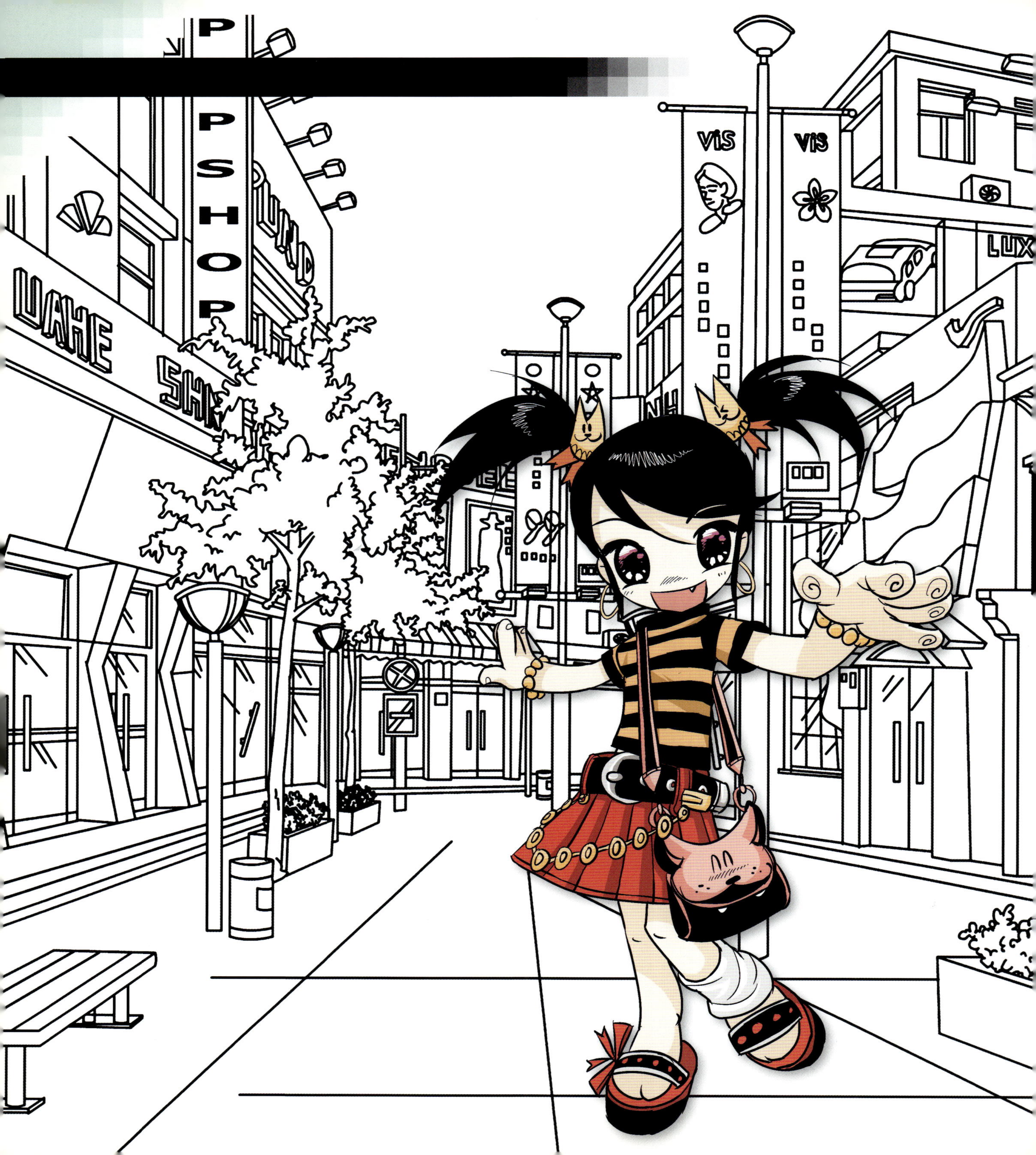
UAHE
ViS
ViS
LUX

INTRODUCTION

"Manga" is simply the Japanese word for "comics," referring solely to printed comics. The word, however, has become internationally recognized as referring to the art style, subject matter, and method of presentation, and manga-style artists can be found all over the world. Manga in its present form has existed for over fifty years, but the origins of Japanese sequential art date back to ukiyo-e painting from the nineteenth century. Hokusai, probably the most famous ukiyo-e artist, is generally credited with coining the term "manga," literally meaning "irresponsible pictures." The development of this style into mass-produced sequential art in the early twentieth century, combined with influences from European and American strip-panel comics, evolved the form into what is now commonly accepted as manga. Anime, referring to Japanese animated films and cartoons, is also a big influence on manga artists. Both manga and anime share many visual traits, so it's natural for the two to be associated. The flexibility within manga is part of its appeal, and there's manga-style artwork to suit all tastes. From the gritty and realistic to the cute and exaggerated, and every step in between, there's always something interesting about every new picture drawn in this uniquely versatile art form. This book offers you a massive selection of manga females illustrated in a wide range of styles, themes, and poses.

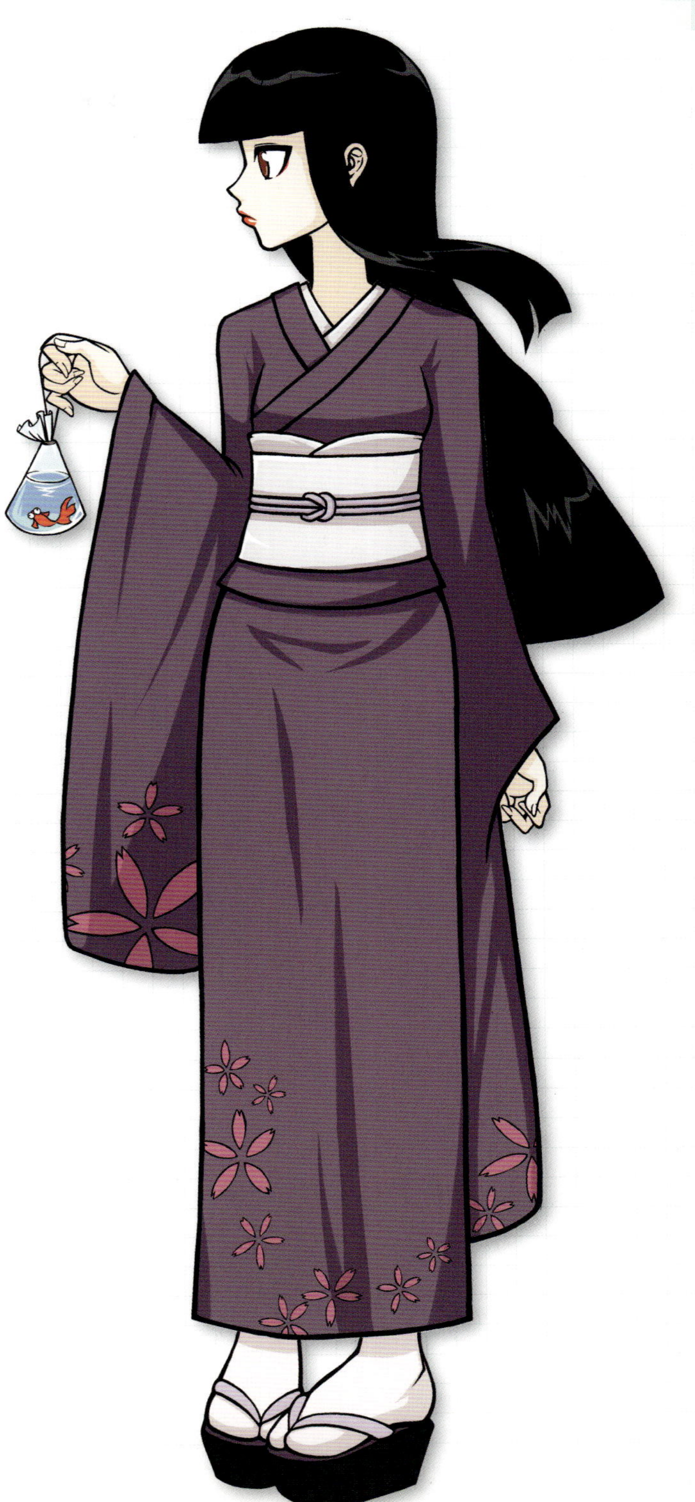

ON THE DISC

On the CD you will find a variety of characters and accessories. Whether you are an experienced artist or trying your hand at manga for the first time, there will be something here for you. We have done most of the hard work for you, so you will be able to create your own characters in a matter of minutes. It's as simple as choosing the look you want, assembling the components of line-art you like, and throwing in a splash of color!

You can use the provided illustrations as building blocks to create your own characters and then add color digitally using your computer. Or you can print off your line-art and use inks, pencils, or paints to bring your pictures to life. The CD enables you to create an assortment of characters ranging from heroic warriors to contemporary fashionistas, with a variety of faces, bodies, and accessories to fully customize your design. A vast array of possibilities lie ahead of you: you can design sci-fi creatures, traditional Japanese females, and kawaii characters. You are only limited by your imagination!

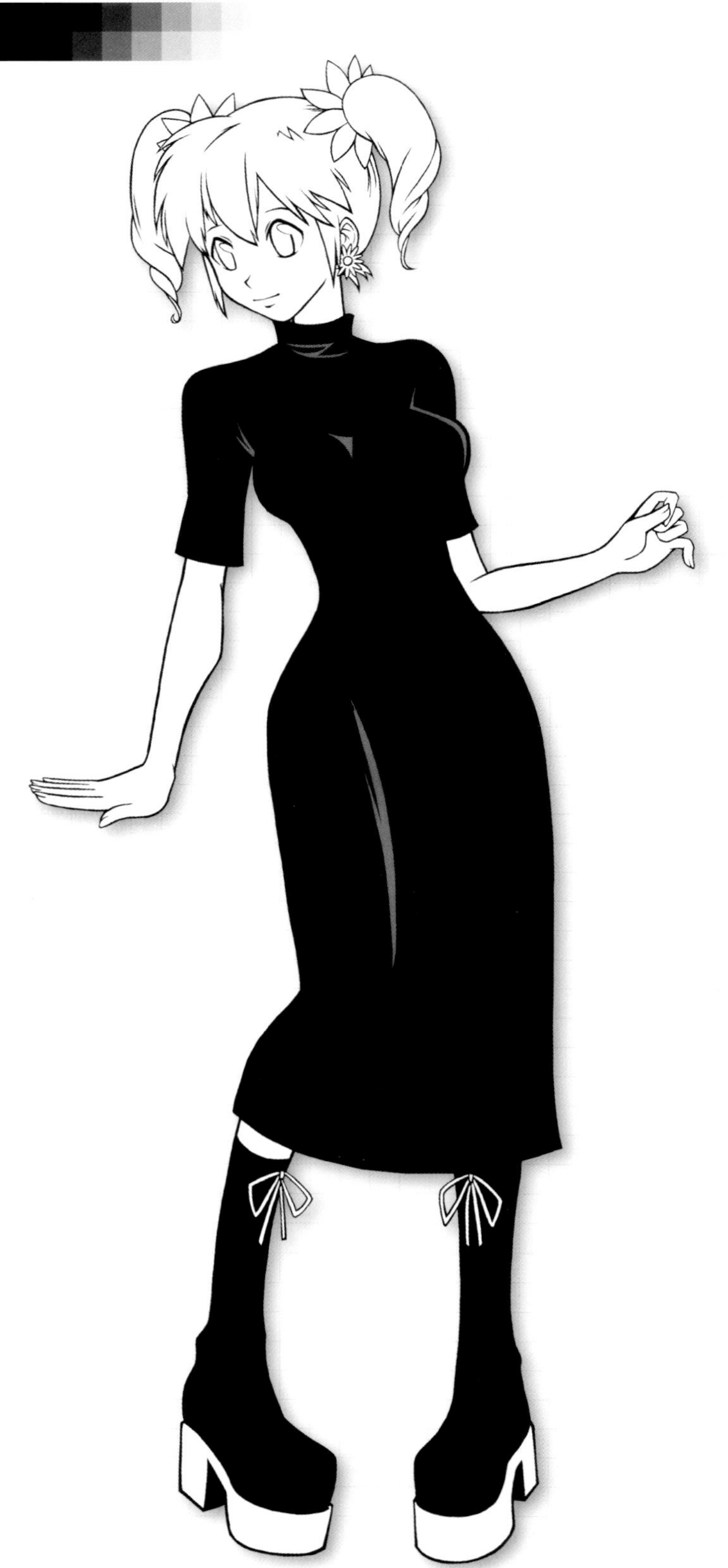

Accessories
Choose from a selection of accessories to add to backgrounds or individual characters. There are instructions for using them on page 24, and they are laid out in a gallery on pages 122–125.

Backgrounds
There are eight backgrounds to add your artwork to. You can choose which one to use depending on the style of your character and each one can be colored to reflect different times of day and weather conditions. See page 25 for the instructions on how to add characters to backgrounds, and pages 112–121 to see them laid out.

Characters
The meat of the disc—21 multilayered character files are provided that can be edited in Photoshop or Photoshop Elements. By turning the layers on and off, you can create hundreds of different characters. Pages 20–25 describe how to create your own manga characters, and the Characters chapter shows some of the variations that can be made using each of the files.

License
You should read this before using any of the files provided on the disc for details of how you can legitimately use the images.

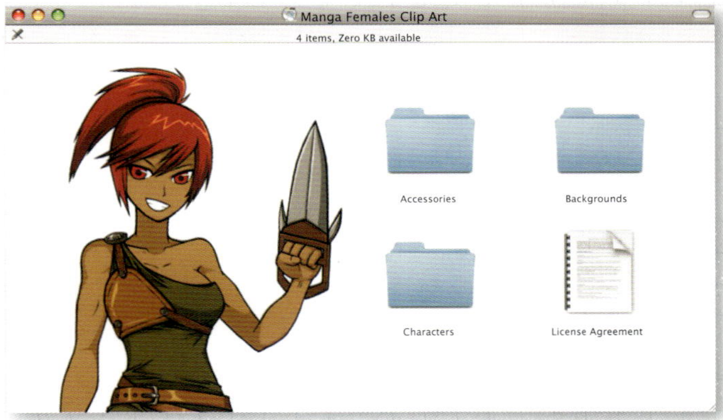

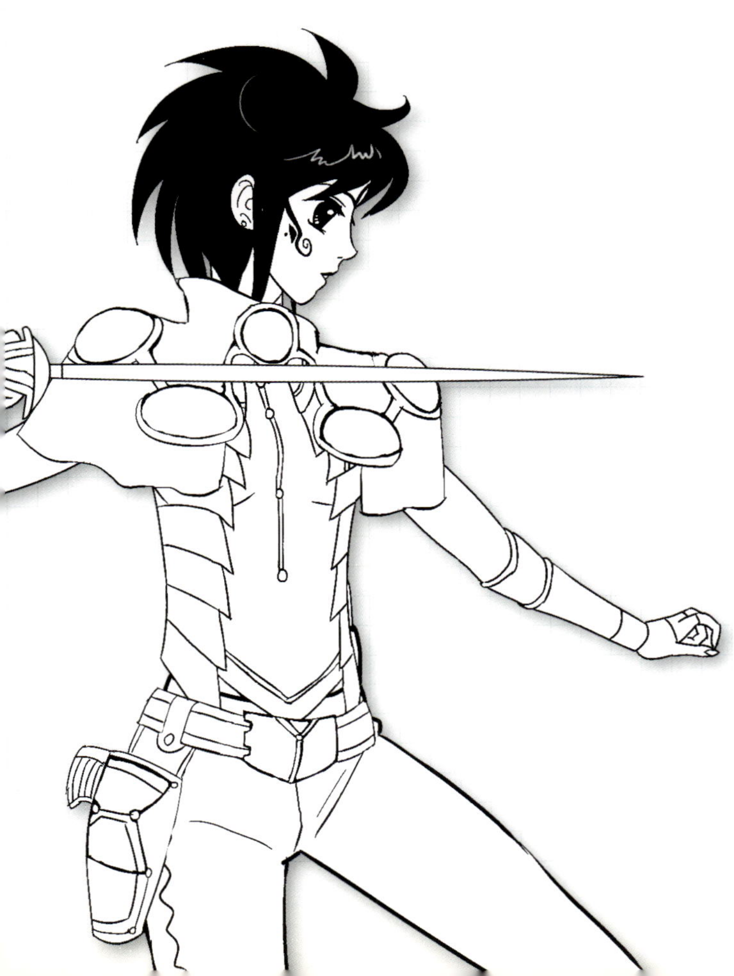

There's no need to feel constrained to using the line-art provided on the disc. In time, you may find that you have your own ideas for characters. Perhaps you will have an accessory in mind that is not on the CD. You can use your experience with this package as a guide to creating your very own line-art with the images provided on the CD to give you even more variety. When you feel confident enough, you may even want to create an entire cast of characters and go as far as putting them into your very own manga story. Either way, you will be able to use this package to gain insight into how a manga character is put together. Enjoy yourself and apply your creativity to what has been provided and you're on your way.

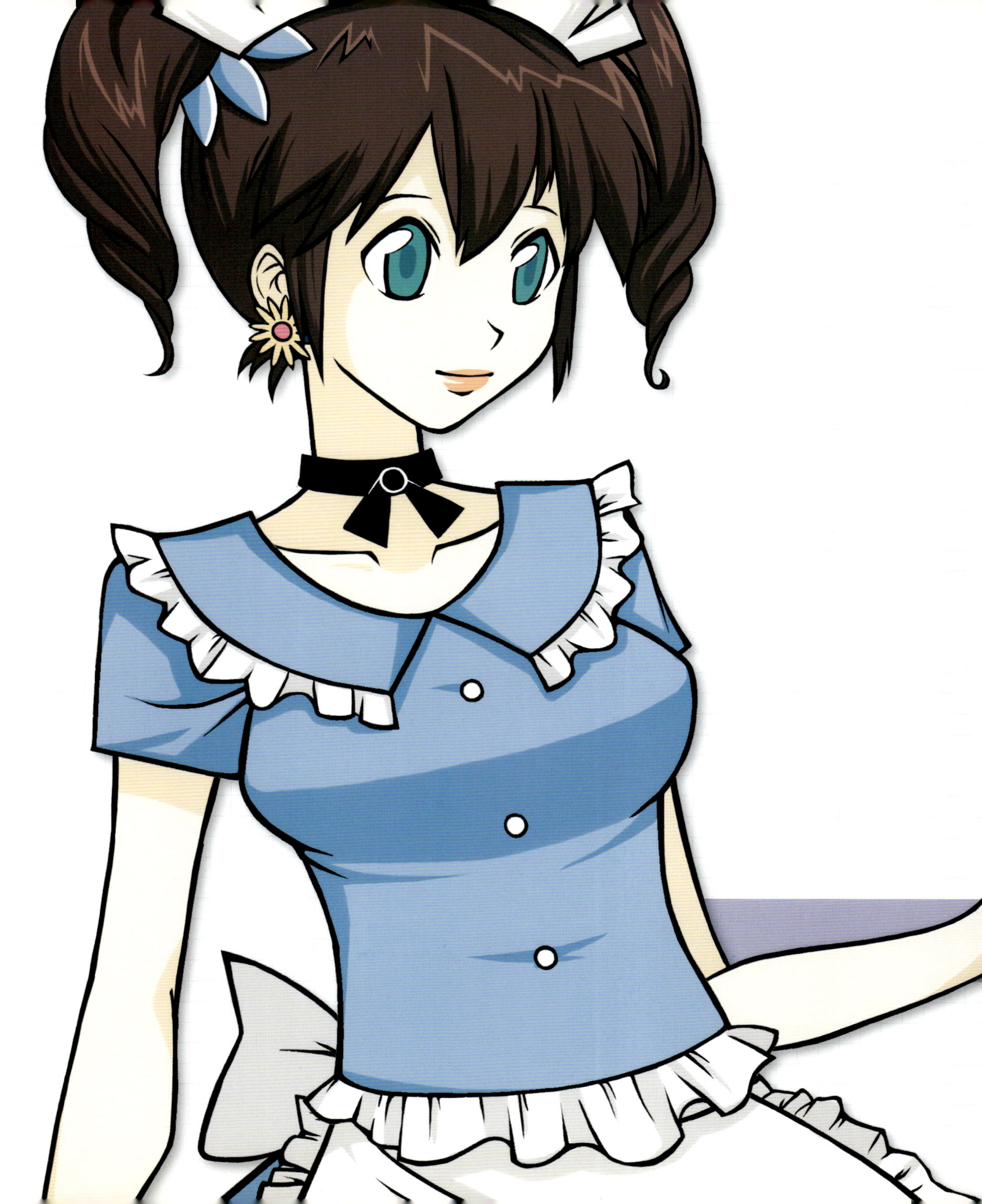

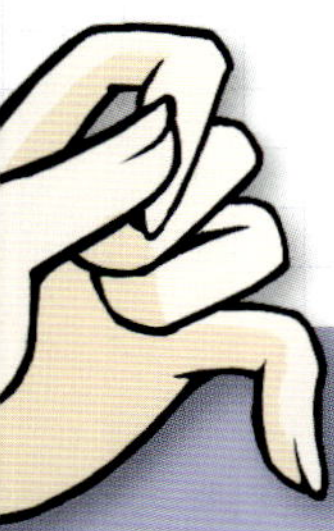

DIGITAL MANGA

INTRODUCTION TO DIGITAL ART

Computers have revolutionized the art world, opening up new avenues for artists to explore and making the production of professional-quality images more achievable. With a speedy computer and the plethora of creative software available, creating slick, eye-catching manga artwork is quicker, easier, and no longer restricted to the professional mangaka.

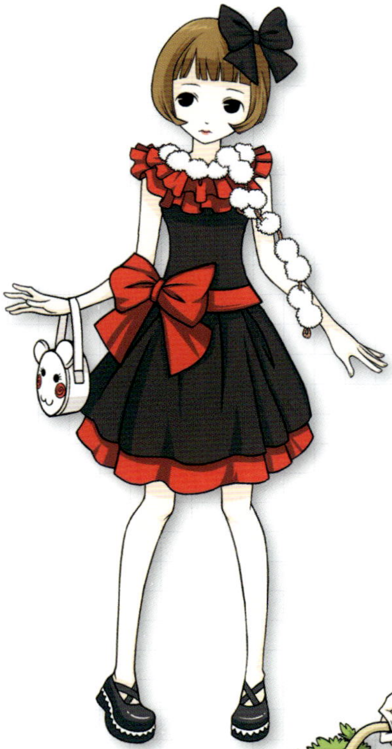

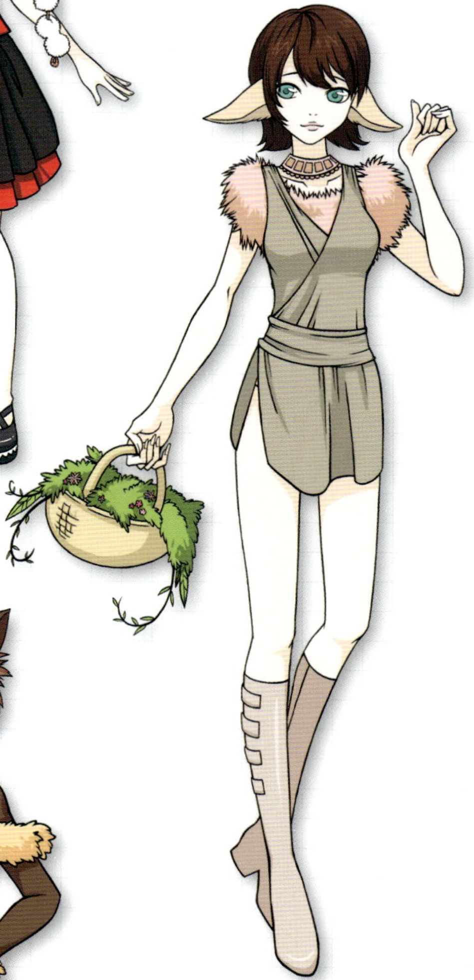

Computers like those shown here are capable of many things—storing music, editing videos, and, most significantly for the artist, editing images. Editing programs have developed significantly and we can use the results—powerful applications like Photoshop—to our advantage. You may already have access to most, if not all, of the equipment shown. If not, it can all be acquired relatively cheaply. Photoshop itself is now available in a cut-down form called Photoshop Elements. For the purposes of this book, everything can be achieved with this significantly less expensive program. Elements will also show you the color-coded layers we've used to make the creation of manga characters as easy as possible. From a professional perspective, the full version's CMYK facilities and masking tools are invaluable, but at home you'll be able to draw, color, and have fun with either.

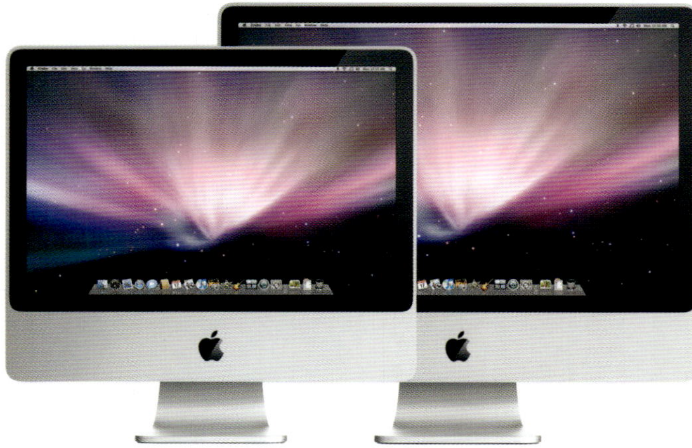

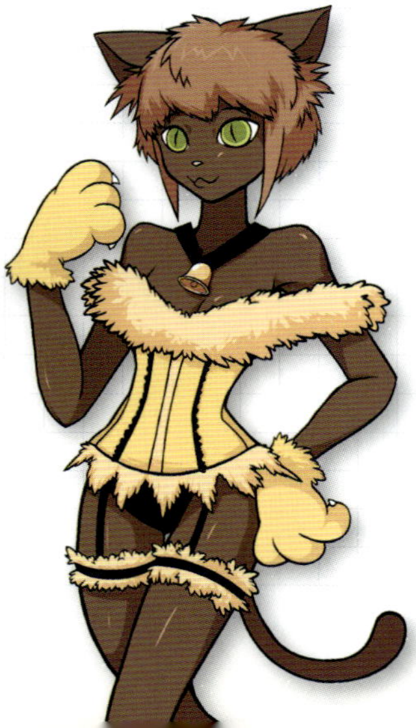

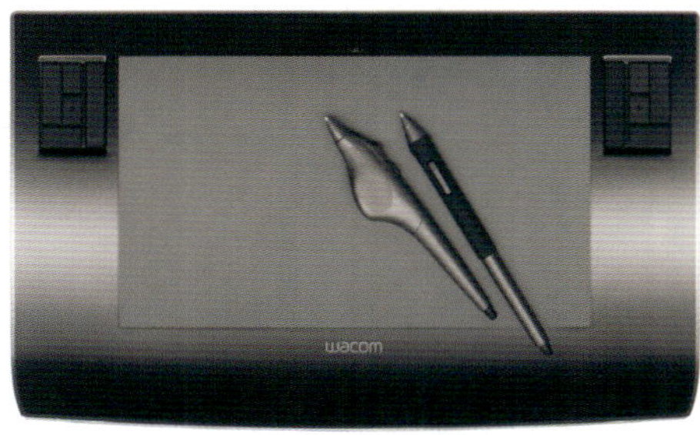

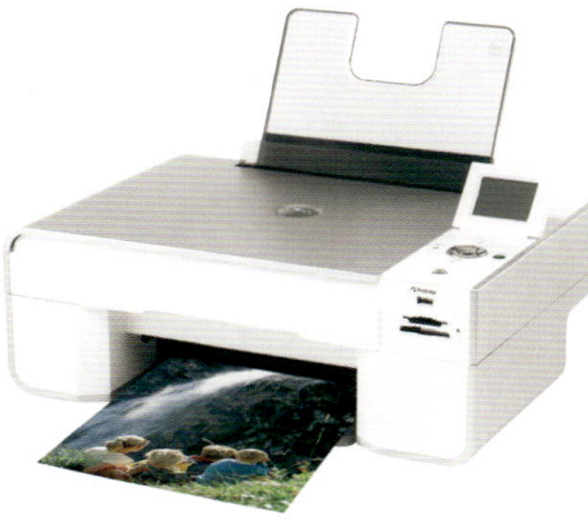

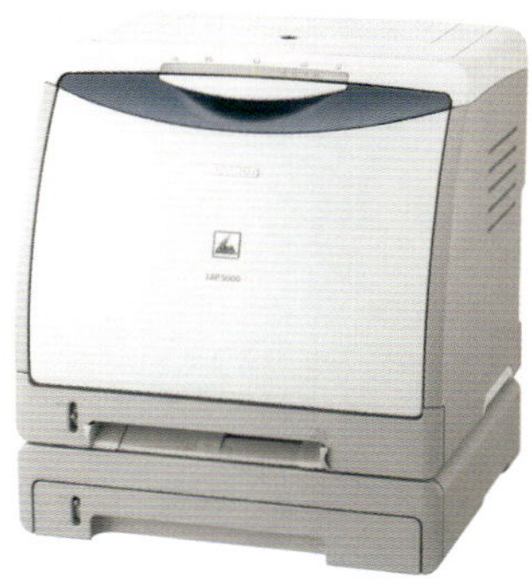

Mouse
Every computer has a pointing device, but it is worth making sure you have a good one if you intend to use it for artwork. Ideally, you should use a laser- or LED-based mouse. These are much more precise than traditional ball-based mice, and won't jam or become slow. Their other advantage is that they don't require such frequent cleaning to operate reliably. The only drawback is that they can be a bit picky about the surface they operate on.

Graphics Tablet
Although it takes a little practice, it's much easier to draw and color on a computer if you're using a graphics tablet. Many different brands and types of tablets are available. When buying a tablet, consider the software that is bundled with it, and whether or not the pen requires batteries. Although some popular brands can be more expensive, their quality and reliability can more than justify the cost.

Inkjet Printer
Color printing is now very cheap and high quality, and it's certainly worth buying a color inkjet to see your creations on paper. Even relatively cheap printers are able to create good quality prints, and quality can be improved considerably with the use of photographic paper (so long as you set the appropriate options in your printer's software). It's worth knowing that certain colors will look different when printed than on a monitor. Many shades of purple will look different in print, as well as bright shades of blue and yellow, but your pictures will look great regardless of this small inaccuracy.

Laser Printer
Although laser printers—particularly the more affordable ones—are usually only black and white, they do have some advantages over inkjets. The lines are often crisper and the printing speed is significantly faster. Most importantly, the ink from a laser printer is waterproof and alcohol resistant. This means that printed pages can be handled without risk of being smudged by fingers, which is great for comic pages. It also means that it is possible to use markers to color in your characters, without risk of the ink smudging. Inkjet inks would mix with the pens and run (one way round this is to use a photocopy).

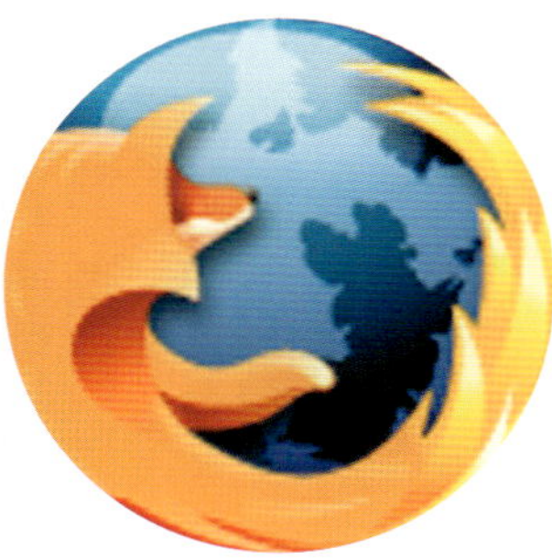

Internet
The Internet has made it much easier for artists to share their work than ever before. By publishing your artwork on the Net, you can get immediate feedback and impressions from other manga enthusiasts. It's also possible to get advice and support when trying to improve your skills. Looking at other people's work can be both inspiring and informative when learning skills like computer coloring, and it's often possible to ask artists questions about how specific illustrations were made. Be sure to make the most of this great resource and allow the whole world to see your manga creations.

PHOTOSHOP AND PHOTOSHOP ELEMENTS

There are many software packages available for digital artists, but Photoshop has become the industry standard for professionals. The immense array of tools and functions makes it ideal not just for editing photographs but for illustration as well. Photoshop enables the manga artist to create full-color characters from scratch and it can handle very high-resolution images. The software comes in two versions: the full version, which is part of the Adobe Creative Suite, and Photoshop Elements, which is a cheaper, cut-down version of its bigger brother. Outlined here are several of the main features available in both versions, but we will look at Photoshop Elements.

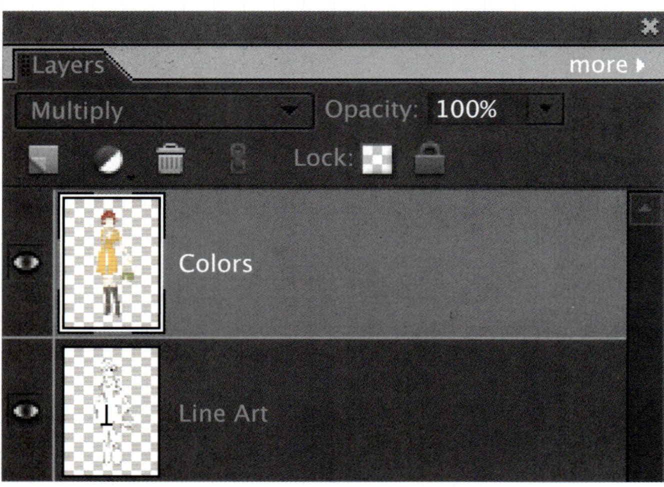

Layers

Layers are one of the most useful features of digital imaging. Imagine each layer is a piece of clear acetate with part of a picture drawn on it, creating the complete image only when the layers are stacked together. Because each layer can be manipulated independently, it is possible to work much more freely, without the risk of spoiling your artwork. You can use layers to experiment, simply turning them off if you don't like them, a process that is essential to building your manga characters.

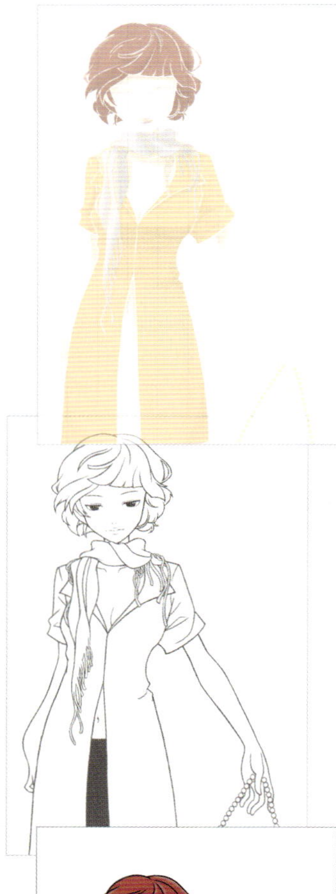

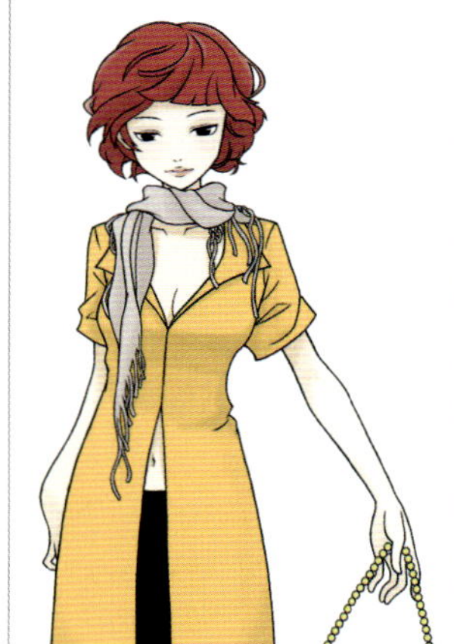

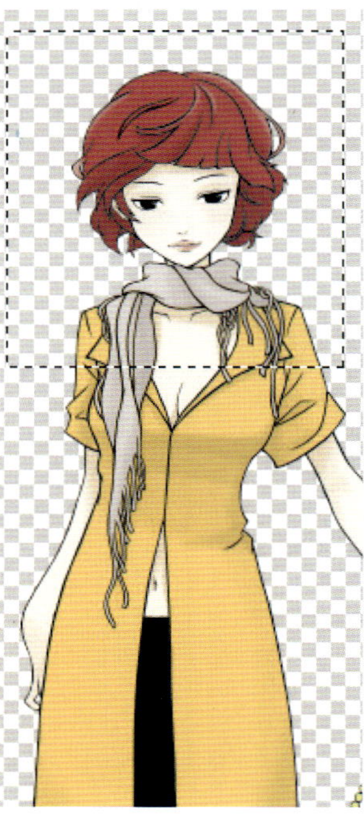

Selection Areas

When working in Photoshop, selections are an important way to control which part of the picture is affected by your painting. A selection is outlined by "marching ants" and changes can only be made within it while it is active. You can define a selection using tools—for example, the Rectangular Selection tool draws a simple box, while the Magic Wand tool selects areas of similar color, whatever the shape. When you have finished with a selection you must remember to switch it off, or "deselect," or you will not be able to edit outside it.

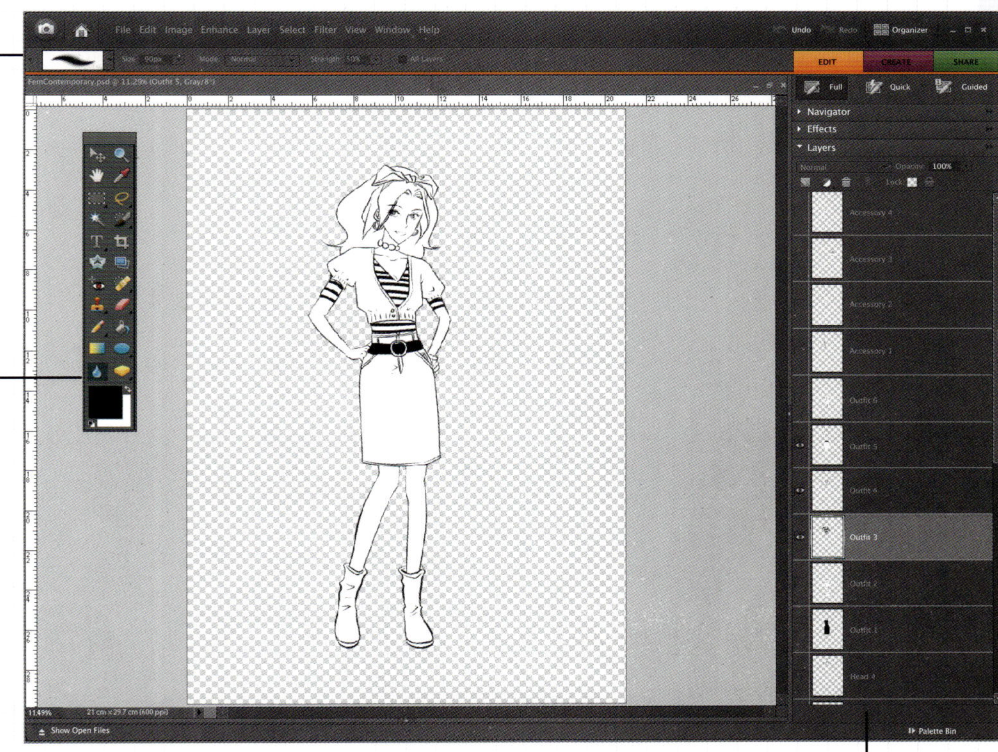

Tool Options bar

While the Toolbox provides access to many different functions, the Tool Options bar allows you to refine the selected tool. If you're using the Brush tool, for example, you can pick different size and texture brushes here.

Toolbox

Though they differ slightly, both versions of Photoshop have a Toolbox that, by default, appears on the left side of the window (in Photoshop Elements it might also be docked to the side of the window as a long single column).

Palettes

Both versions of Photoshop equip you with a number of floating windows, known as "palettes." Perhaps the most useful is the Layers palette, where you can switch on and off the alternative elements in the characters supplied in this book. This is done by clicking in the box to the left of the layer. An eye logo indicates that the layer is visible, or "on."

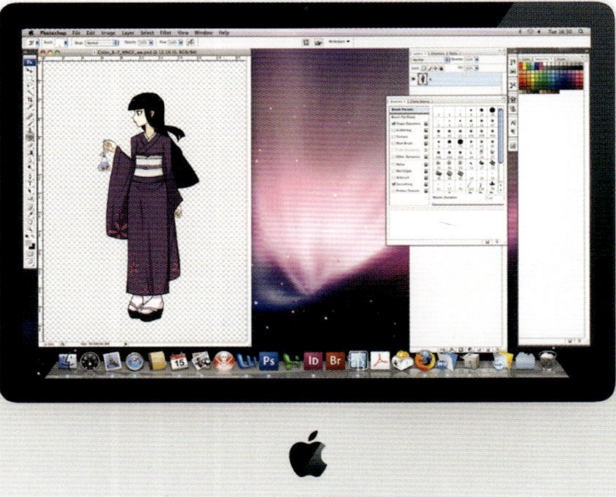

Here, Adobe Photoshop CS3 is shown running on an Apple iMac. If your computer has a large monitor, you'll find yourself with more room for your palettes. You can also zoom in and out of your image, but you should always check your artwork at 100%. That's because only at that size are the pixels in the file seen 1:1 with the pixels on your monitor. At other sizes, false pixels can create a less pleasing, and less accurate, simulation of the final printout.

PHOTOSHOP TOOLS

The Photoshop Toolbox contains all the key functions you need to create your own digital manga artwork, regardless of which version you use. It enables you to zoom in and out, move individual parts of the character and accessories around, as well as color them in as you wish.

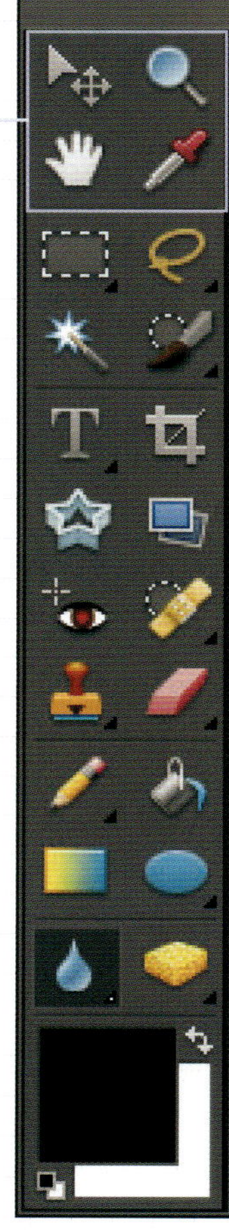

Navigator Window

This window will enable you to move around your document quickly without using the Toolbox or keyboard. This is especially useful if you're using a graphics tablet and prefer to avoid using the keyboard.

Navigation

The ability to move around your image easily is an important part of working digitally. Whether it's to focus on small details, a different part of the body, or to zoom out and see the big picture—moving around the image quickly will help you to work more efficiently.

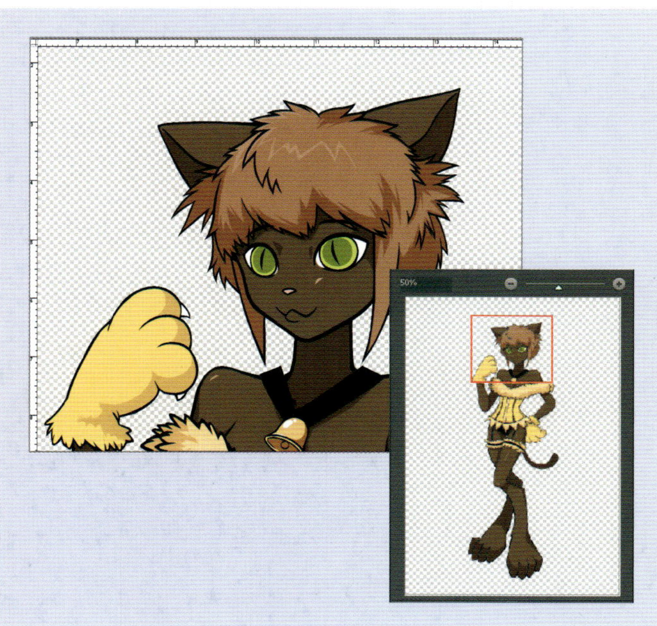

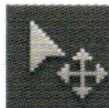

Move

Click and drag to move the currently active layer or selection.

Zoom

Using the Zoom control will let you enlarge and reduce the preview of your image. Holding *Ctrl/Cmd* and pressing the "+" and "– " keys will allow you to zoom in and out at any time.

Hand

The Hand tool lets you pan (or scroll) the image around, making it possible to see different sections of the image.

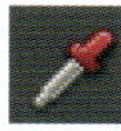

Eyedropper

The Eyedropper tool selects any color you click on and makes it the foreground color (as shown at the foot of the Toolbox). Set the mode to "point sample" to ensure precise color picking. The *Alt* key has the same effect when you're using the Brush tool.

Tip

Holding the *Shift* key when using a selection tool will let you make more than one selection at a time, which you can "add" together to make a single selection. If you hold down the *Alt* key it allows you to delete areas from the existing selection. Next to the mouse cursor, + and – signs show whether you'll be adding or subtracting.

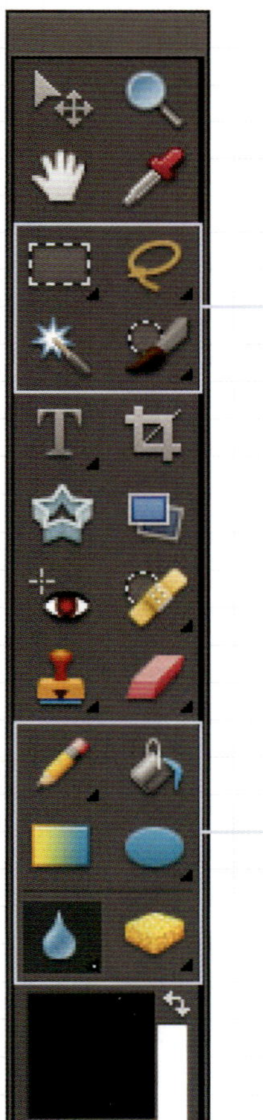

Selection

Accurate selections help you make professional-looking artwork. Luckily, there's a tool for every situation.

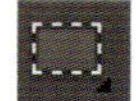

Marquee tools
These are the simplest selection tools enabling you to highlight a simple rectangle or ellipse by clicking and dragging. Hold *Shift* as you do so for a perfect square or circle.

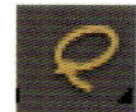

Lasso tools
These tools allow you to select any shape you wish. The Freehand Lasso allows you to quickly define a shape with the mouse, but it can be difficult to control precisely. The Polygonal Lasso creates a selection by drawing a series of points to define a shape.

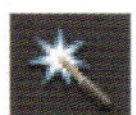

Magic Wand
The Magic Wand tool allows you to select areas of a specific color in the image.

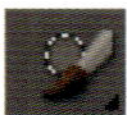

Selection Brush
The Selection Brush allows you to "draw" the areas of selection directly onto the page. The Selection Brush is exclusive to Photoshop Elements, but Photoshop uses the Quick Mask feature, which allows other tools to be used to "paint" the mask.

Paint Tools

The paint tools are used to draw lines and add color to an image. Different shapes and sizes of brush will affect the way the lines appear on an image. See page 18 for more information on different brushes.

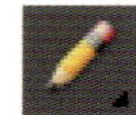

Pencil
A special variation of the Brush tool, creating pixel-perfect (or "aliased") lines. This is very useful for cel-style coloring (*see page 34*), since by default the computer tends to soften edges.

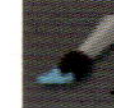

Paintbrush
The standard painting tool, useful for soft edges and smooth lines. This is a great coloring tool, and there are many stylistic options in the Tool Options bar.

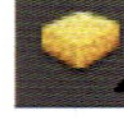

Dodge, Burn, and Sponge
These brush-like tools adjust the color in different ways. Dodge lightens the current color, while Burn makes the color darker and richer. These tools can offer easy ways to shade images, but most artists prefer to use layers and other methods of shading. The Sponge tool, on the other hand, absorbs the color and turns the image to gray.

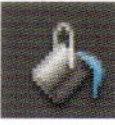

Paint Bucket
This tool fills an area with a selected color or pattern, and is perfect for laying block colors on an illustration. Click on an area and it will be filled to its edges (the level of contrast required to define an edge is called "Tolerance"). To make a selection in this way, without filling, use the Magic Wand tool.

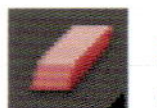

Eraser
The Eraser deletes color from the currently selected layer. The Eraser works in exactly the same way as the Paintbrush, but removes the color instead of adding it.

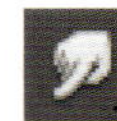

Smudge, Blur, and Sharpen
These tools have no color of their own. Instead, the Smudge tool will smudge the colors around in the direction in which you move the cursor. Blur and Sharpen will alter the contrast of neighboring pixels to soften the definition, or increase sharpness.

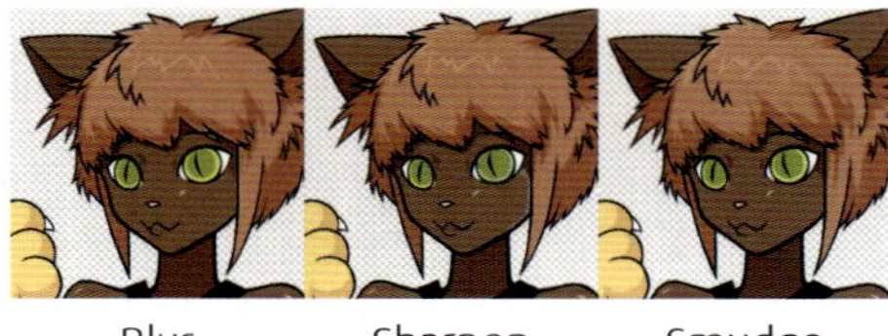

Blur Sharpen Smudge

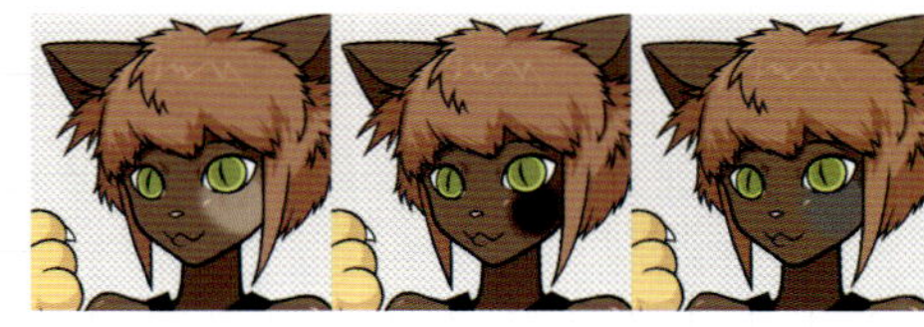

Dodge Burn Sponge

PHOTOSHOP BRUSHES

When you start drawing your own manga, or editing some of the creations on the CD accompanying this book, the Brush and Pencil tools will be your main allies. They represent the most basic method of adding lines and colors to an image. By changing the brush shape and other settings, you can set the Brush tool to be opaque like a paint, translucent like a marker pen, or even remove color like an eraser. The nib can be blunt like a piece of chalk, sharp like a pencil, or even vary in width like a paintbrush or nib pen. Learning how to easily change and control these settings will give you much more freedom when working in Photoshop or Photoshop Elements.

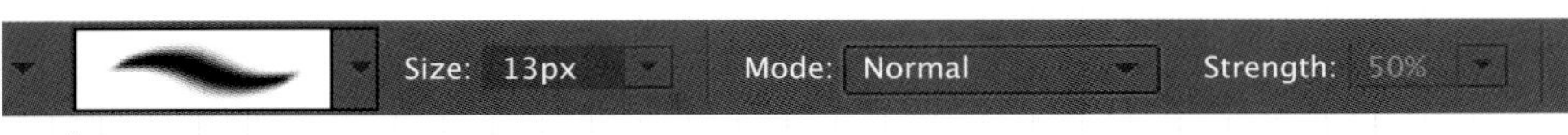

Brush
Choose the type of brush you want to use from this menu. Pressing "<" and ">" will cycle through the range of brushes.

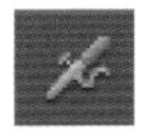

Airbrush
This changes the brush to Airbrush mode, which gives you a gradual flow of paint (depending on the Flow setting). Although this is useful, many people just use a soft brush instead.

Size: 13px

Size
This adjusts the size of the currently chosen brush. You can use the "[" and "]" keys to perform the same function.

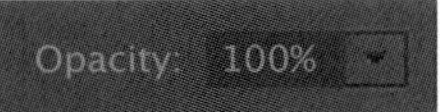

Opacity
Changes how transparent the ink or paint will be. At 0% the paint is completely invisible, at 50% it's half-transparent, and at 100% it's completely solid.

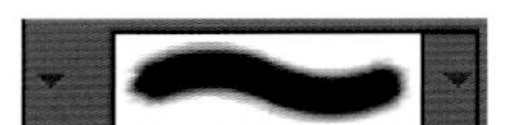

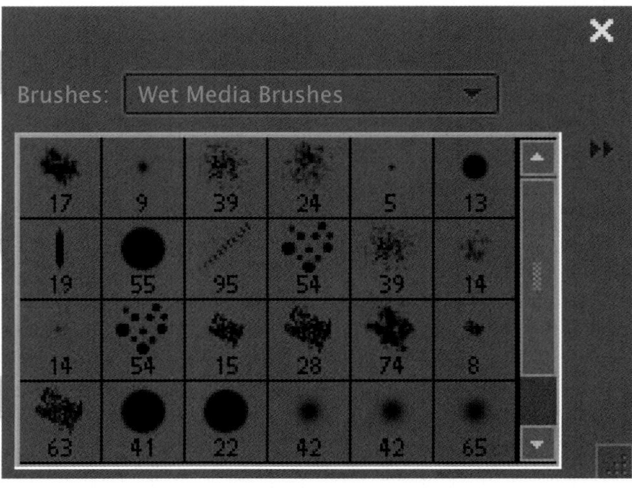

Brush Shapes

Hard brush
These brushes give you a solid shape and smooth outline. Although the edge is anti-aliased (softened), it is still sharp enough to give a convincingly hard line.

Soft round
These brushes have a gradient of density, and their opacity is reduced toward the edge of the basic shape. They are perfect for soft, airbrush-style coloring.

Natural brushes
A selection of irregularly shaped brushes are available with the intention of emulating "natural media" such as paints, pastels, and charcoal. This style is covered later in the book (*see page 44*).

Brush Spacing

A simple setting in the Brushes palette, this can make a big difference in the quality of your lines, as well as the performance of your computer. By reducing the brush spacing, the dots will be drawn closer together, resulting in a smoother line (in most instances), and translucent areas of the brush will appear darker. However, as more dots will be drawn it also means that your computer will have to work harder. Also, when using a graphics tablet it is often crucial to increase the spacing in order to avoid the line breaking when the pen is moved very quickly.

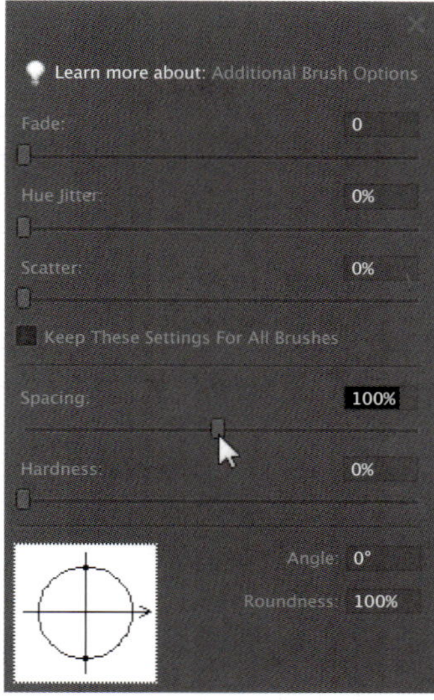

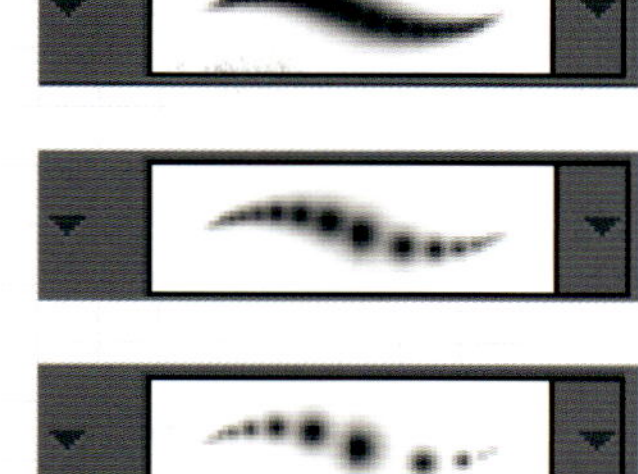

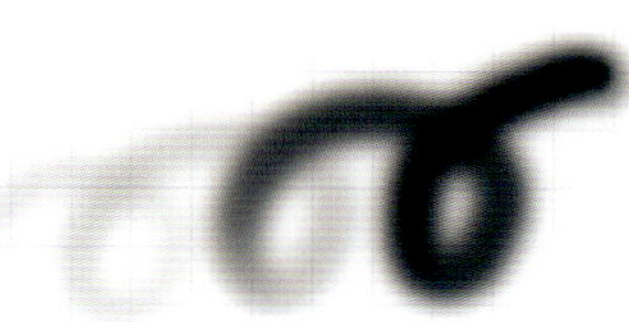

Pressure = Opacity

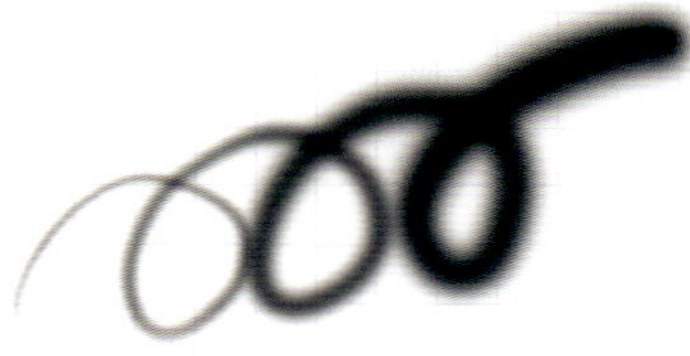

Pressure = Size

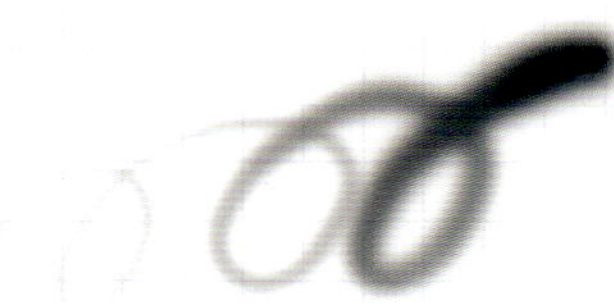

Pressure = Size + Transparency

Keyboard Shorcuts

Quick Brush Resizing

The "[" and "]" (square bracket) keys allow you to quickly resize your brush (holding down the *Shift* key at the same time also alters the hardness). By making the most of this you can quickly adjust the level of detail you're working with. This is especially useful when using soft brushes to color your images.

Quick Color Changes

When working with the Brush or Pencil tools, you'll often want to change color quickly. By holding the *Alt* key and clicking over a pixel of the color of your choice, you pick up that color from the canvas. (You might even want to keep a "palette" area of dabs of color on your image, until you're finished.) Also worth noting is the "X" button, which will quickly alternate between your foreground color and background color.

Painting with Opacity Controls

The number keys along the top of the keyboard act as handy shortcuts for adjusting the opacity of your brush. Press 1 for 10% opacity, 2 for 20% opacity, etc. If you press 2 and 5 quickly, you will get 25% opacity. This is useful if you want to introduce subtlety to your coloring, but don't want to change color. Combined with the "X" button it can allow for very fast monochrome illustrating.

Graphic Tablet Pressure Settings

One of the biggest advantages of using a graphics tablet over using a mouse is the fact that the pen is pressure-sensitive. This allows you to change the way a Photoshop tool behaves, depending upon how firmly you press the tip of the pen against the tablet. Usually you'll want to set the pressure control to Size when drawing inks and block colors, and to Opacity when shading or adding color.

Some more expensive tablets (such as the Wacom Intuos series) also allow for pen tilt recognition, which allows for additional settings to be adjusted relative to how close the pen is to being held vertical. This is a handy feature, but not as useful as the pressure control.

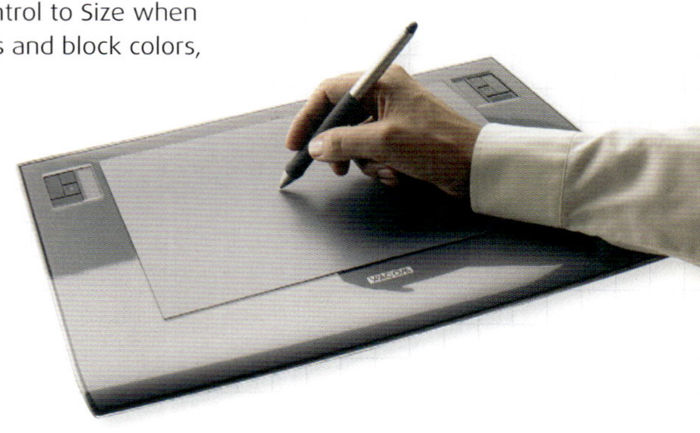

CREATING CHARACTERS

Building a character from the files supplied on the CD is simple. There are numerous possibilities so be sure to experiment and try out lots of different combinations. The files have been designed to be as flexible as possible, so you can mix and match to create your own customized manga characters.

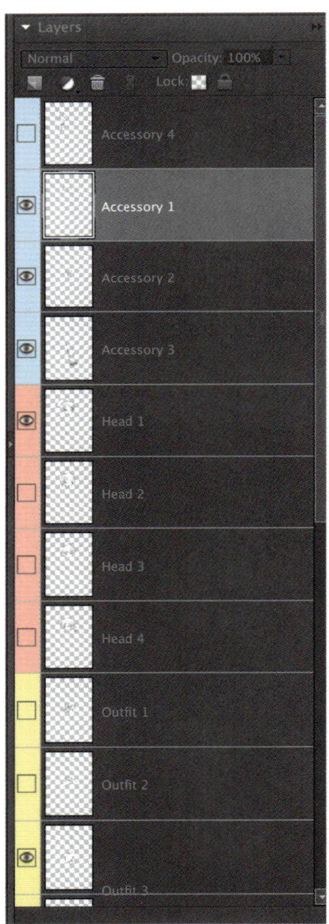

1 Insert the CD-ROM supplied with this book. It doesn't matter what kind of computer you're using—Mac or PC—you should find a folder labeled "Characters." Inside this you'll find a layered .PSD, or Photoshop, file for each character type in this book. Copy the folder onto your computer so that you can save any changes you make to the files. Go to *File > Open* in Photoshop or Photoshop Elements, then choose the character you want to work with.

The layers within the files act like a traditional animator's acetate films—all we need to do now is put the elements together to form a character. This process is achieved by turning the visibility of some layers on and off—their status is indicated by the eye icon to the left of the layer in the Layers palette.

Merge Layers

To "merge" the layers, make sure they are all selected and click More (which is the double-arrow icon) in the top-right corner of the Layers palette. Alternatively, select all the layers and press *Ctrl/Cmd* and the "E" key.

2 Turn to the corresponding pages of this book to see the options for your character, including a full listing of the layers available. To help you, the layers have been color coded, and generally you will not want to turn on more than one head, legs, or torso at once.

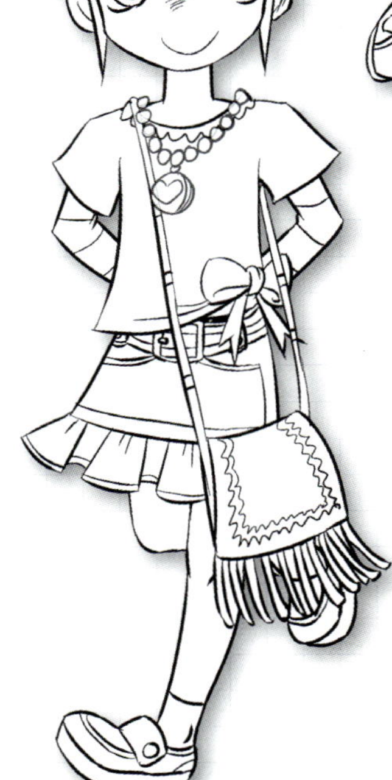

3 When you are happy with your character, simply select all the layers and "merge" them together to create one, single layer. Then save the image onto your computer using *File > Save As* from the menu. Make sure you are always working from files copied onto your computer as you will not be able to save over the original file if it is on the CD. If you find things just aren't right, then try the tricks on the next few pages to perfect your character.

Adjusting the Layers

You may want to adapt the look of a character by changing the layer order. For example, underneath the dress layer this wrap adds detail to the overall outfit, but by moving it above the dress layer (outfit 5) it becomes a shawl and you can see the leaf brooch. Simply drag the layers up and down on the Layers palette to change the order.

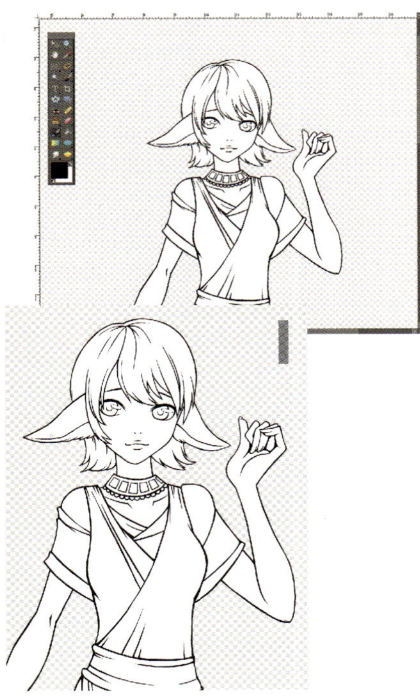

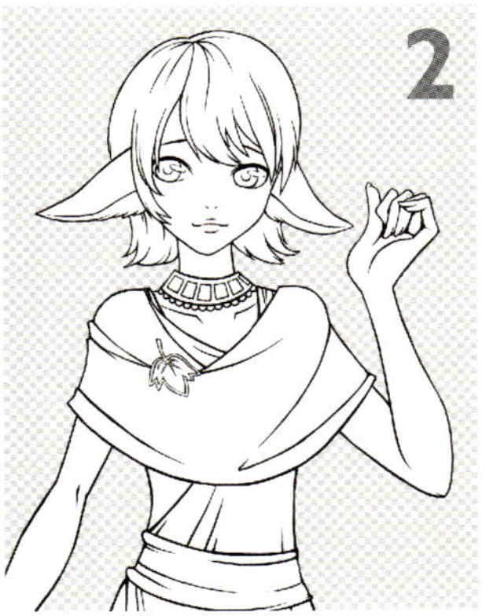

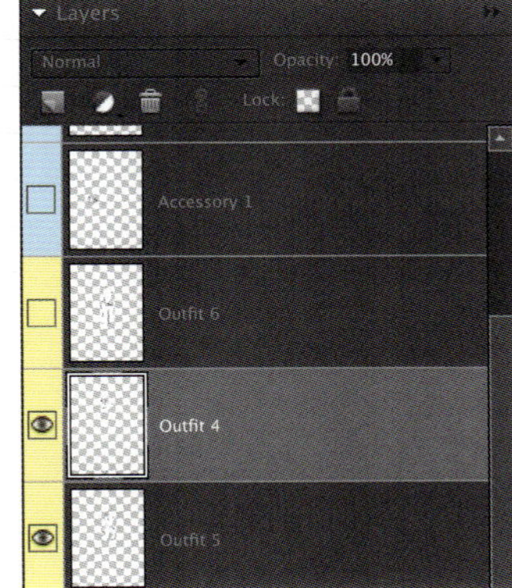

This technique allows you to create more variations for each figure. In the example below, by moving the skirt layer (outfit 3) above the dress layer (outfit 6), a completely new look is created.

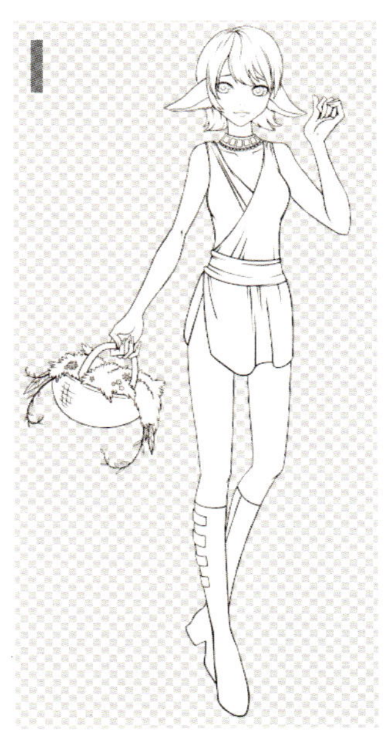

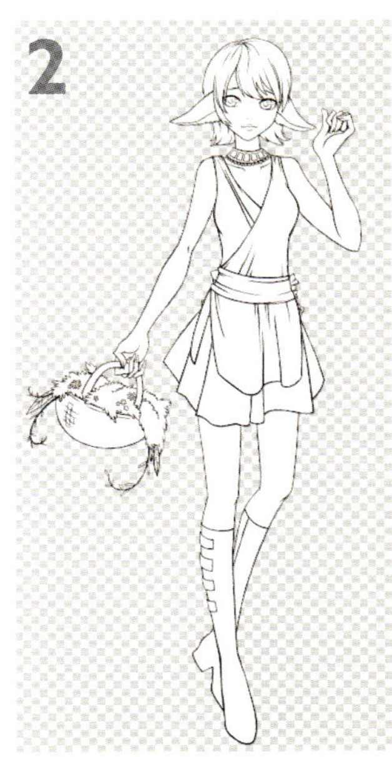

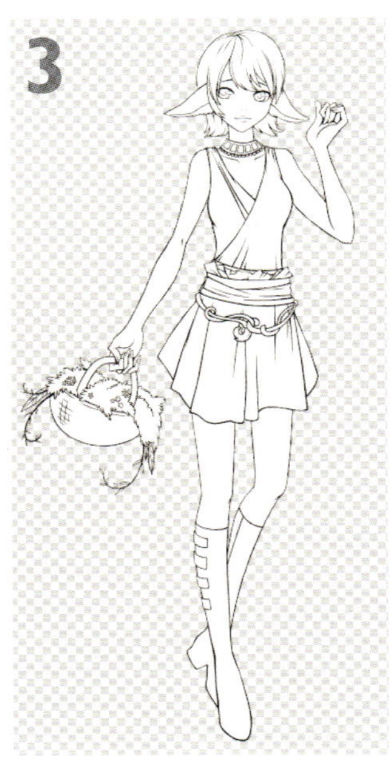

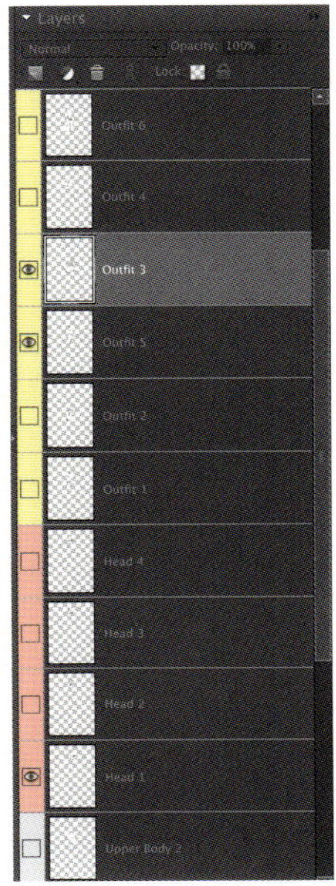

Mixing Costume Sets

Many of the costume sets allow you to experiment with different combinations from other characters, rather than just layers on the same file. By interchanging parts from different sets, you can create some truly unique and diverse characters.

This character is a mix of Kawaii and Child components, with an accessory borrowed from one of the Traditional Asian figures.

Select the files (costume sets) you wish to mix. If you open them both in Photoshop Elements, the files appear in your Project Bin and you can switch between each one easily.

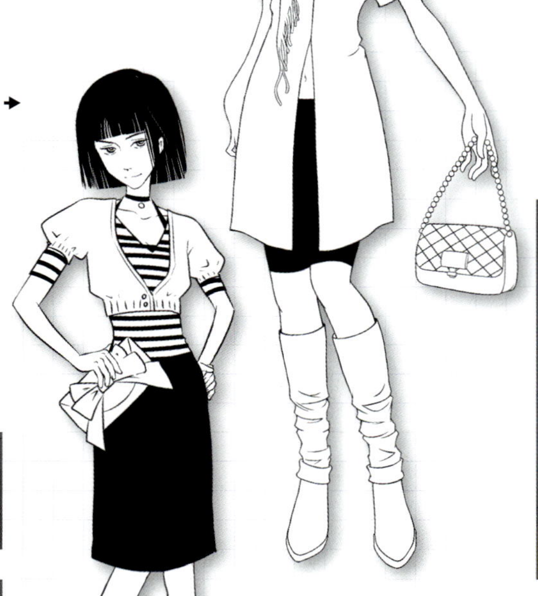

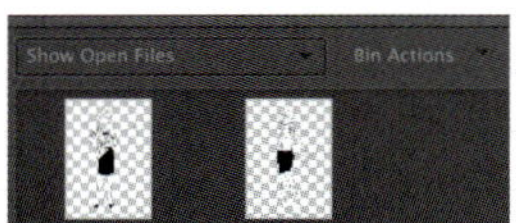

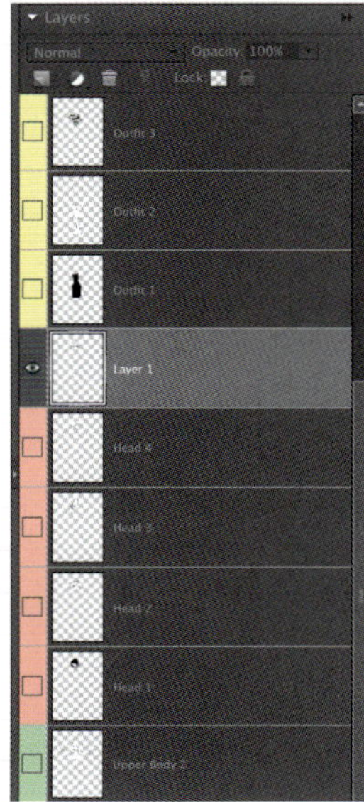

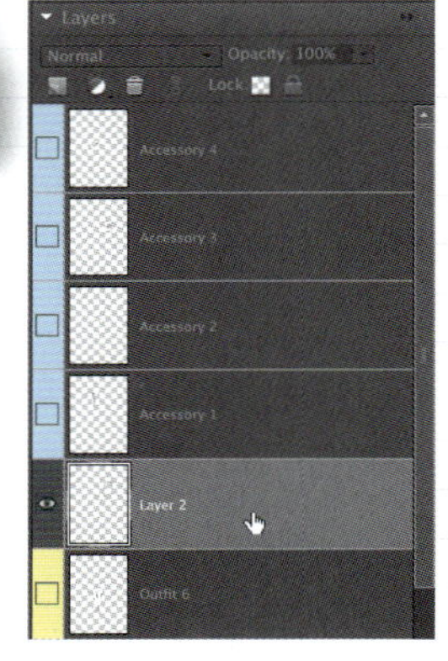

If you copy and paste the item directly onto the main figure, a new layer is automatically created.

When mixing costume sets, you will need to adjust the added feature to fit the new figure. You can do this by following the techniques shown in the examples on the next page.

If you select the layer you want to use, either copy it by clicking *Ctrl* + "A" and then *Ctrl* + "C" (*Cmd* + "A" and *Cmd* + "C" for Mac) and then paste it onto the main figure you want to use (*Ctrl/Cmd* + "P"), or simply drag the layer from the one figure to the next, as shown right.

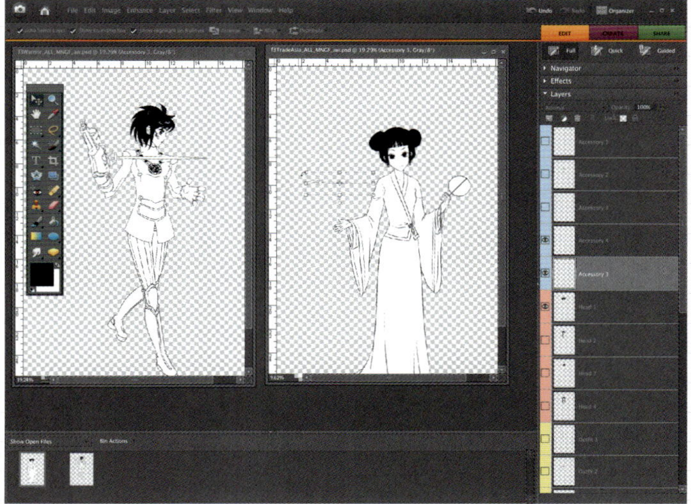

Rotating or Resizing

You may want to try rotating or resizing certain accessories—or even heads—to alter the appearance of your character, but you will need to do so when mixing costume sets. This is very easy to achieve using the Free Transform tool either in Photoshop or Photoshop Elements.

To rotate or resize, select the layer you wish to adjust in the Layers palette, then go to *Edit > Free Transform* (or use the keyboard shortcut *Ctrl* + "T" / *Cmd* + "T"). A box will appear around the selected layer.

To rotate, hover the pointer just outside the box; it should change to a curved, two-sided arrow. Now click and drag to rotate the selection. (When doing this, you can also move the object by dragging inside the transform box.)

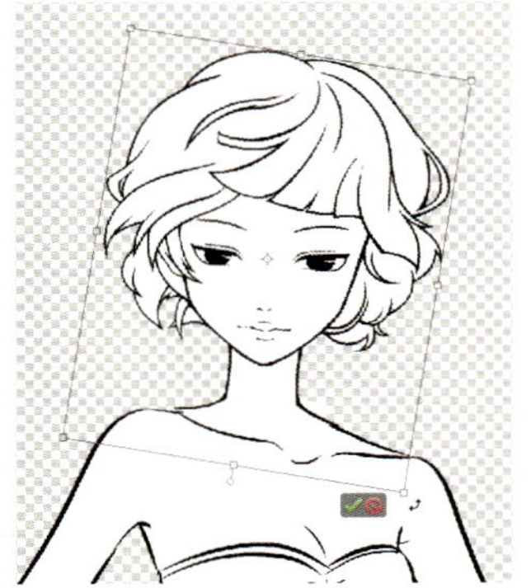

▲ To scale, click and drag on the corner square. If you hold down *Shift* while you drag, it maintains the scale of the width and height proportionally. Avoid using the side handles, as these will stretch the object.

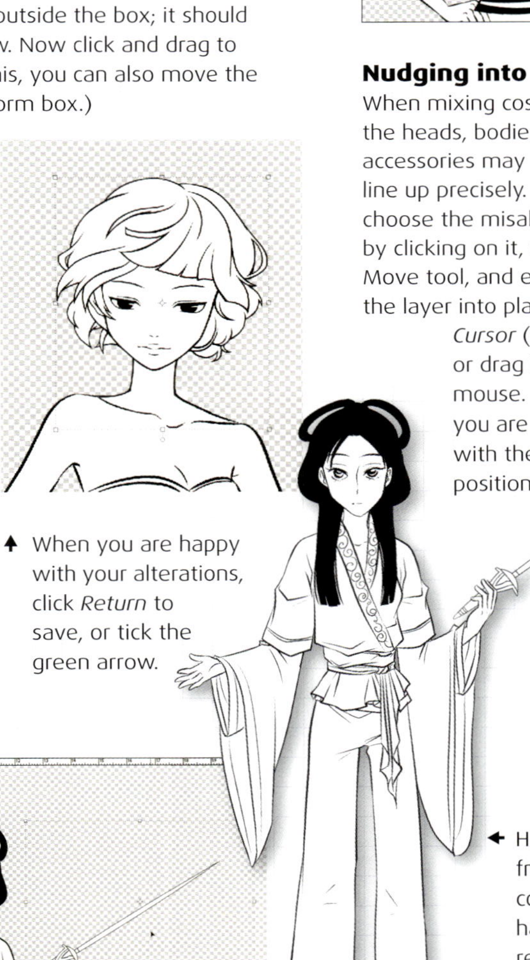

▲ When you are happy with your alterations, click *Return* to save, or tick the green arrow.

◀ Here a sword from a Warrior costume set has been resized, rotated, and moved to fit in the hand of a Traditional Asian figure.

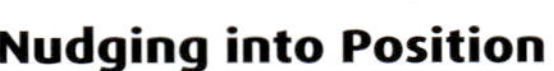

Nudging into Position

When mixing costume sets, the heads, bodies, and accessories may not always line up precisely. In that case, choose the misaligned layer by clicking on it, select the Move tool, and either nudge the layer into place with the *Cursor* (arrow) keys or drag it with the mouse. Stop when you are happy with the new position.

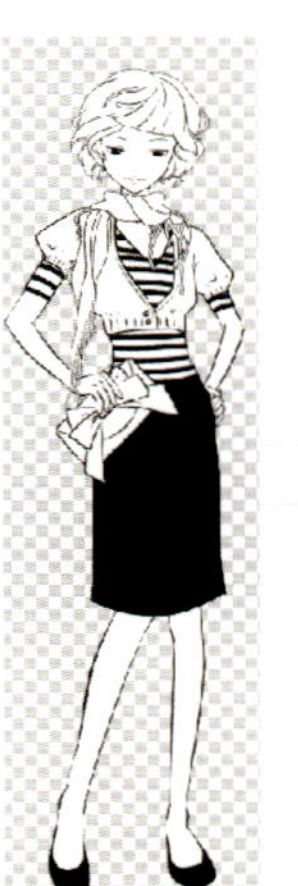

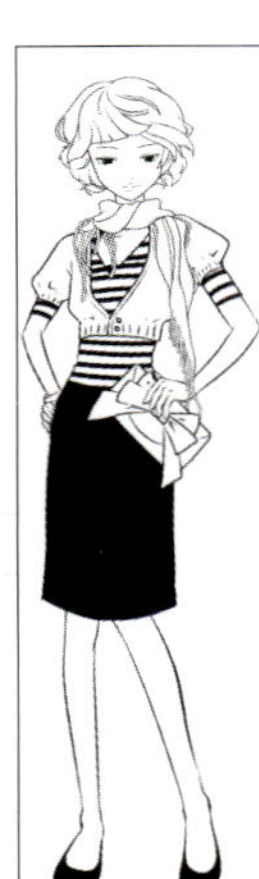

Flipping

To get a whole new angle on your fantastic creation, try flipping the image. This can be applied at any time—before or after coloring—and is an ideal way to fit a second character into a scene when it doesn't initially seem to work. Simply click *Image > Rotate > Flip horizontal*. It is also a good technique to use when adding new accessories to characters.

Adding Accessories

To add accessories to your character, open the accessory file alongside the character. Then simply drag that layer onto the main character image and close the accessory file again.

Position the accessory using the methods described on the previous page. If necessary, reduce the accessory layer's Opacity temporarily and erase certain sections so that, for example, the thumb appears "above" the umbrella's handle.

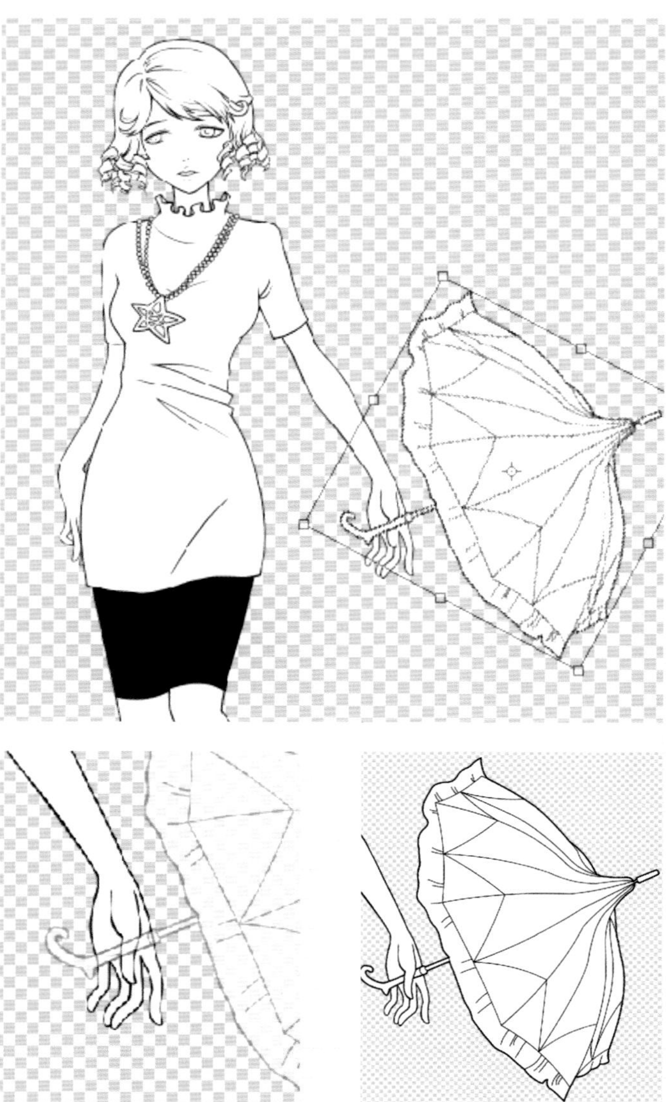

Additional Clothing

The suggestion of additional clothing can be introduced to the characters with simple lines added to the character after construction. Think about how the final image will be colored, and areas that could suggest extra clothing or layering simply with the use of an extra line. You can also create new looks by erasing certain lines of existing artwork. Try some of these:

- Stockings
- Leggings
- Long socks
- Sleeves
- Gloves
- Vests and tight clothing
- Collars and chokers
- Straps

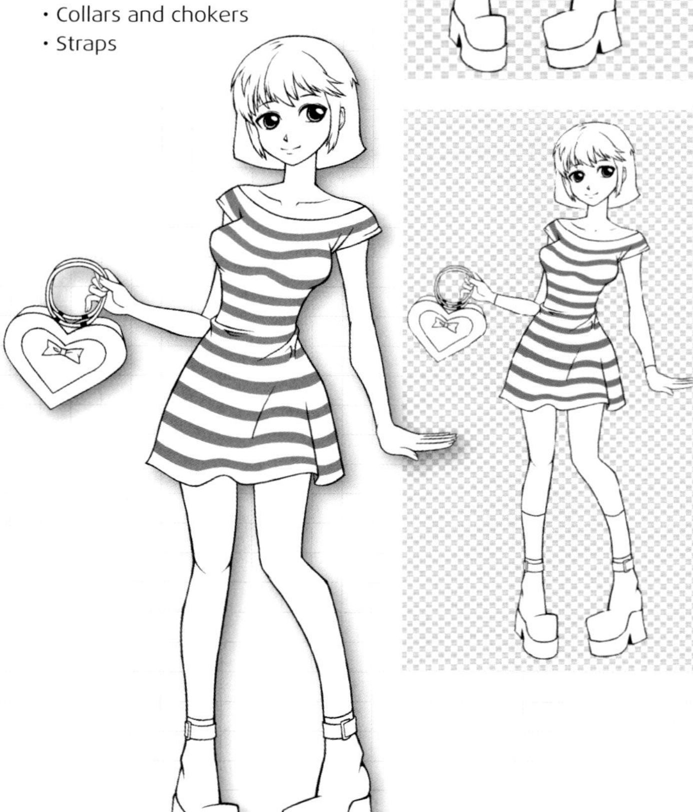

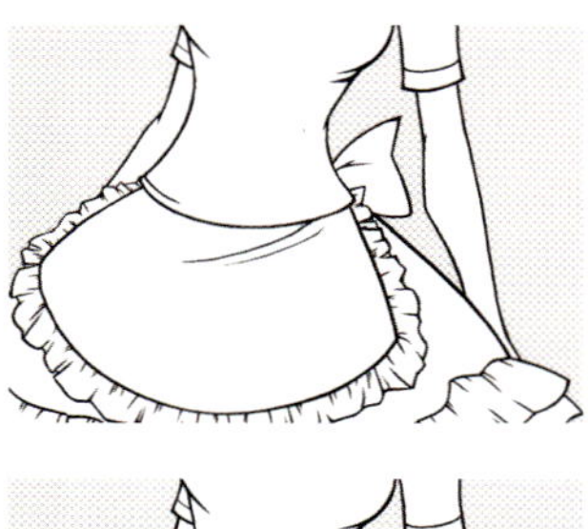

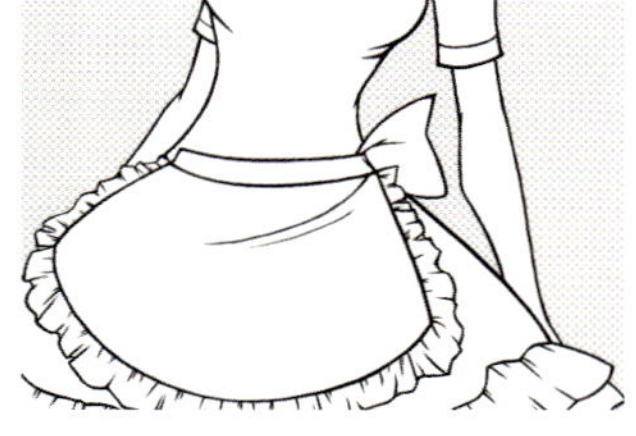

You can adjust outfits by erasing lines as well. For example, by moving the layer with the T-shirt below the skirt layer, it gives the impression it's been tucked in. However, it doesn't look quite right.

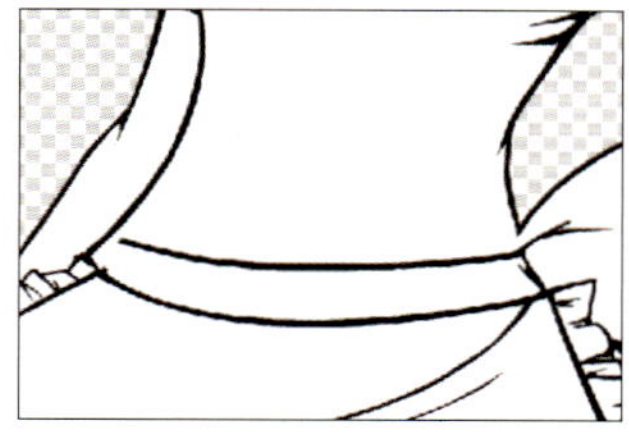

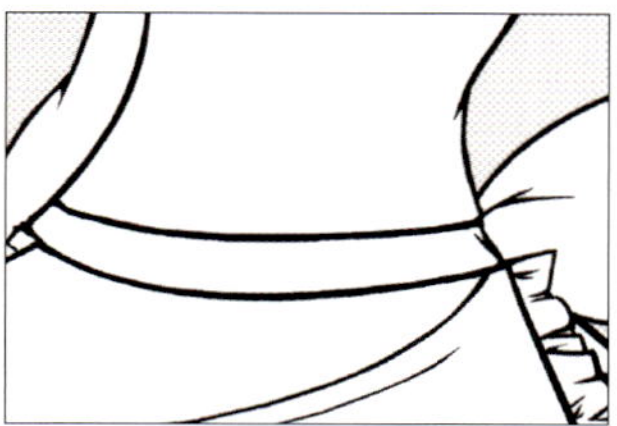

By erasing the sides of the waist of the skirt, and then joining up the lines so they reach the side of the T-shirt, it now looks like it was originally drawn that way.

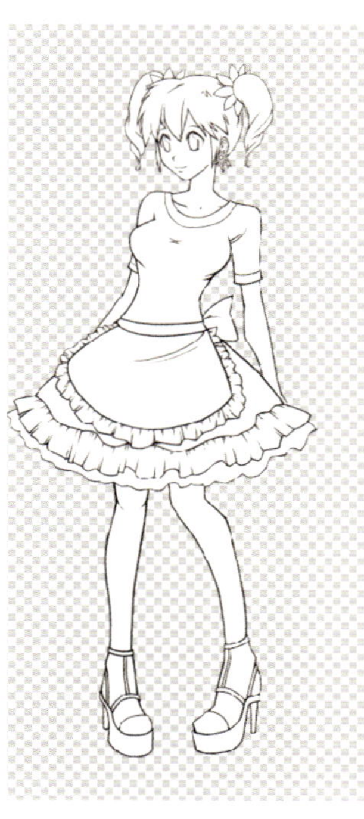

Adding Characters to Backgrounds

You can do this the same way you would add an accessory or mix costume sets. Again, just either copy the figure and paste it onto the background, or drag the layer of the figure onto the background file. To do this make sure you have merged all the layers so that the figure is only on one layer. You can do this by highlighting all the layers, going to the options for the layers palette and selecting "Merge" (or shortcut *Ctrl* + "E"/*Cmd* + "E").

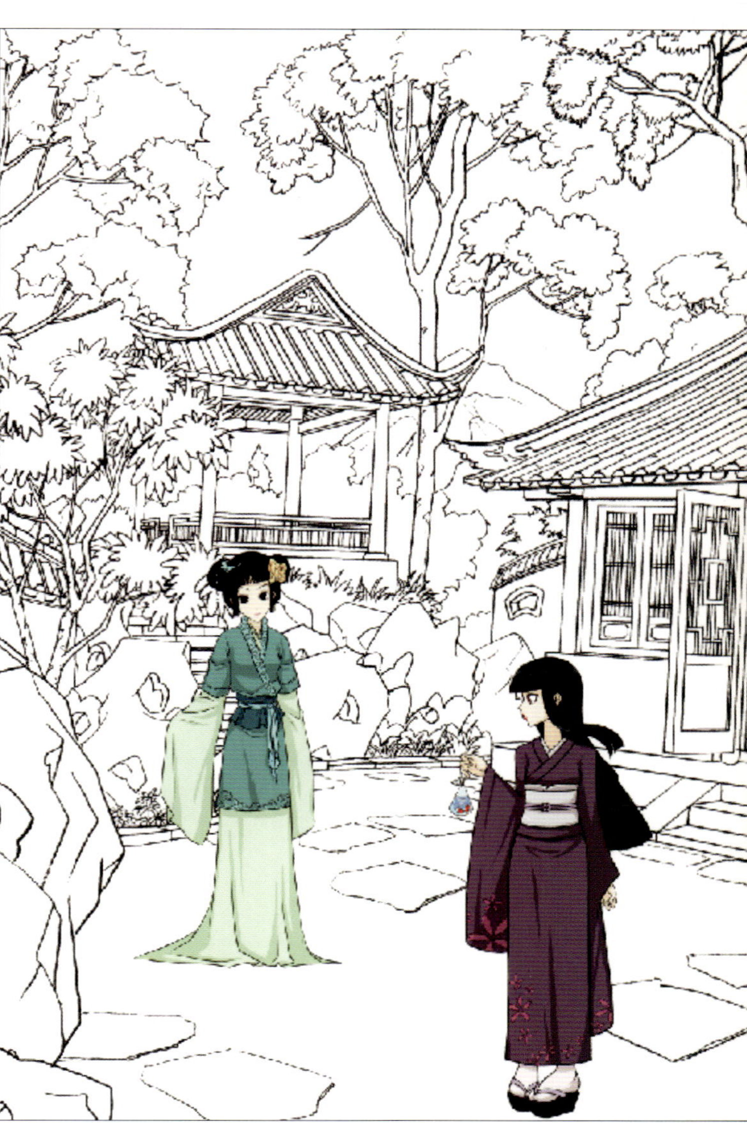

Mixing Costume Sets and Accessories

Using the methods outlined on the previous pages, you can create lots of different characters. You can add details to characters by using accessories, or you can create whole new figures by mixing costume sets. Below are a few examples of how you can mix and match the files included on the CD.

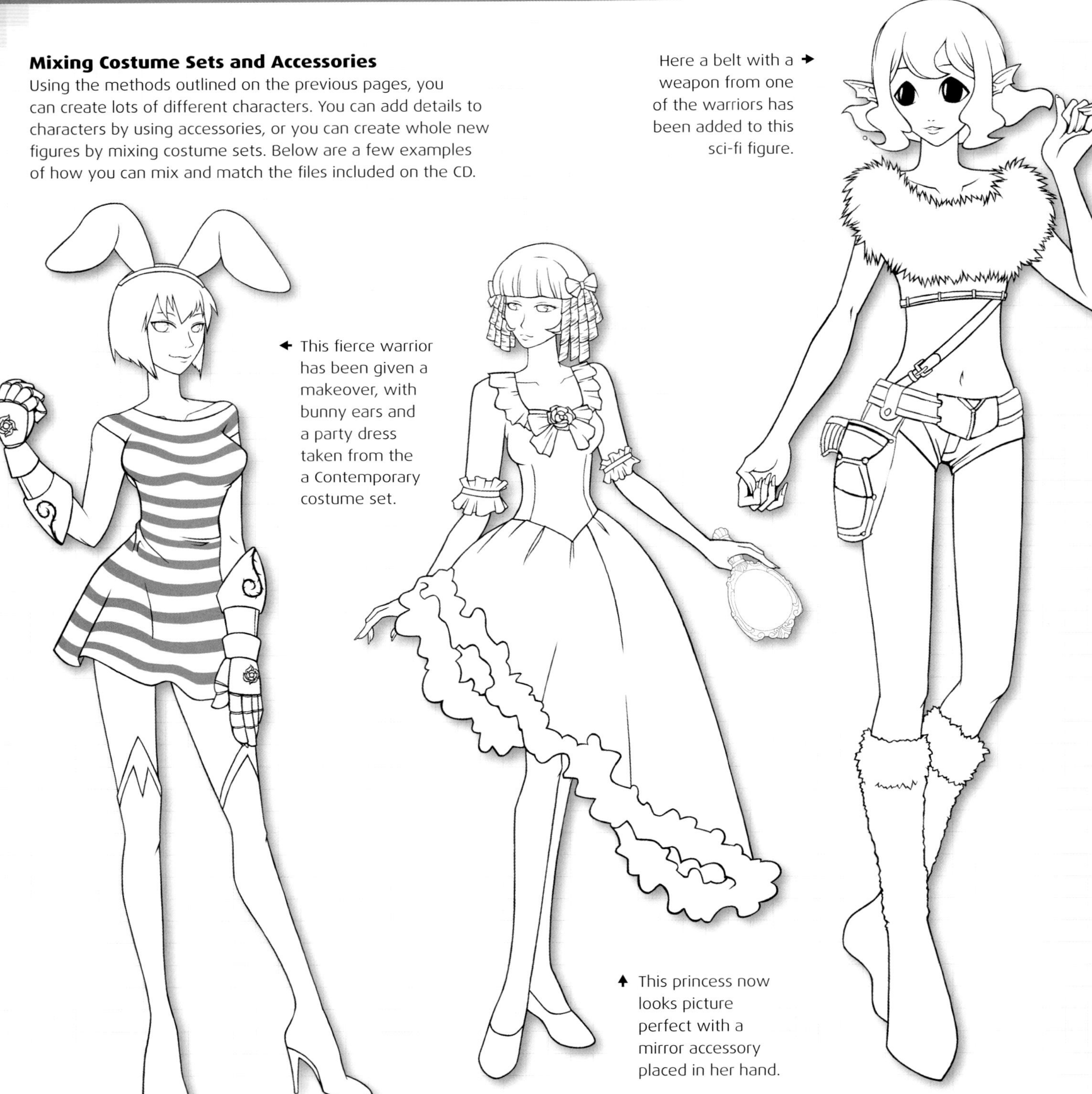

Here a belt with a weapon from one of the warriors has been added to this sci-fi figure.

This fierce warrior has been given a makeover, with bunny ears and a party dress taken from the a Contemporary costume set.

This princess now looks picture perfect with a mirror accessory placed in her hand.

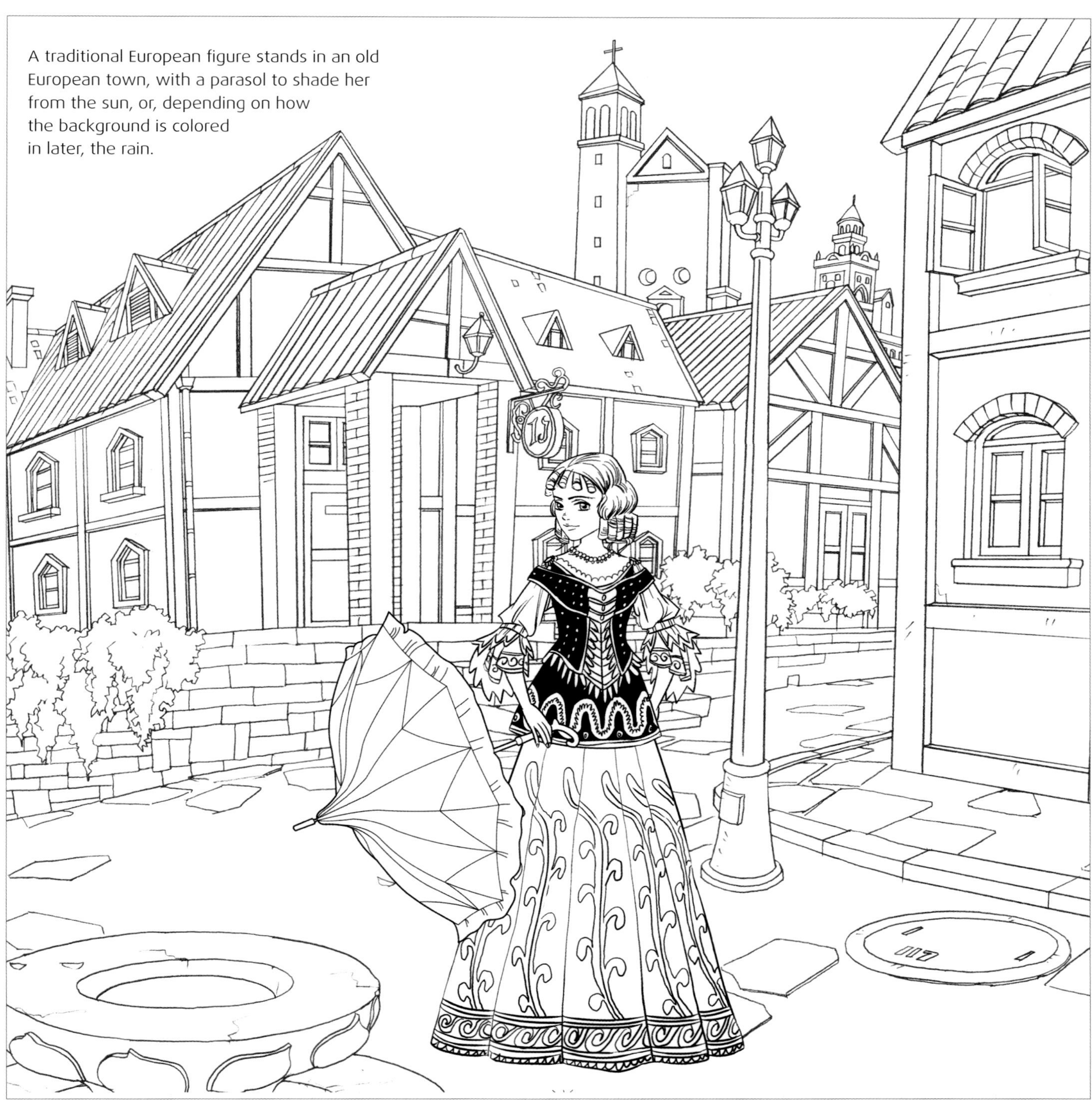

A traditional European figure stands in an old European town, with a parasol to shade her from the sun, or, depending on how the background is colored in later, the rain.

CHOOSING COLORS

No matter how attractive your line-art, if you choose the wrong colors to go inside those lines, your image can be ruined. Your choice of color and the effect it can have on a piece in terms of composition, design, and mood is key to creating professional-looking manga artwork.

One of the first choices you may come across when coloring your artwork is whether you should choose colors that are realistic and believable, or colors that simply look the part. Of course, in the world of manga, these lines can often become blurred. Take hair for example: in the context of manga, bright pink hair doesn't seem odd at all!

However, no matter how radical (or how realistic) your tastes, it's always helpful to know a little of the theory behind the color process. Certain colors will naturally complement others, and these will make your images more successful.

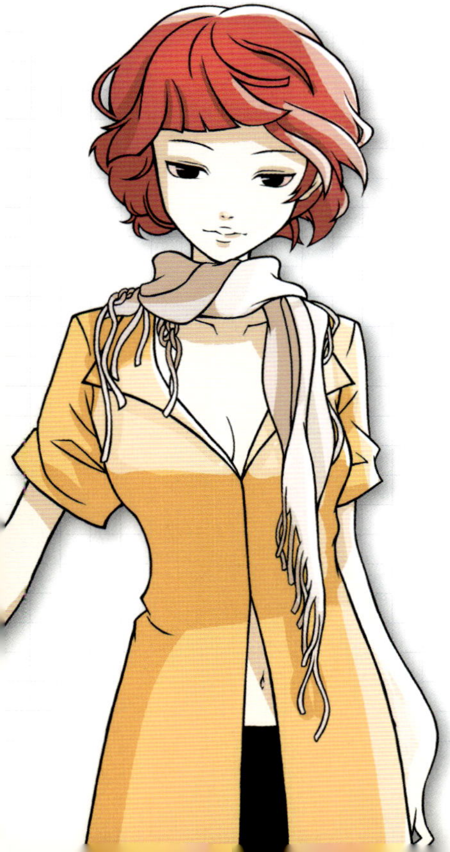

The effect of a chosen color can range from evoking basic emotions to stimulating thought. For example, mixing red, white, and blue in a piece—even when not in the shape of a flag—subtly suggests British, American, or French nationality.

The colors in your piece can also speak volumes about the mood of the character captured within. Here are just a few examples of how colors can directly reflect or provoke a mood: **Red, orange, and yellow** are warm colors. They tend to suggest warmth, passion, or even danger. Our mind associates them instantly with fire or the sun. The color red, however, can suggest far more. It is the color of choice for warning signs, and neon lighting in certain morally dubious areas of town.

Blue, green, and purple are the cool colors. They can be soothing because of what they represent; green makes us think of nature, blue can denote the sky or the sea. However, blue can also show coldness, loneliness, and depression. It can sum up many negative emotions. Purple tends to represent something with more of an "edge" and is a relatively eccentric color. It can also be a symbol of wealth or nobility.

Finally, the neutral colors (**gray, beige, and brown**) can create a subtle and toned-down image. However, they are sometimes more effective when used to contrast the more vibrant colors in an image.

Design

How you choose to combine colors is one of the main factors in giving your work a unique style. Sometimes you may simply want your character to wear a realistic, modern outfit. In that case, you are unlikely to want to use any color scheme that is too garish or clashing. Other times (and more frequently in manga) you may want to try something radical!

Don't feel that you should even be limited to conventional coloring styles. Try coloring an entire image in varying shades of just one color and see what kind of effects you can create.

The Three Golden Rules of Coloring

Research

If you are attempting to create a realistic piece, be sure that your colors suit the genre or timescale of your image. If your piece is a historical one, you will need to consider the common color schemes of the era.

Design

When coloring an outfit, try to make sure that a design element is present. For example, if a character wears a red scarf, perhaps she would have matching red shoes or ribbons on her socks? A little consistency, even in the craziest color scheme, can add professionalism to an image.

Have Fun!

What you see here are the theories and starting points to help you choose which colors you want to use. Experiment and capture your own style and remember that coloring can be a long process, but very rewarding in the end.

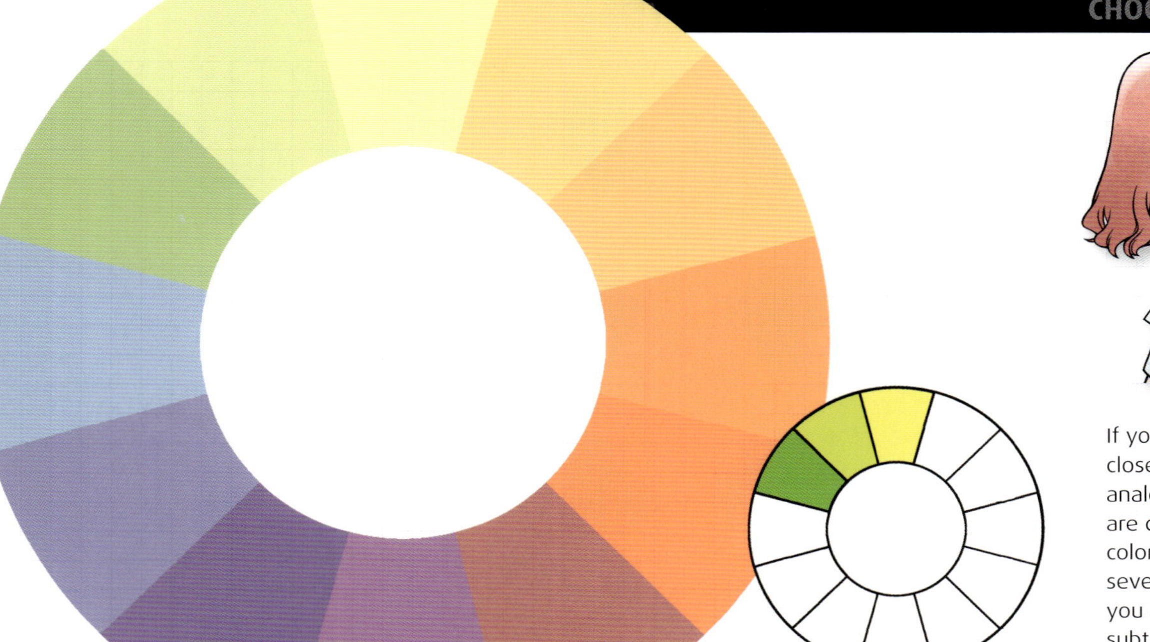

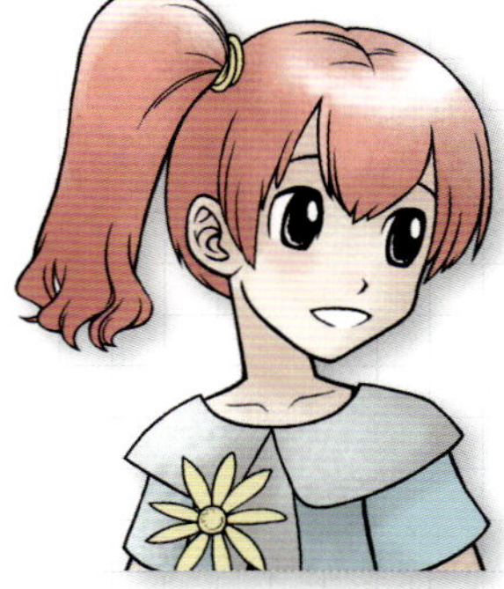

Primary
Most people think of the primary colors as red, blue, and yellow. More accurately, they are cyan, magenta, and yellow. These colors can be combined to create any single color of the spectrum.

Secondary
Fewer people may be aware of the secondary colors: orange, purple, and green. Each can be made by mixing two of the primary colors together.

Tertiary
Finally, we move on to the tertiary colors: yellow-orange, red-orange, red-purple, blue-purple, blue-green, and yellow-green. Each of these colors can be created using one primary and one secondary color.

By putting all of these colors into a color wheel, we are given a simple overview of color and can quickly see which colors should be used in conjunction with others.

If you want colors that relate closely to each other, choose analogous colors—colors that are close together on the color wheel. By choosing several analogous shades, you can achieve a more subtle color scheme.

For something a little more daring, try complementary colors. By choosing two colors that are directly opposite each other on the color wheel, you can achieve some incredible contrast and vibrancy. However, be careful not to make your scheme too garish when trying out this style.

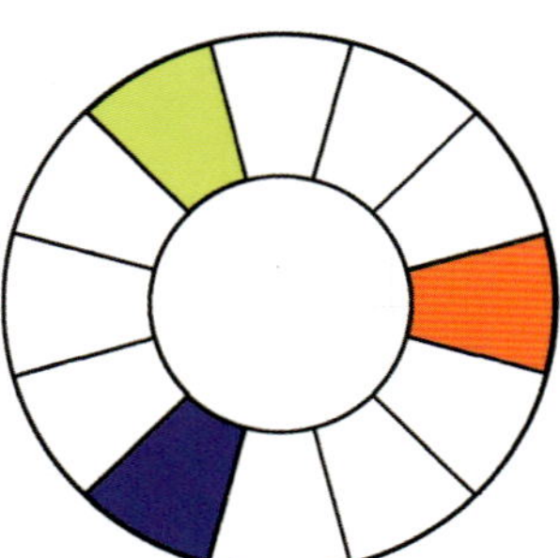

Lastly, there is the triadic color scheme. As the name suggests, the idea here is to choose three colors that are evenly spaced on the wheel. One way to use this is to choose two colors to form the basic color scheme, and add a third as an occasional highlight for accent and depth. This works well because that third color will be equally different to each of the base colors.

BLOCKING IN BASE COLORS

Once you've created your character, the next step is to block in the base colors. Filling in base colors is the first and most important stage of coloring as it is when you pick the dominant shades to use in your picture. Think about the kind of mood you want to create. Do you want to use lots of soft, pale colors, or strong, bold hues? The colors you choose now will affect the shades you use for shading and highlights, no matter what coloring method you choose to follow afterward. These colors create a foundation, or in some cases can be all the picture needs to look complete.

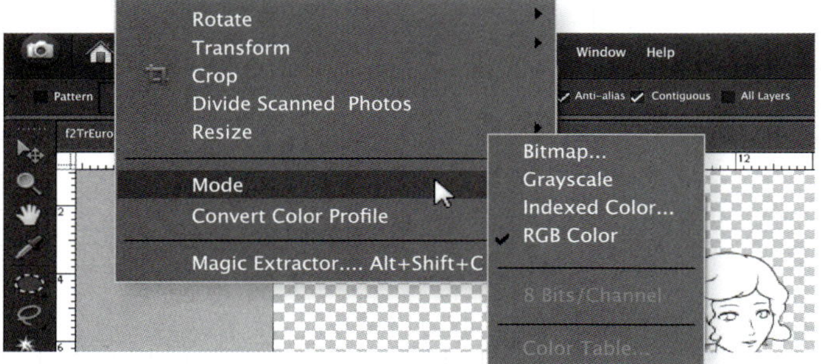

1 You might find that your line-art is in Monochrome or Grayscale mode. In either case, you will not be able to apply color or, if you do so, it will appear as a shade of gray. To solve this, click *Image > Mode > RGB Color*, which will give you a theoretical palette of 16.8 million colors.

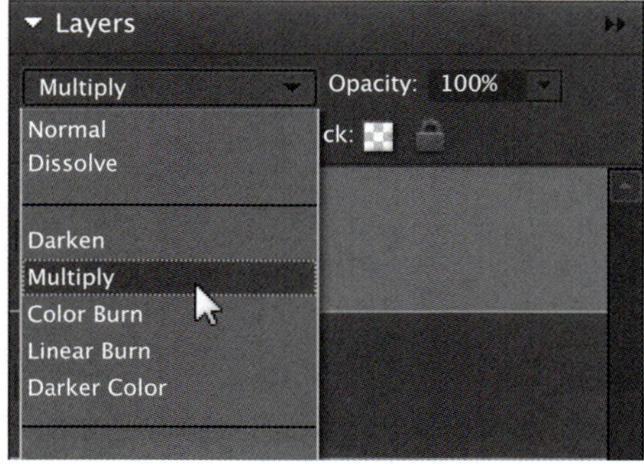
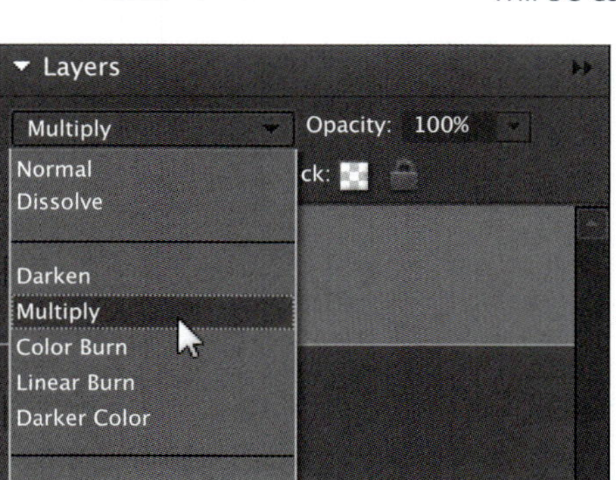

2 Save your file somewhere on your own computer's hard disc using the *File > Save As* command.

3 Prepare your line-art by first copying it to a new layer. Set this layer's blend mode to Multiply. This will allow the colors on layers beneath to show through the layer above.

4 Create a new layer beneath the line-art layer, and keep the blend mode set to Normal. This will be used for colors.

5 Make a new layer and place it beneath the base color layer. Fill the entire page with a pastel color (light blues and greens are often best). This will help make it easier to spot any gaps in your coloring.

6 Choose the Paint Bucket tool, and make sure the settings have Anti-aliased unchecked, Contiguous checked, and All Layers checked. Set the Tolerance to a small amount (such as 32) so that neighboring areas are not filled in by mistake.

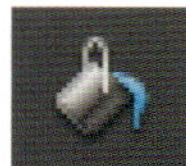

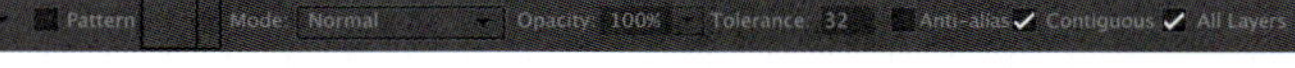

Tip

Rapid Color Swapping with the "X" and *Alt* Keys
Most of the time when you are coloring, you will only be using two colors at a time. By using the "X" button to alternate between foreground and background color, you can have a "spare" color available at any time. Also, it's often worth using the *Alt* key to quickly pick up colors from other areas of the picture—this can help to make sure your picture is coordinated, and also minimizes the need for the Color Picker window.

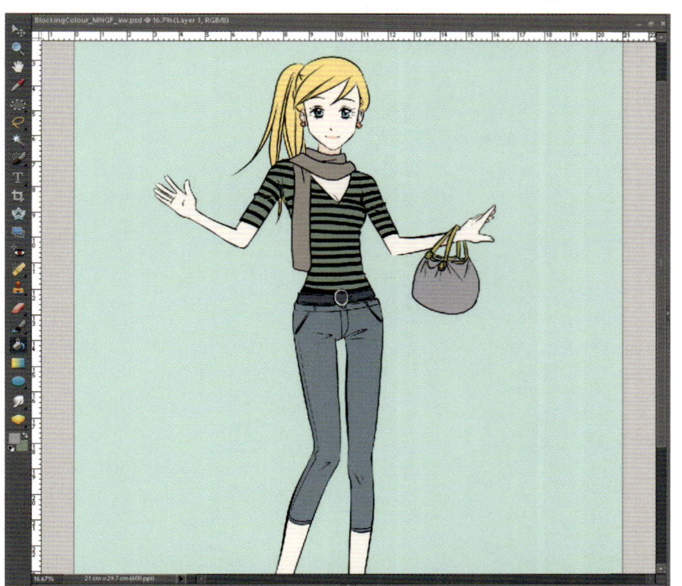

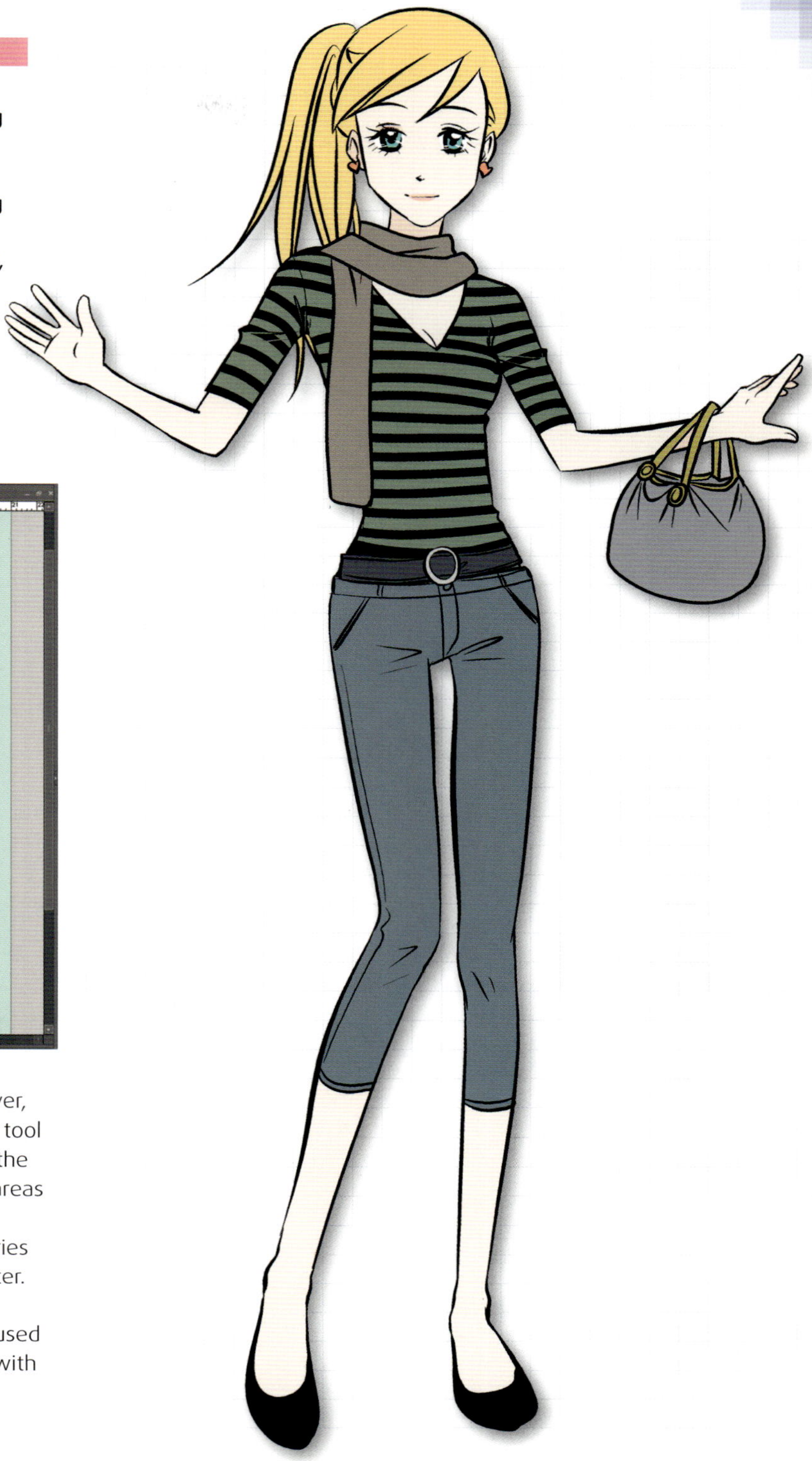

7 On the base color layer, use the Paint Bucket tool to color each section of the image. Color the larger areas first, like hair, skin, and clothes, leaving accessories and other extras until later. This way it's easier to complement the colors used on the clothes and hair with the accessories.

8 Now select the Pencil tool to begin adding detail. If there are any difficult-to-fill areas or small gaps in coloring, use the Pencil tool to color them carefully. Often eyebrows and strands of hair are problem areas.

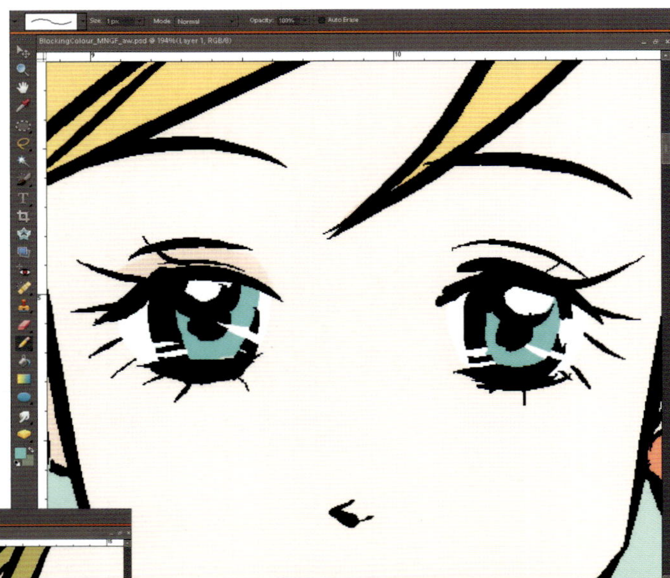

9 Some parts of the image may not have each part of the body fully defined in the line-art. By using the Pencil tool, you can add colors to the image very precisely, sectioning off parts of the picture or making areas more vivid.

10 When your base colors are complete you can proceed to add shading to the image.

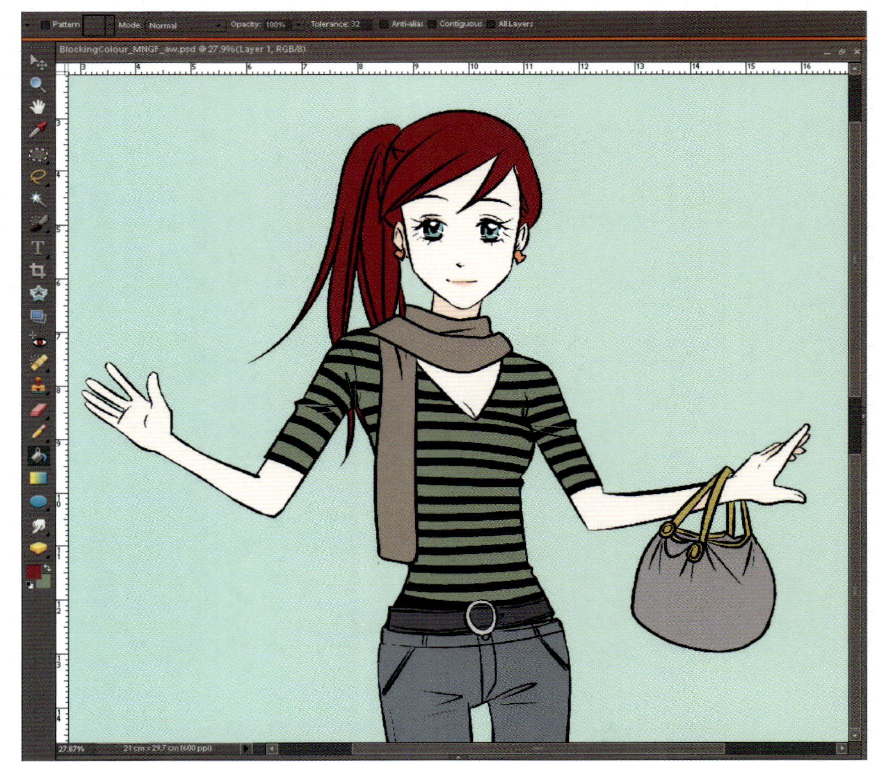

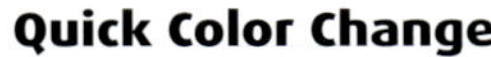

Quick Color Change

If you decide you don't like a color you've used, but you've already finished the base colors, you can still change it easily with the Fill tool. Uncheck the Contiguous box on the toolbox, and with one click you can replace the unwanted color with a different shade.

Using Contiguous to Speed Up Coloring

Some image areas can be quite complicated to color, with many small areas that would take a long time to fill in with a Brush or the Paint Bucket. The Contiguous setting in the Paint Bucket options can make this easier. By turning Contiguous off, you can fill entire areas with color very quickly, even though it will flood outside of the area you wish to color. Using the selection tool to choose small areas of the image, you can use the Paint Bucket without Contiguous to fill an area, then turn Contiguous back on to correct the areas where the color was not wanted.

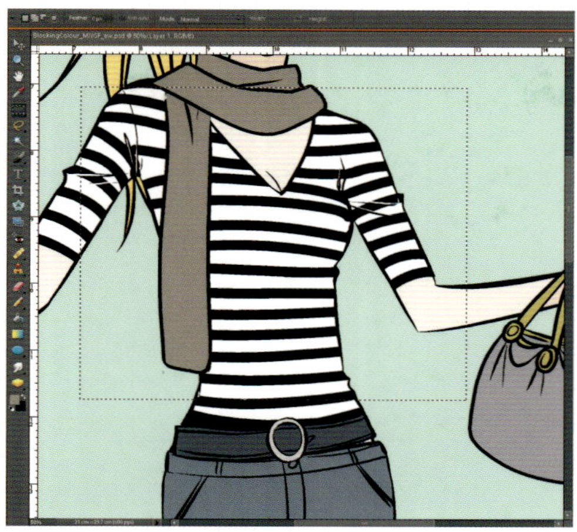

1 Select the rough area you wish to fill in using one of the selection tools—here I've used the Rectangular Selection tool.

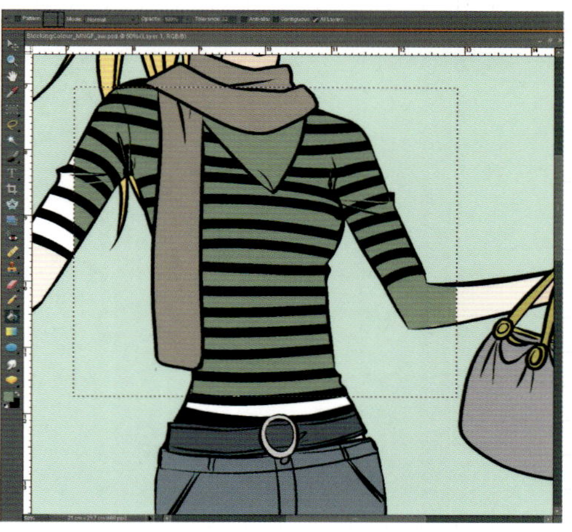

2 Use the Paint Bucket with Contiguous unchecked to fill in the green.

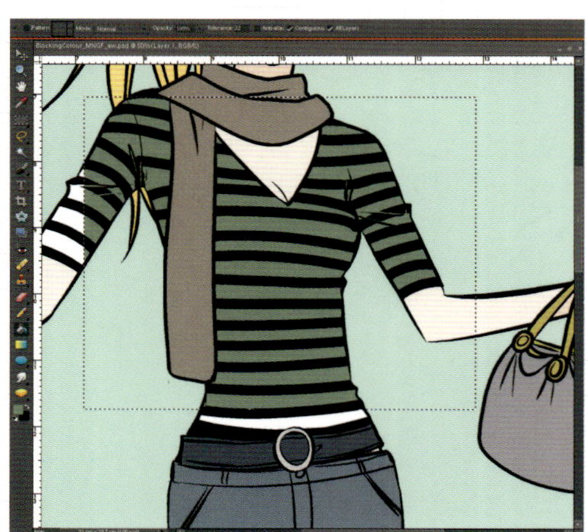

3 Turn Contiguous back on, and fix the excess green. This way we've avoided clicking between every contiguous shape in the stripy T-shirt, and only clicked once to fill the larger green area.

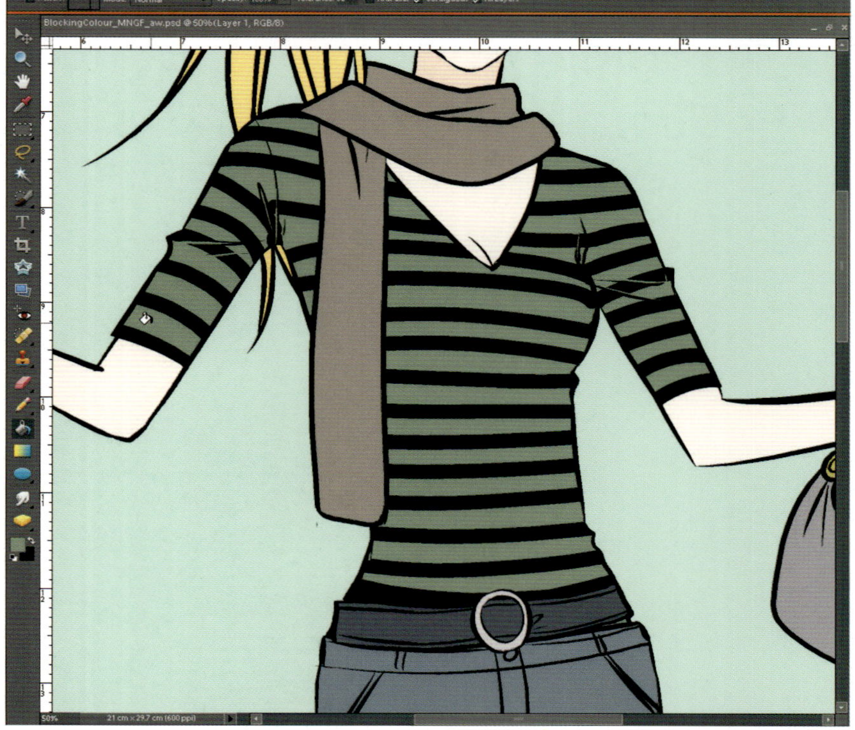

CEL SHADING

Cel shading refers to the style of using flat block colors to represent areas of light and shadow on a picture. This relates to the use of animation cels in Japanese anime, and the way that colors are used to define depth. The use of darker and lighter tones to define shape and shadow was so unique and distinctive that it became intrinsically associated with Japanese animation. Although some Western studios have adopted the technique since, it is still something that helps to make authentic-looking anime-style characters.

The appearance of cel-style shading is very easy to emulate using Photoshop. By making the most of layers, it is possible to achieve a high-quality look very quickly. The time can be spent focusing on the details rather than getting the overall cel look to work effectively.

Finally, cel shading is often the basis for many other visual styles, such as airbrush or natural media, and acts as the basis of lighting for most images. Time spent on the cel-shading process will improve the look of any image, regardless of the style you use for the final piece.

Original
This snowman has no shading, just simple base colors. The most important aspect of cel shading is understanding how light falls, and how the shape of an object will affect the shading.

Shading
The lightest parts of an object are those that face the light source, and the darkest parts are those that face away from the light. Unless the light source is very small and weak (such as the glow from a TV screen or a flickering flame) the light will affect the object equally. In other words, about the same amount of light falls on all the areas that point toward the light. The light source on this snowman is originating from the top left, so any areas facing away from there have been shaded more darkly.

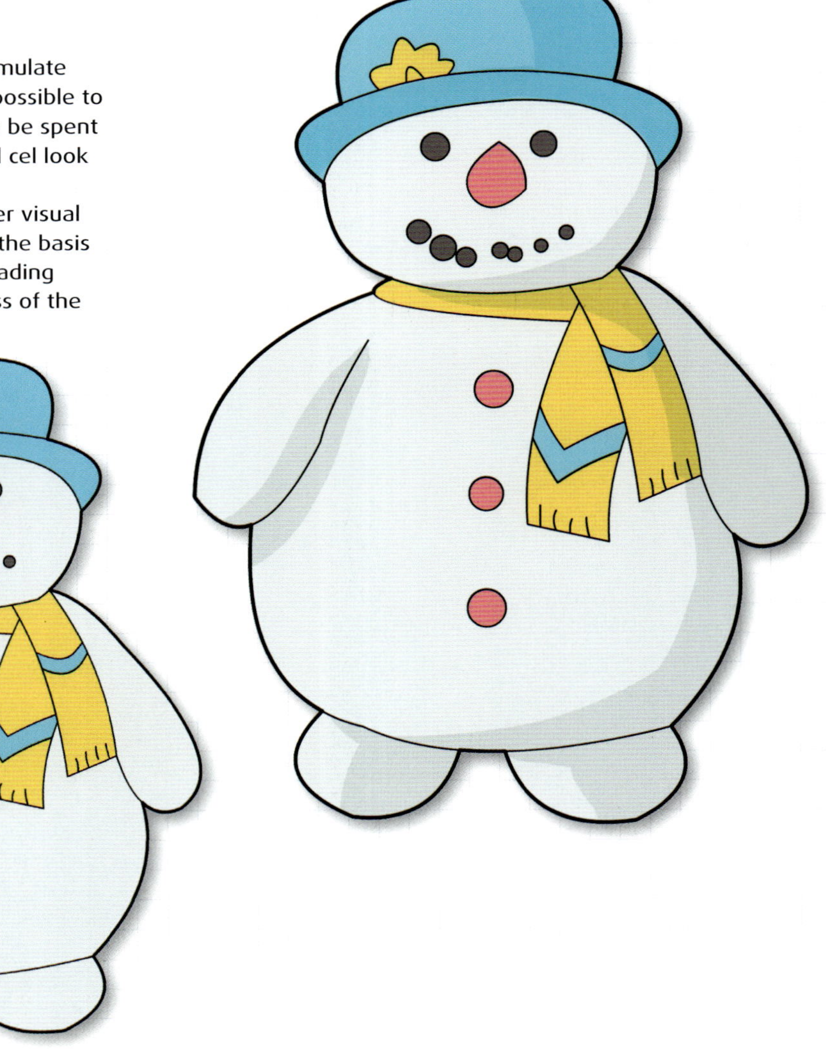

Shadows

Effective definition of shadows can make all the difference to how "solid" your picture looks. When objects in a scene are obviously affecting one another, your picture becomes more believable.

Firstly, the snowman now casts a shadow onto the floor. The shape of his body has been defined, and the arms can be seen in the shadow too. Secondly, the snowman is also casting shadows on himself. You can see how the facial features are blocking the light from his face and the two legs are not directly lit at all. It's easy for objects to cast shadows on themselves, so you need to be aware of this.

Highlights

Highlights are only necessary on shiny materials, and can be used to a greater or lesser degree depending on the effect that is desired. In this image, highlights have been added from the main light source. However, some additional highlights have been added in the opposite direction, implying some sort of other light source nearby. This style of "backlight" is quite a popular method to give an object more volume.

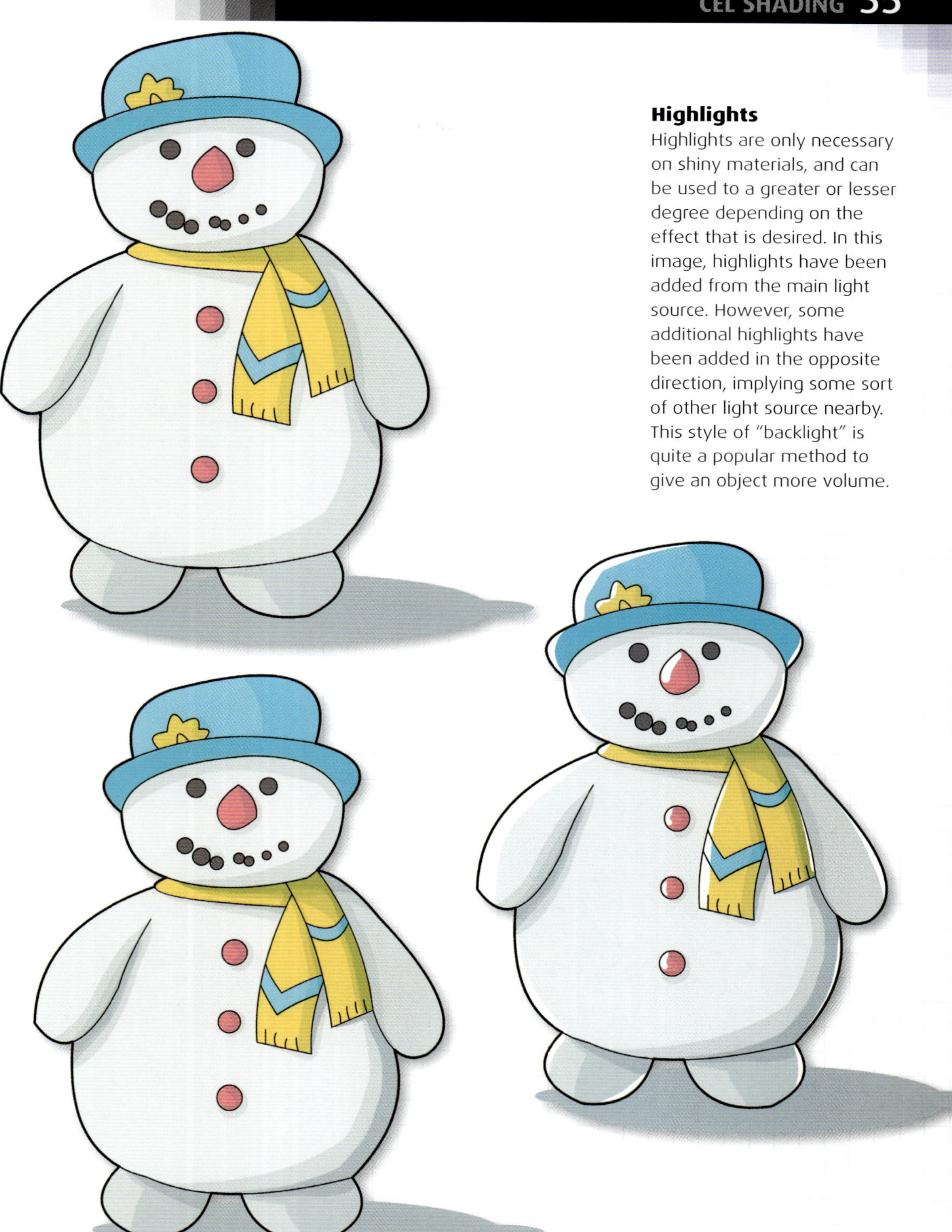

Dark Shadows

With shiny materials such as plastic or skin (in some instances), you may wish to further define the shadows. Giving these areas a heavier shadow can help to define the shape of the object more vividly.

Applying Basic Cel Shading

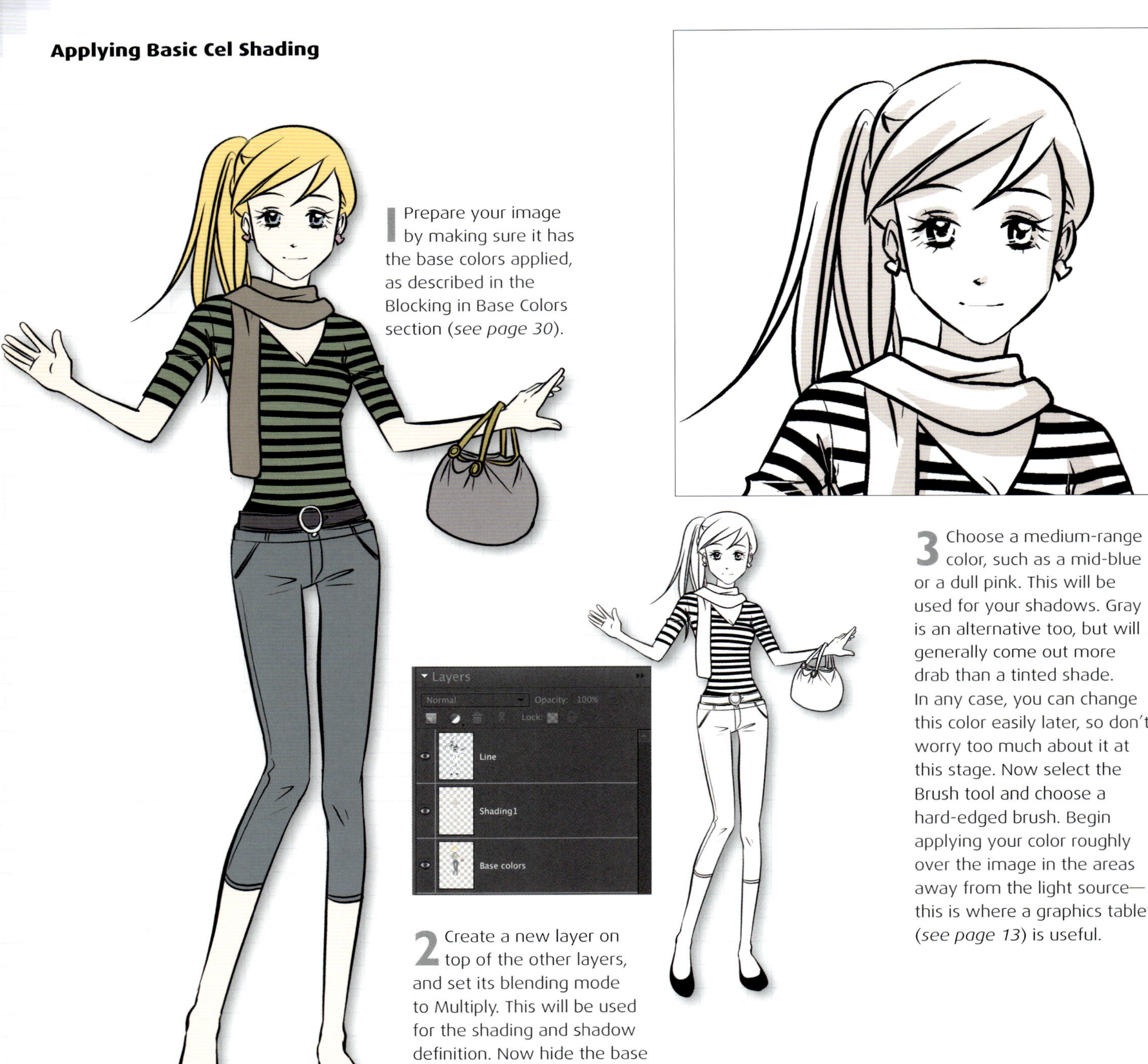

1 Prepare your image by making sure it has the base colors applied, as described in the Blocking in Base Colors section (*see page 30*).

2 Create a new layer on top of the other layers, and set its blending mode to Multiply. This will be used for the shading and shadow definition. Now hide the base color layer of the image, so the line-art is visible against a white background.

3 Choose a medium-range color, such as a mid-blue or a dull pink. This will be used for your shadows. Gray is an alternative too, but will generally come out more drab than a tinted shade. In any case, you can change this color easily later, so don't worry too much about it at this stage. Now select the Brush tool and choose a hard-edged brush. Begin applying your color roughly over the image in the areas away from the light source—this is where a graphics tablet (*see page 13*) is useful.

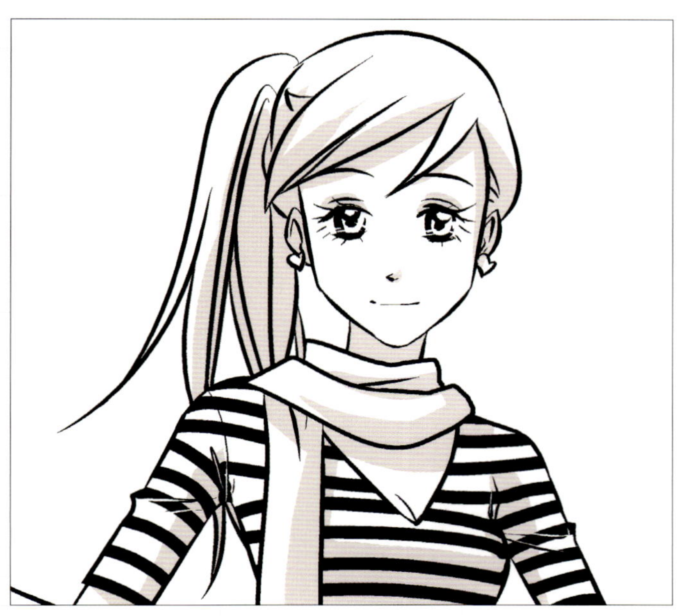

4 Using either the Eraser tool or the Brush tool set to white, clean up the image and add definition to the shading. Remember to pay close attention to areas that cast shadow, such as the nose and eye sockets.

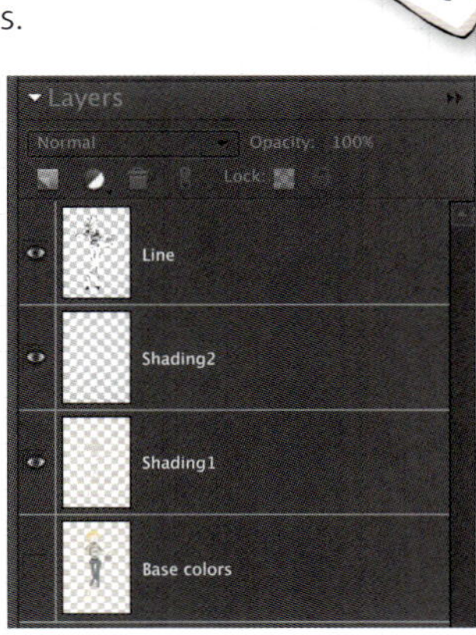

5 By choosing a darker shade of the same color, certain dark areas can be defined more heavily.

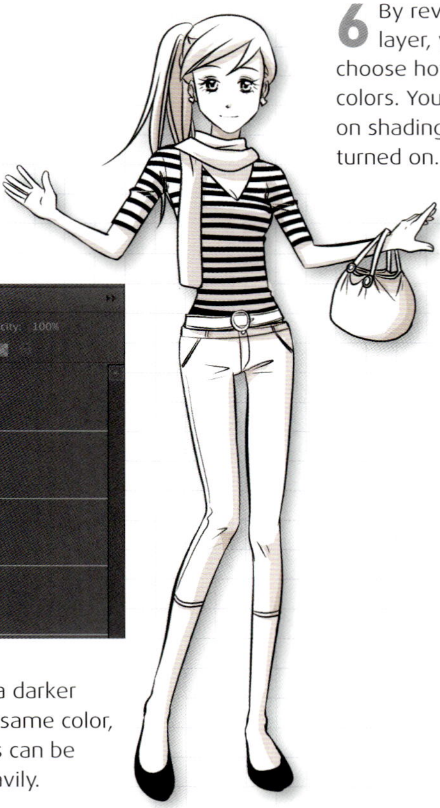

6 By revealing the color layer, you can now choose how to adjust your colors. You can easily work on shading with the colors turned on.

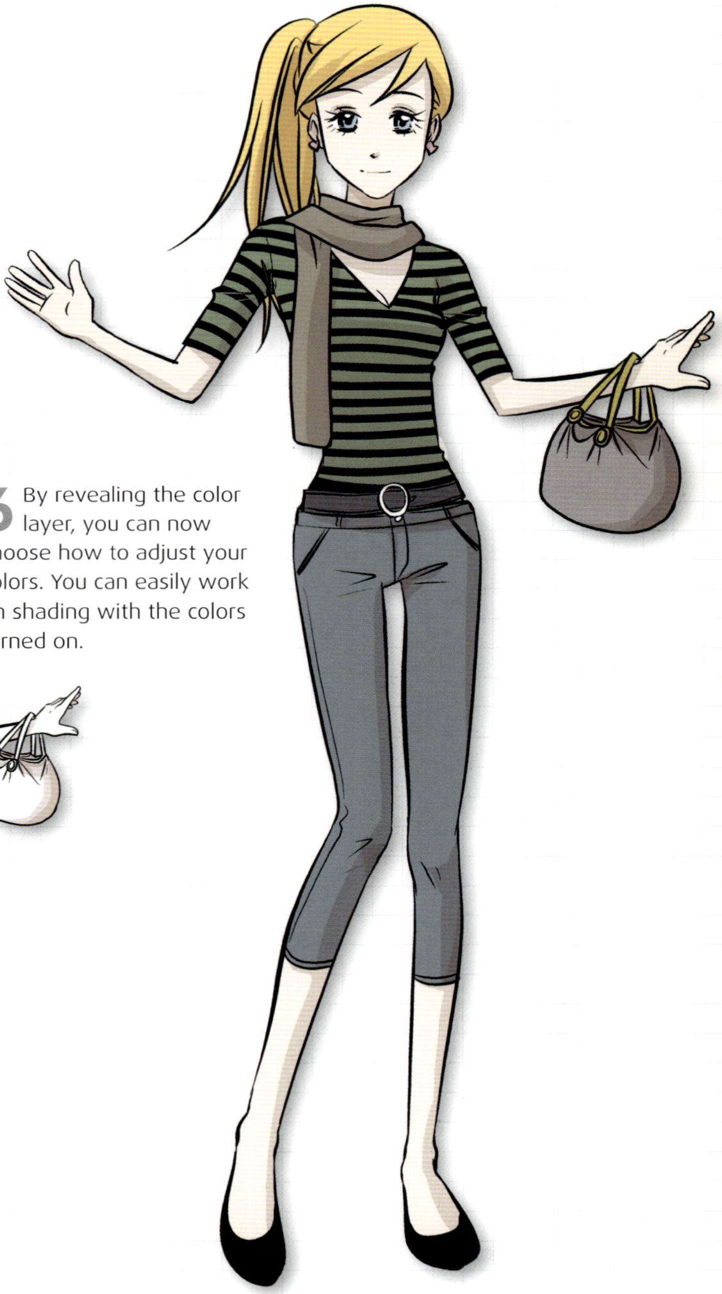

Adding Highlights

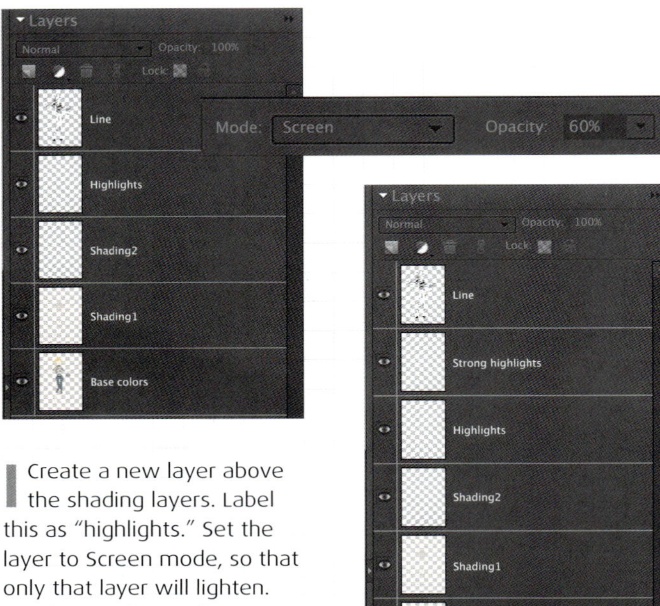

1 Create a new layer above the shading layers. Label this as "highlights." Set the layer to Screen mode, so that only that layer will lighten. Set the opacity to about 60%.

3 Create another layer, labeled "strong highlights." Leave this at 100% opacity.

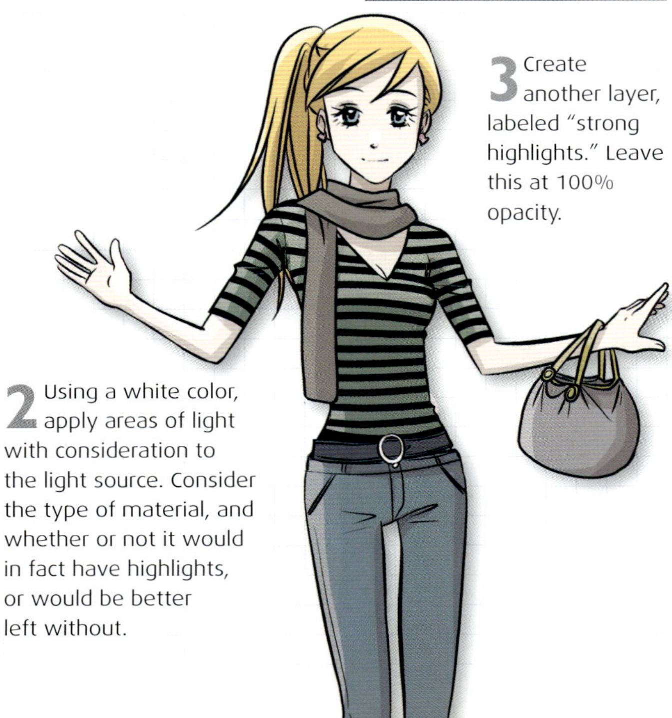

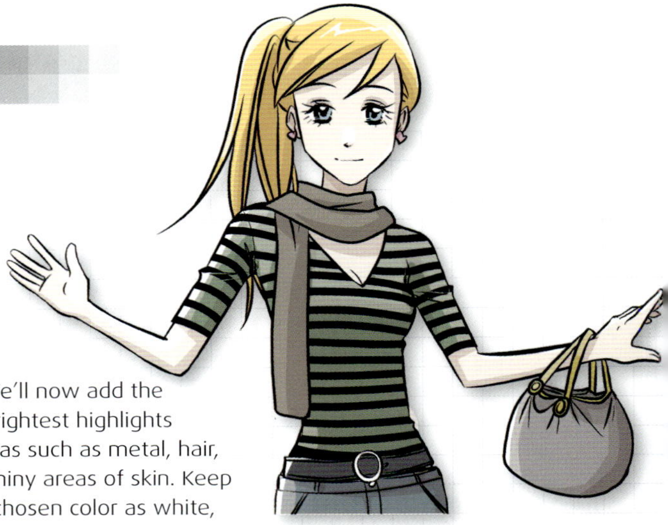

2 Using a white color, apply areas of light with consideration to the light source. Consider the type of material, and whether or not it would in fact have highlights, or would be better left without.

4 We'll now add the brightest highlights to areas such as metal, hair, and shiny areas of skin. Keep your chosen color as white, and begin to add small dots, lines, and "glints" of white light to areas that would especially pick up the light.

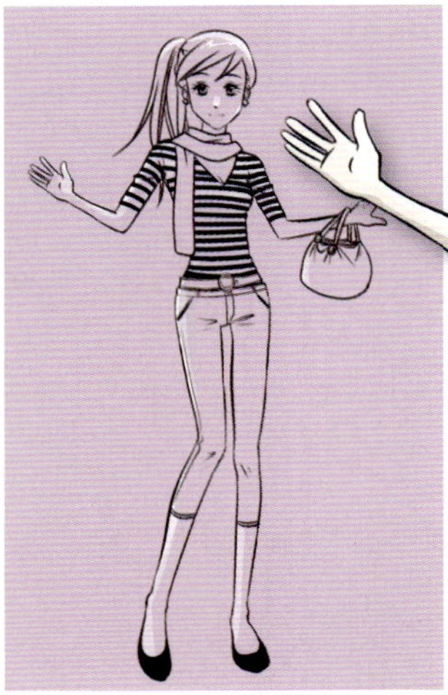

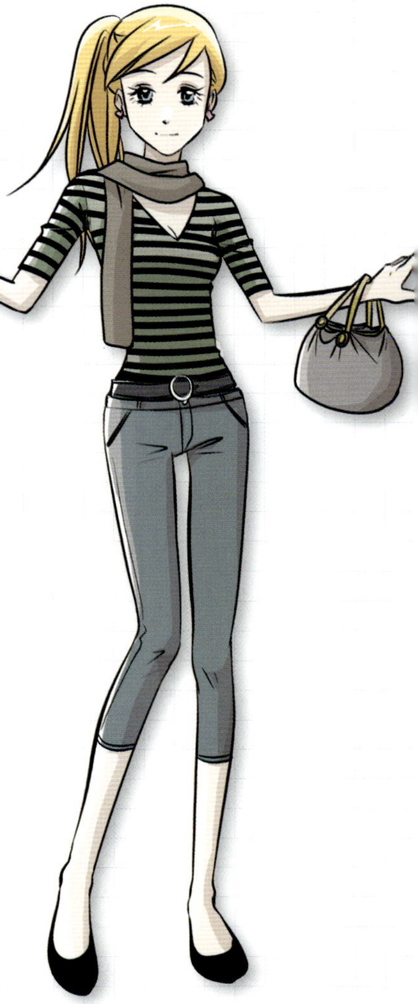

5 As with the shading, it is possible to turn off the color layer's visibility to check that your shading is accurate and that no areas have been accidentally missed. You can create a background layer filled with a pastel color to check this.

6 Finally, turn on all the layers to see it finished.

Fine-Tuning Your Colors

Although using layer types such as Screen and Multiply is great for speeding up the process of shading and highlighting, sometimes the results aren't entirely satisfactory. You can fine-tune the colors afterward.

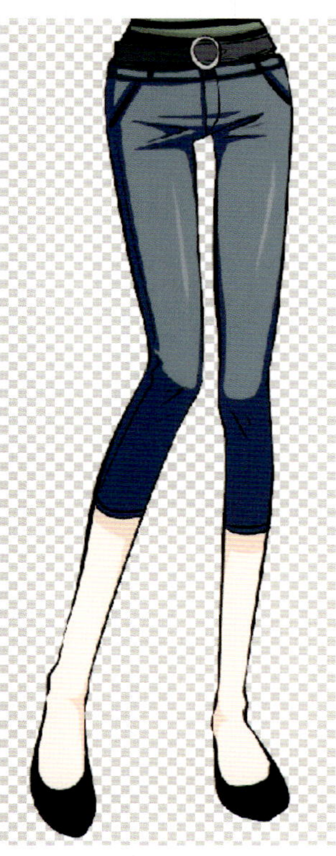

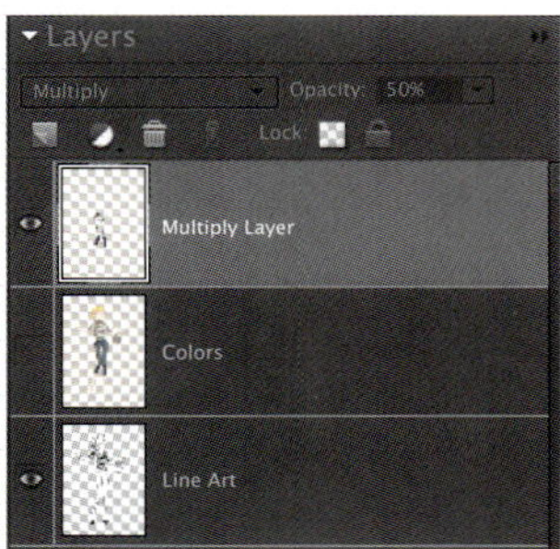

Change the Shade of Your Multiply Area to Contrast with the Color Beneath

Although a blue Multiply layer (the shadows layer) will look very striking against purple, sometimes it simply won't have the same impact against similarly toned areas (such as blue shading against blue jeans).

Tolerance: 5 anti-alias Contiguous All Layers

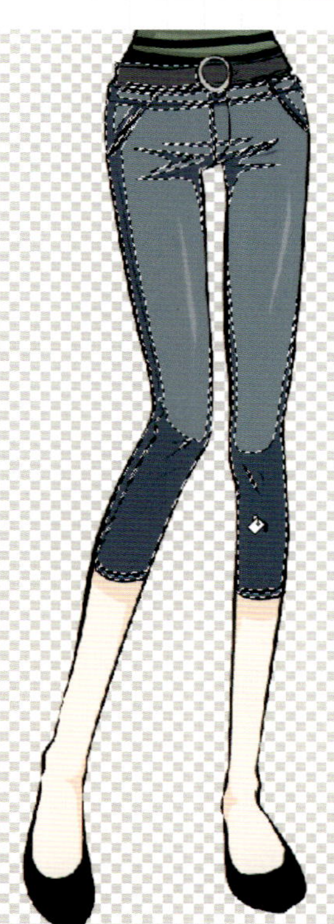

Select the shading layer, choose the Paint Bucket tool, and turn on Contiguous and All Layers, with the Tolerance set very low. Choose a color to contrast with the area and fill in the area. You can repeat this until you find a color that creates the right effect. Selecting the section with the Magic Wand and then altering it with the Adjust Hue slider can also be a great way to achieve this effect.

Tip

Using Additional Layers

If you use separate layers for each level of highlight, you can easily fine-tune the results by using the Opacity setting to make some layers more "see-through."

Highlights for Eyes

The representation of eyes in manga is possibly the most striking aspect of the genre. Typically renowned for its characters' glossy, saucer-sized eyes, even manga styles with smaller eyes devote of lot of attention to this area. Highlights and detail on eyes can make all the difference to any manga-style picture. Even a flat-colored picture can be improved hugely with some extra detail in the eyes.

- The center of the eye should be a darker color than the rest of the eye, giving a sense of depth.
- Highlights should be drawn at both the top and the bottom of the eye, just as you would with a glass or metallic object.
- You may wish to create a layer above the line-art, and draw your highlights over this. Failing that, you can just delete parts of your line-art if you think the definition is too heavy.

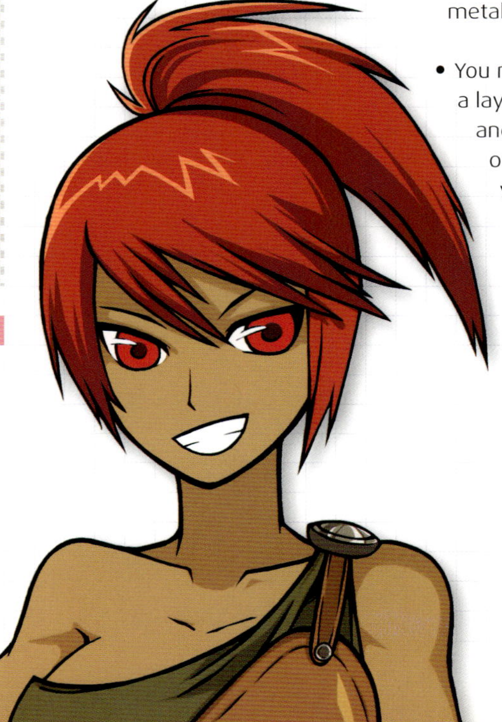

AIRBRUSH TECHNIQUE

Before computers were used to produce artwork, people often used airbrushes to create gradients and soft transitions between different colors. Rather than just using solid tones, lighting can be represented as a smooth blend between light and dark.

Thankfully, this method of painting is very easy in Adobe Photoshop, Photoshop Elements, and other digital painting software. By using "soft brushes" (with or without the dedicated Airbrush setting) it's possible to emulate this look accurately, yet still allow for the artwork to be adjusted.

1	3	5	9	13	19
5	9	13	17	21	27
35	45	65	100	200	300
9	13	19	17	45	65

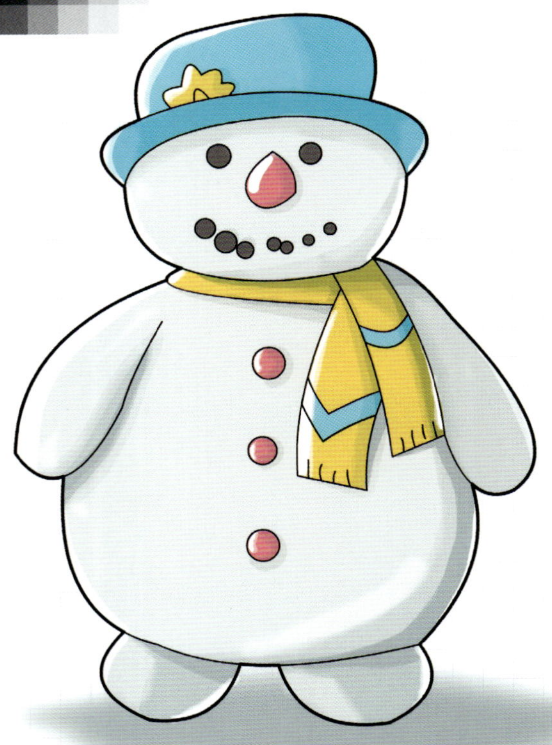

Using Cel Shading as a Basis

As airbrush technique follows the same fundamental rules as cel shading, often it is best to start off with the same solid shading. Remember to pay attention to the direction of light, and define the volume of the character.

Soft Brushes

For an airbrush technique the use of soft brushes is crucial. These are represented as circles that become lighter toward the edge. The larger the brush, the softer the gradient will be. Therefore changing the size of the brush using the "[" and "]" keys can have an apparent effect on the presently selected brush's softness, though holding *Shift* and pressing "[" or "]" will affect it without changing the size of the brush (*see page 18*).

Use of Airbrush Style

An airbrush style is typically used to soften the highlights based upon the direction of the main light source. This is achieved by using a soft brush and going over the shaded edge. A larger gradient implies a more gently curved surface. To see this effect in the real world, just look how the light falls on a cylinder—say an aerosol can—as opposed to a more angular item.

A popular technique is to use "rear lighting" when using airbrush methods combined with cel-style coloring. This retains the hard edge of the cel shading, but benefits from some of the softening of the airbrush, as though to imply ambient light. Using very subtle shading to simulate a rear light can be very effective in introducing curve and volume to an image without losing the charm of cel style.

By combining these two looks, an interesting use of shade can be captured, especially as the front light is much more obvious than the rear light.

Begin by softening off the shading. To do this, it's often worth creating a duplicate of your shading layer, and hiding it. This creates a backup of the color work, just in case you make any large errors.

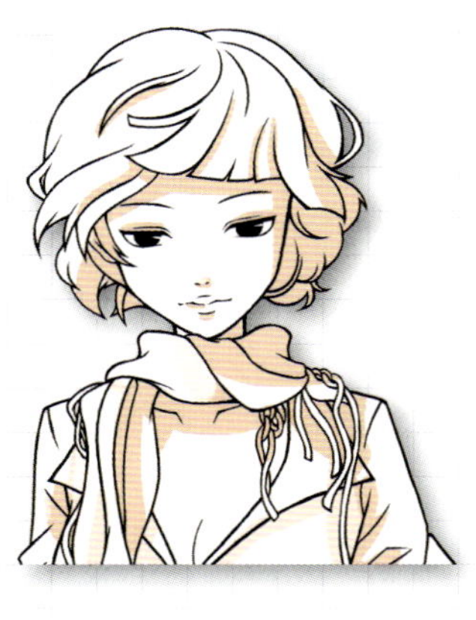

2 Using a soft white brush, or the Eraser tool with a soft head, work over the existing shading layer to lighten the edges where light falls. Hard or shiny materials will have heavy contrast, whereas soft materials such as skin will often have very soft shadows, unless they are wet.

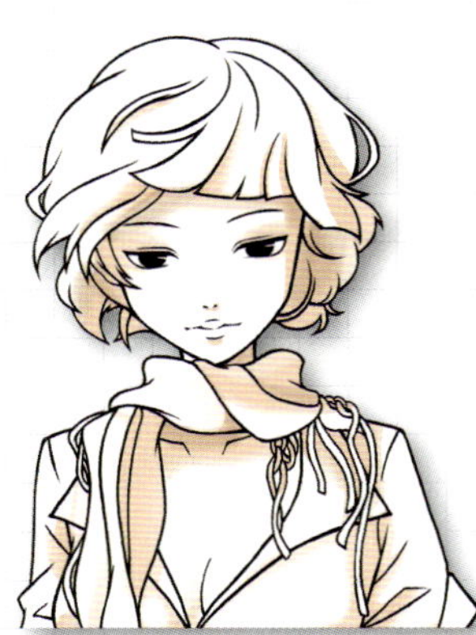

3 Adjust the opacity of your brush with the Opacity slider, or by using the number keys at the top of the keyboard. This will allow you to control how subtle your brushstrokes will be.

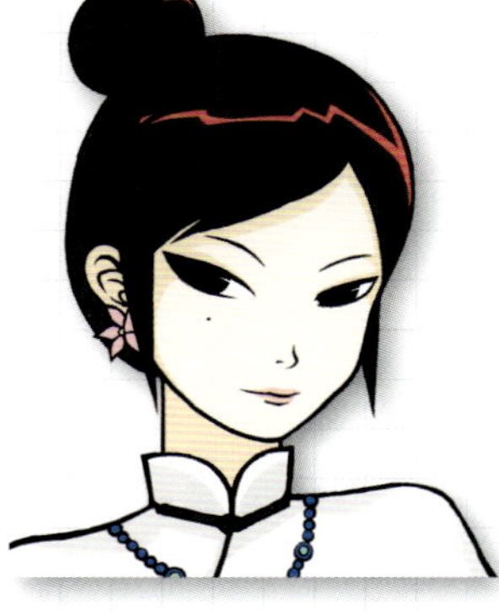

4 Shiny highlights with airbrush pictures are done in a very similar way to the highlights on a regular cel-shaded picture. By combining the methods of highlights from cel style with some of the airbrushing, you can end up with something that appears even more striking. First draw a solid block of highlight, without the definition of fabric or hair.

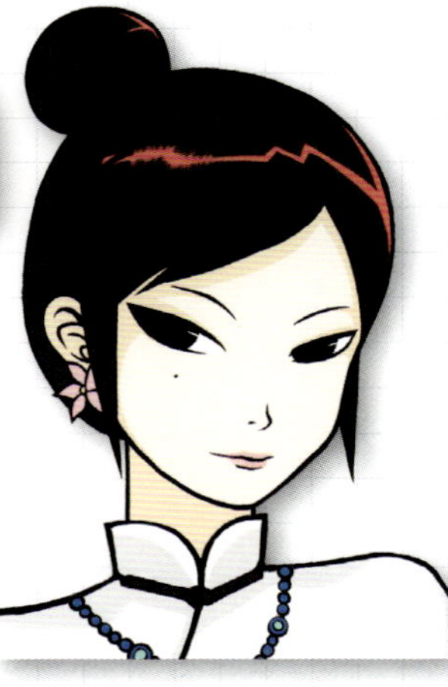

5 Use the Smudge tool to create a point in the highlight area.

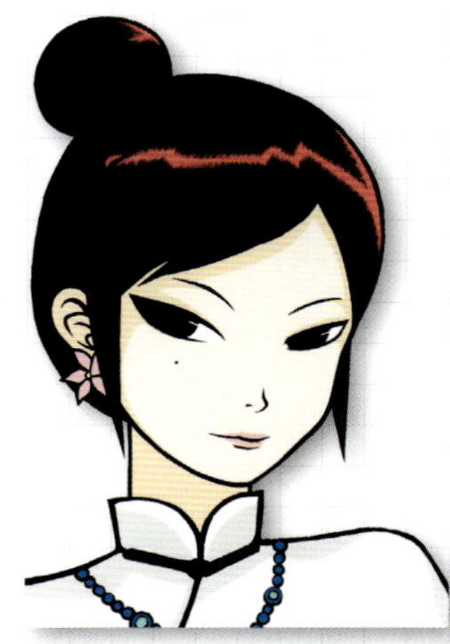

6 Move the cursor backward and forward to represent the shape of the hair.

Tip

Alternatively you can use the same cel-shaded highlight technique as before, but use a large, soft brush eraser to create a gradient. This creates a very clean and stylish look, which can even add to the shininess of the image style.

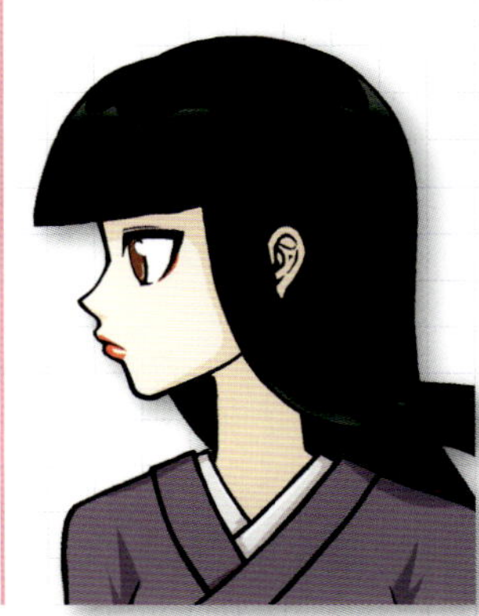

Using the Blur Filter to Soften Shading

The filters in Photoshop are very powerful tools, but overuse can often lead to an image being ruined. However, when used with subtlety and careful application, they can add greatly to the atmosphere of an image.

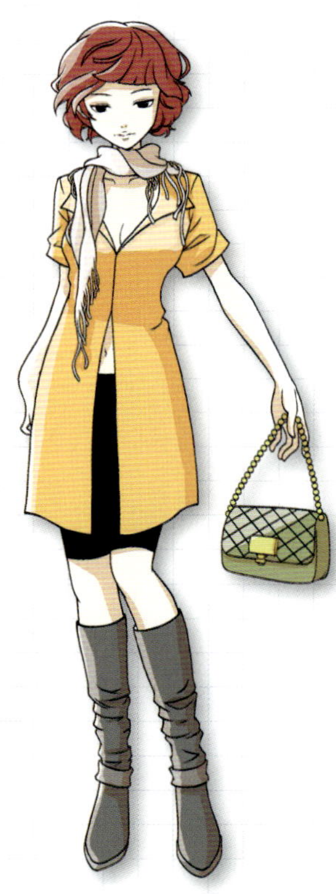

1 Choose the shading layer, use the Magic Wand selection tool and select all the white areas of the image. This will roughly select all the parts of the image that haven't got shadowing applied to them.

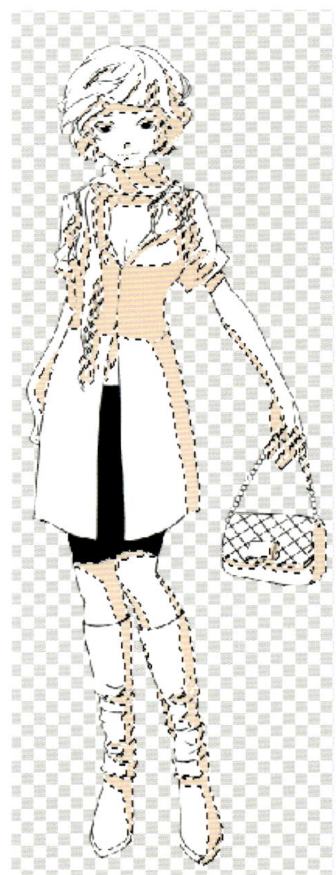

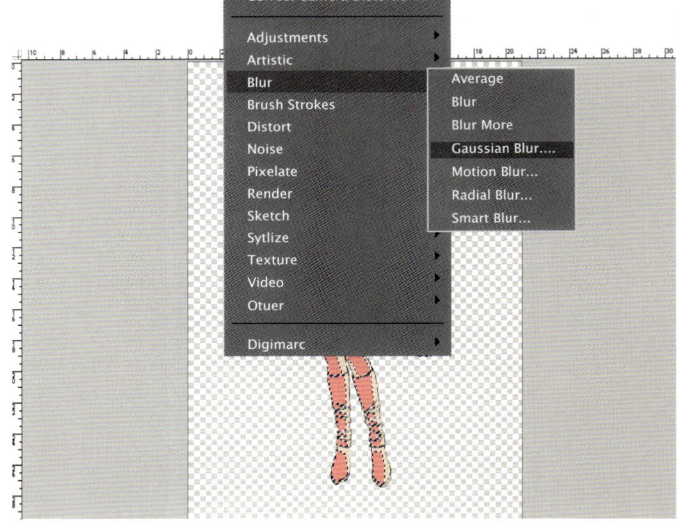

2 Create a new layer, with the layer style Overlay. Fill in the area with a color such as yellow, pink, or white (make sure All Layers and Contiguous are unchecked).

3 Using the Gaussian Blur filter, adjust the layer until it spreads out significantly. The amount you wish to blur this highlight will depend upon the look you wish to achieve. Below, for example, a radius of 75.4 is ideal for the soft light effects.

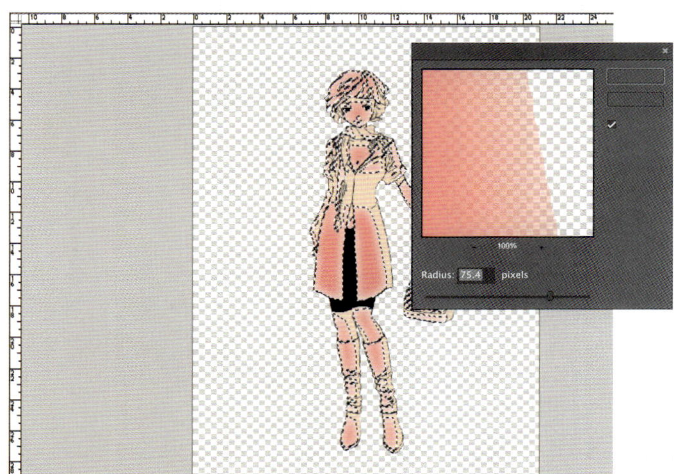

4 You can change the opacity until you're happy with the effect. It's also possible to create interesting soft shadow results by duplicating the shading layer and blurring it. You will have to experiment with the opacity of the blurred and unblurred shading layer until you get the right look, but the results can appear quite soft and interesting.

Using these airbrush techniques, you end up with a cool and stylish image.

Different Looks

With Photoshop it is very simple to quickly see different looks for your artwork. Remember that there's no correct way for your artwork to look, and try to experiment as much as possible to find the style that suits you most. (You can always go back to the previous state by pressing *Ctrl* or *Cmd* + "Z" or by using the History palette.) By adjusting the opacity of different layers, you can completely change the way that shading, highlights, and colors will affect the overall image. You can also drastically change the image by changing the color of your shading layer, using multiple blur layers, or by experimenting with the Hue, Saturation, and Lightness of the layers.

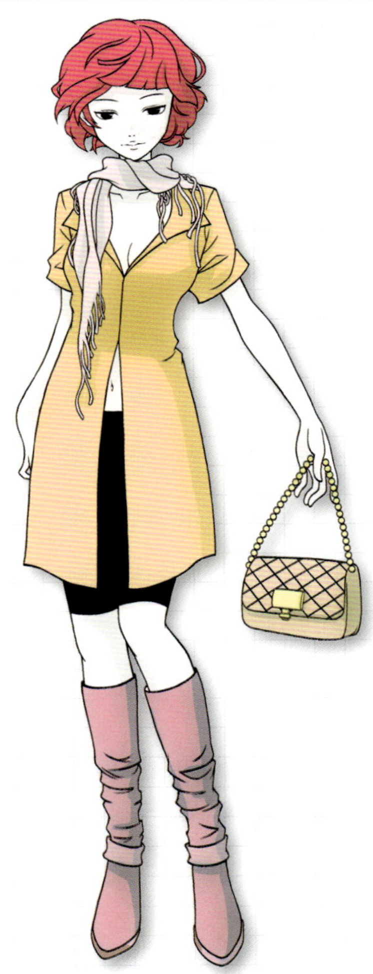

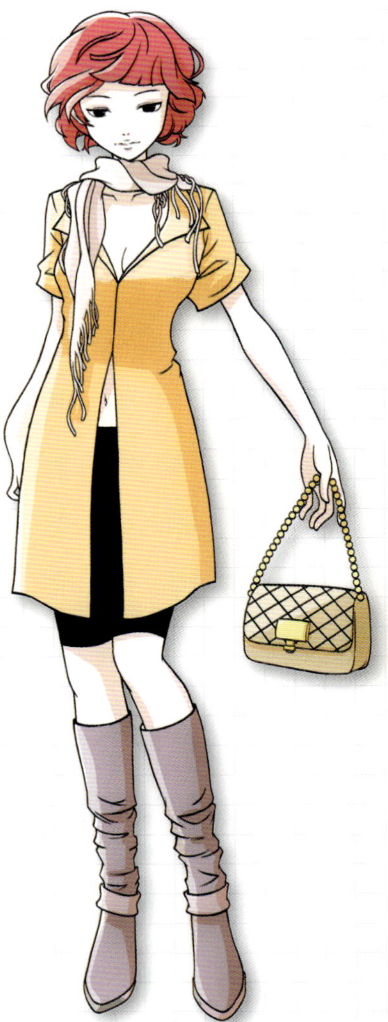

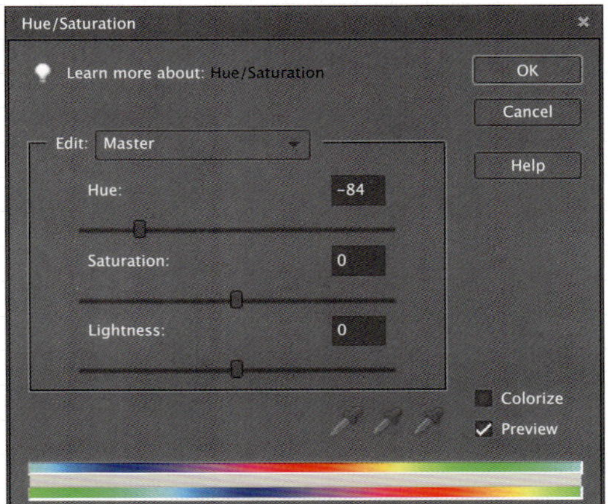

NATURAL MEDIA

Simulated natural-media coloring is popular with manga artists in both Japan and the West. Computer-generated (CG) images are generally recognized as being pixel-perfect, but natural media is a move away from that perfection, adding the textures and flaws of real paintings. As computers have become more powerful, it has become easier and more desirable to recreate complex, realistic-looking techniques that still have all the benefits and the malleability of CG artwork. There are several programs available specifically for natural media simulation, notably Corel's Painter, but you can also create similar effects in Photoshop or Photoshop Elements.

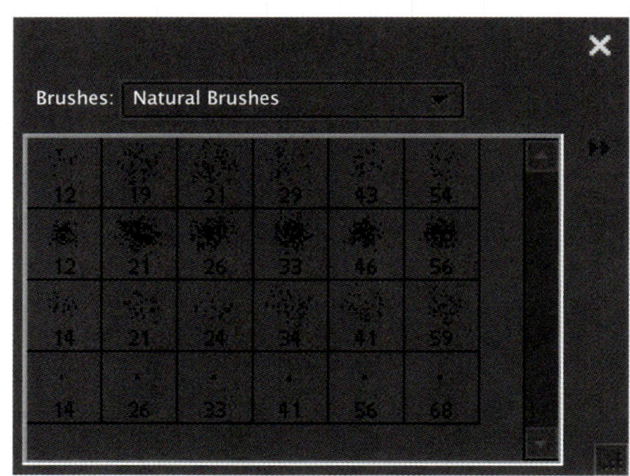

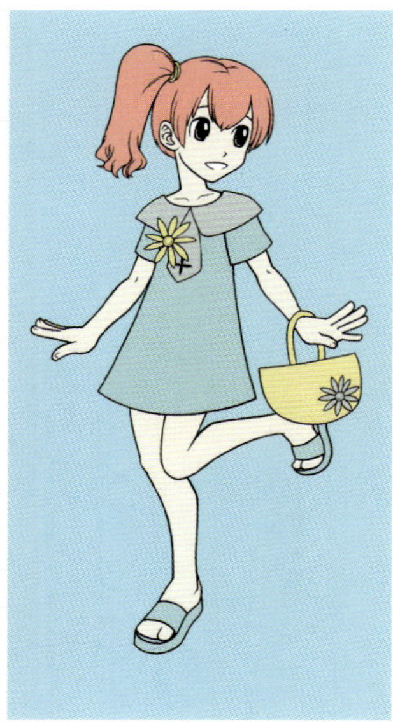

1 Start by coloring your base colors using the method outlined on page 30. Make two new layers, one called "palette" and one called "shading." You can use as many or as few layers for shading as you like.

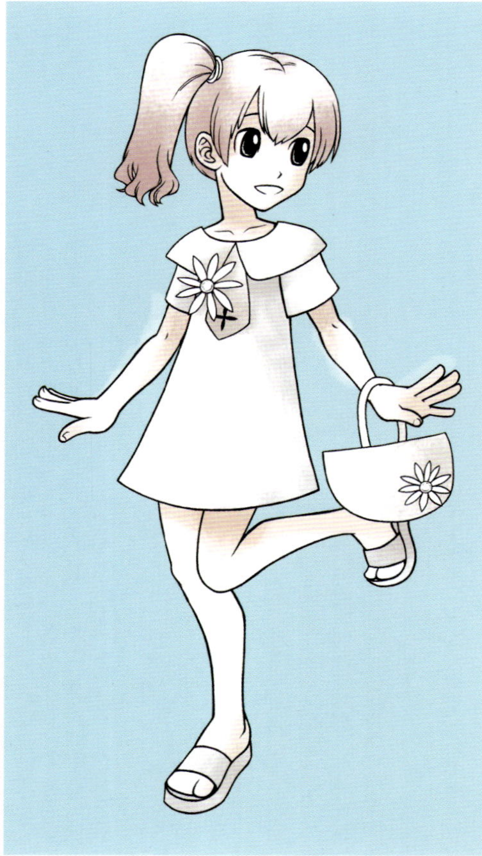

2 Select the Pencil tool from the Toolbox, then choose a natural-looking brush from the drop-down palette in the Tool Options bar. This is the media you'll use to color the image. When coloring in natural-media style, it is best to start with the darkest shadows first, then blend them out with increasingly lighter colors. Set the brush to 15% opacity, and build up the color with many small, quick strokes. This will create more texture than using longer strokes.

3 Next, a lighter color is applied to blend out the shading gradually.

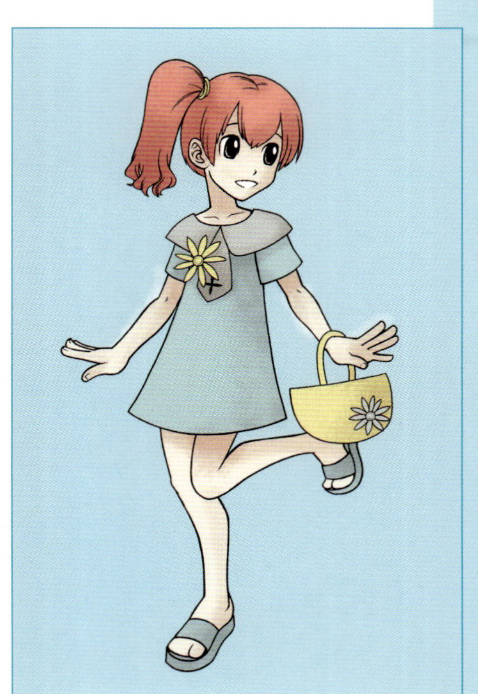

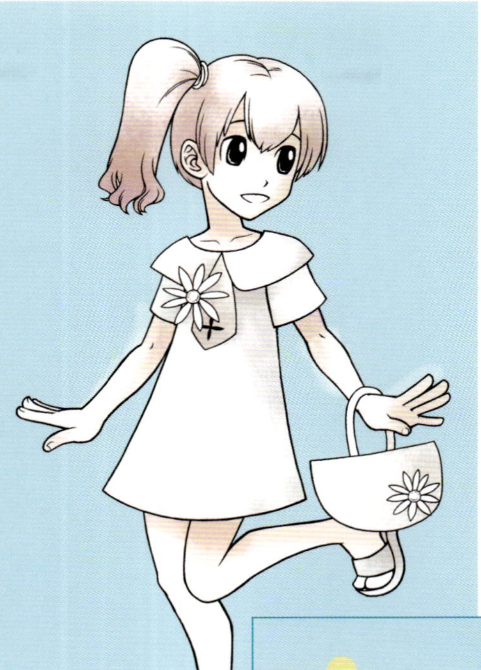

4 Now add some highlights. As with the rest of the coloring, you should still work from dark to light, so blend the highlights toward the lighter shades as you go along. For shiny areas like hair and eyes, make the highlights brighter for more contrast. When the hair is finished, press *Ctrl* or *Cmd* + "D" to deselect the area, and move on to coloring the rest of the image.

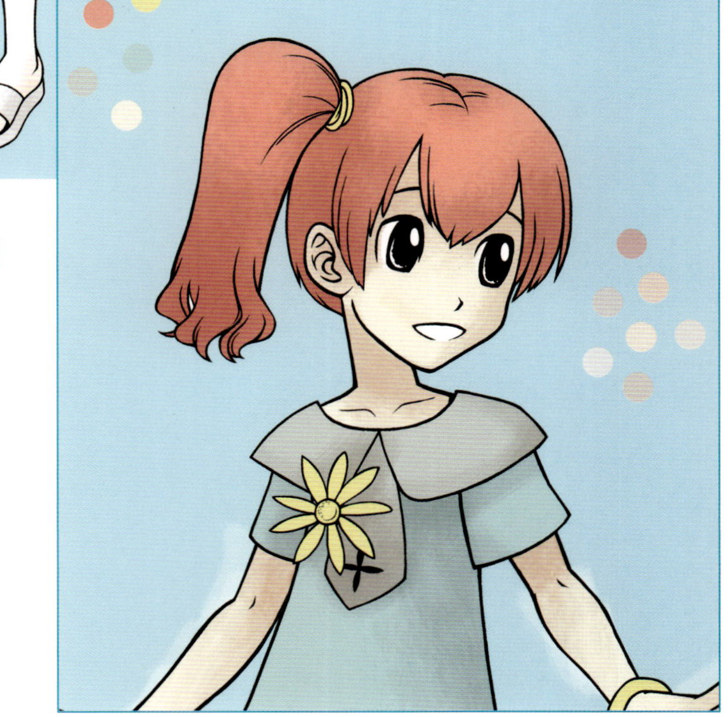

Tip

Using a Palette Layer

When you've finished shading with one color, it's wise to keep a note of it in case you need it later. With natural-media style images, it can be difficult to pick the color from the image with the Eyedropper tool, as there's so much blending and texture that the color becomes diluted. So, to keep the color clean and close to hand, it's useful to have a palette layer containing a dot of each color you use, which you can easily delete when the image is finished. If you need to add a color to your palette layer, but you have a selection you wish to maintain, simply invert the selection by pressing *Ctrl* or *Cmd* + *Shift* + "I" (or *Select* > *Invert*). This will literally turn your selection inside out, meaning you can now color on the areas you couldn't previously. When you're finished adding colors to the palette, simply invert the selection again and continue coloring on the shading layer.

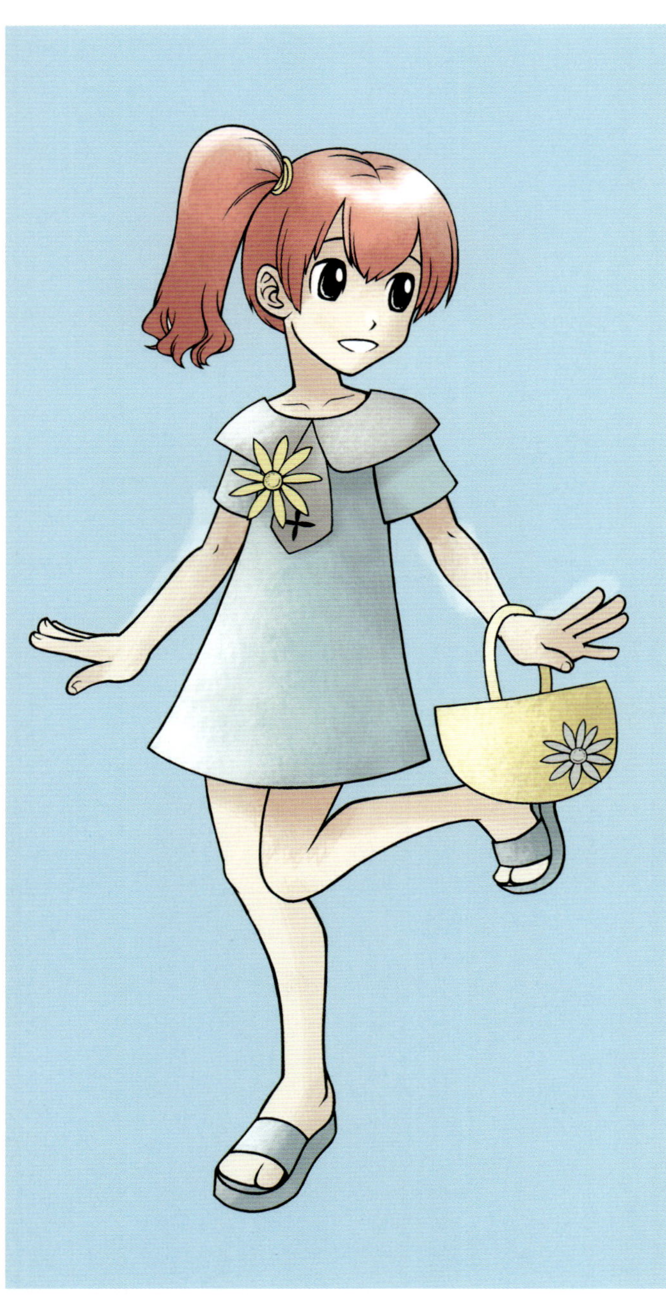

5 The base color is used to blend the shading completely.

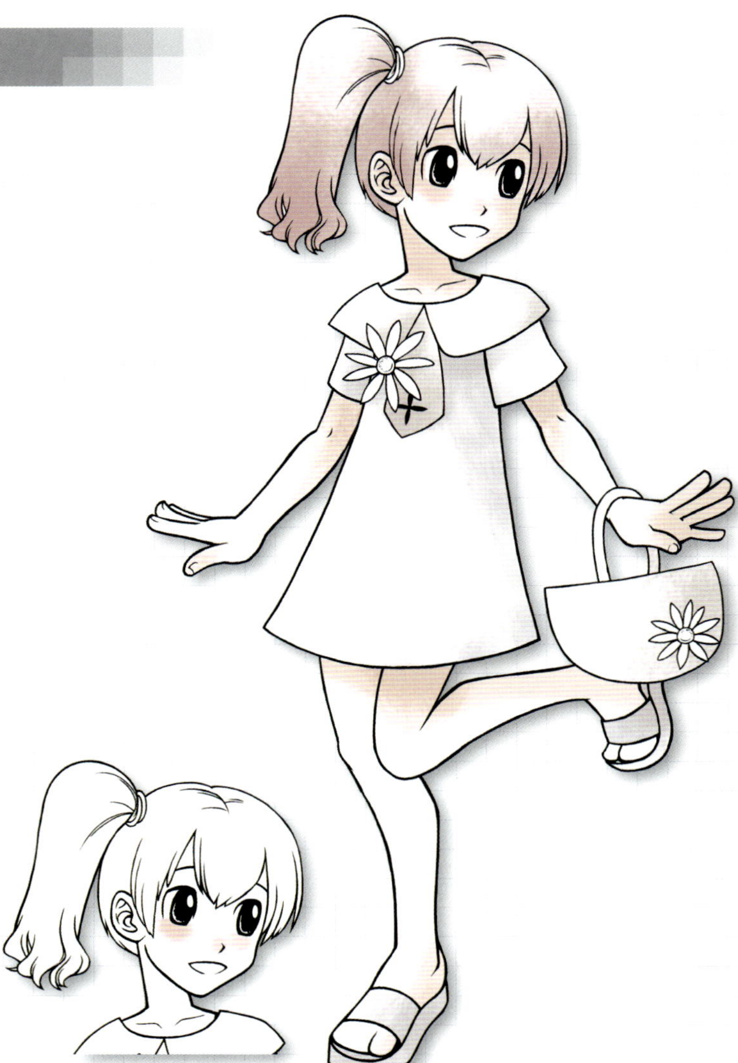

6 Color the small details last, such as cheeks, as you can more accurately work out the lighting and shading to coordinate them with the rest of the picture.

Create a new layer and call it "details." Set its blending mode to Multiply so anything you paint onto the layer will overlay lighter shades underneath. Using a very light, bright pink color, shade the cheeks to give them a rosy glow.

For the white dots, create another new layer—call it "speculars"—and add soft, white dots on the side where your light source is. The speculars need to be on a new layer, as you cannot paint white onto multiply layers; white is effectively transparent with the Multiply setting since the stronger color always takes precedence. Now the image is complete.

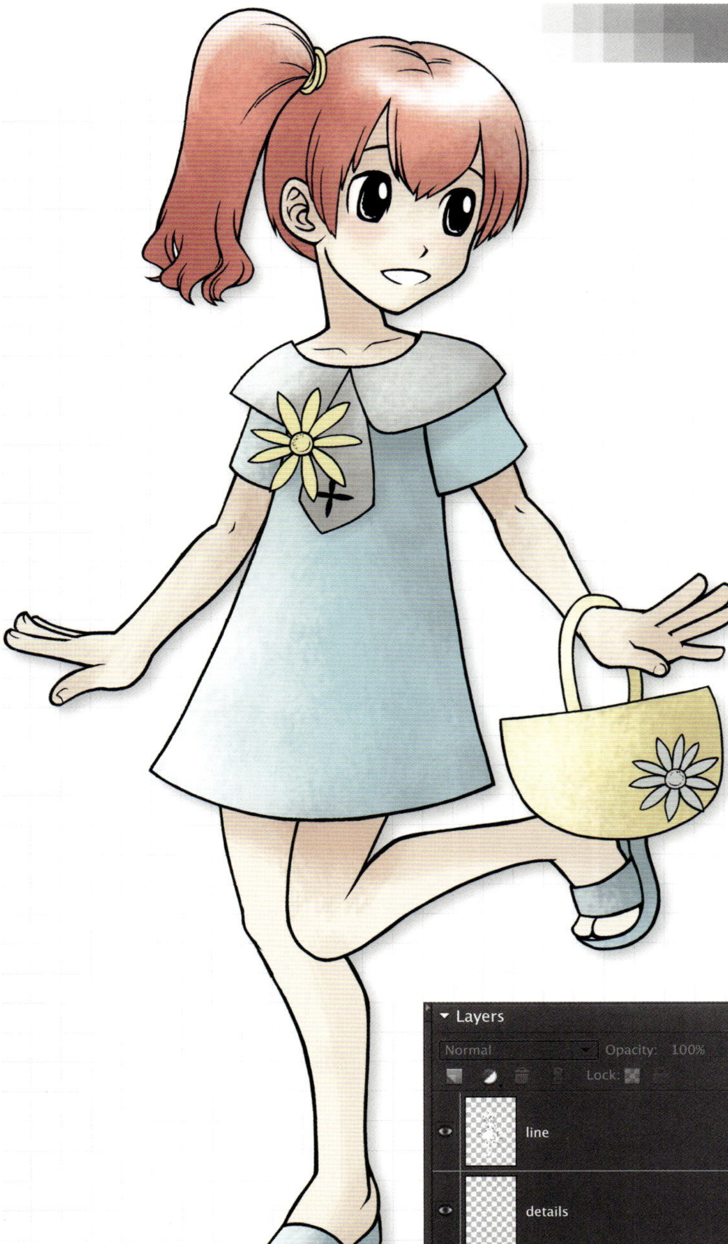

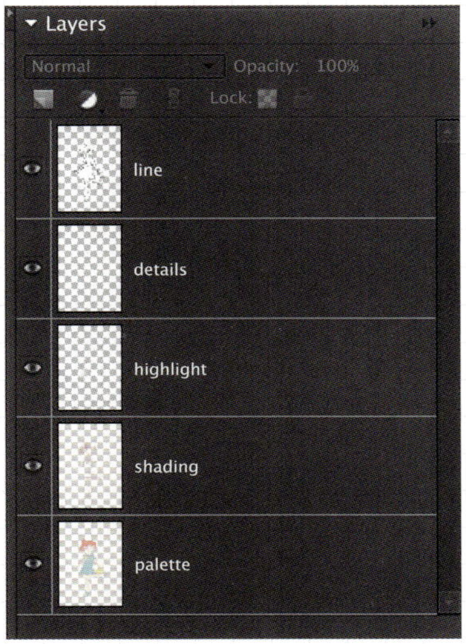

Layers
Normal Opacity: 100%
Lock:
line
details
highlight
shading
palette

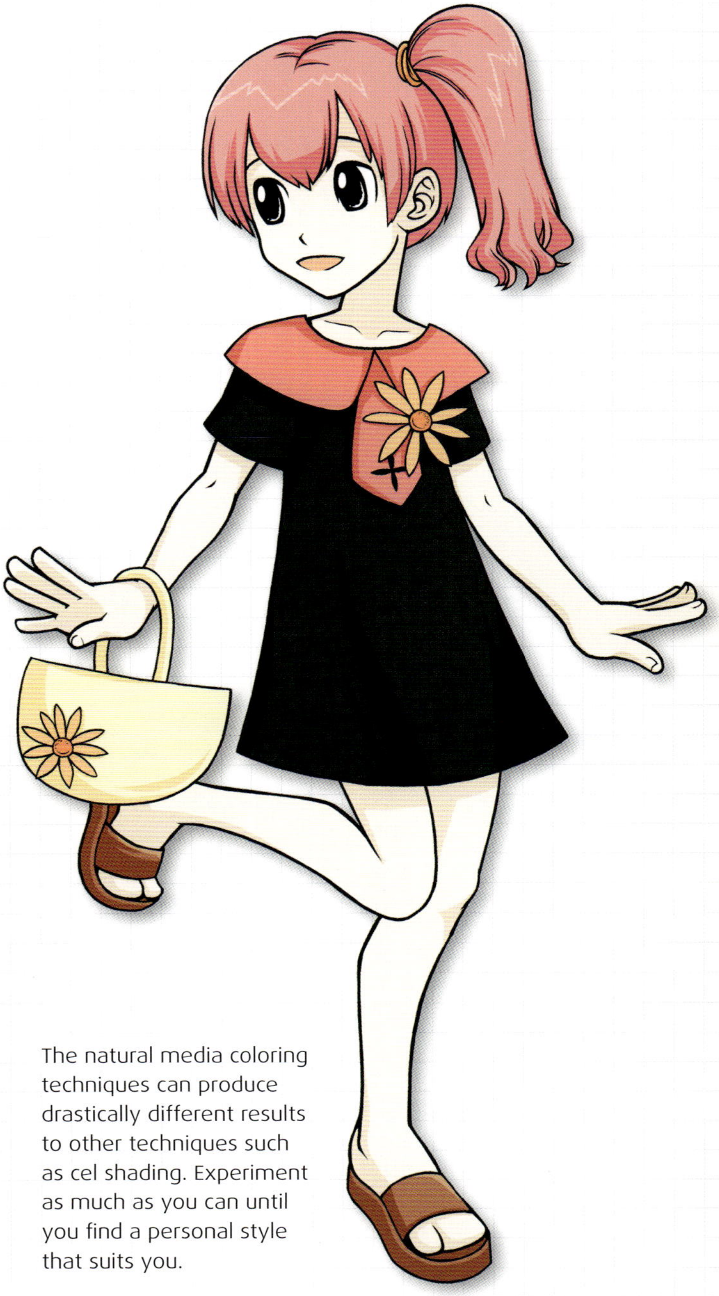

The natural media coloring techniques can produce drastically different results to other techniques such as cel shading. Experiment as much as you can until you find a personal style that suits you.

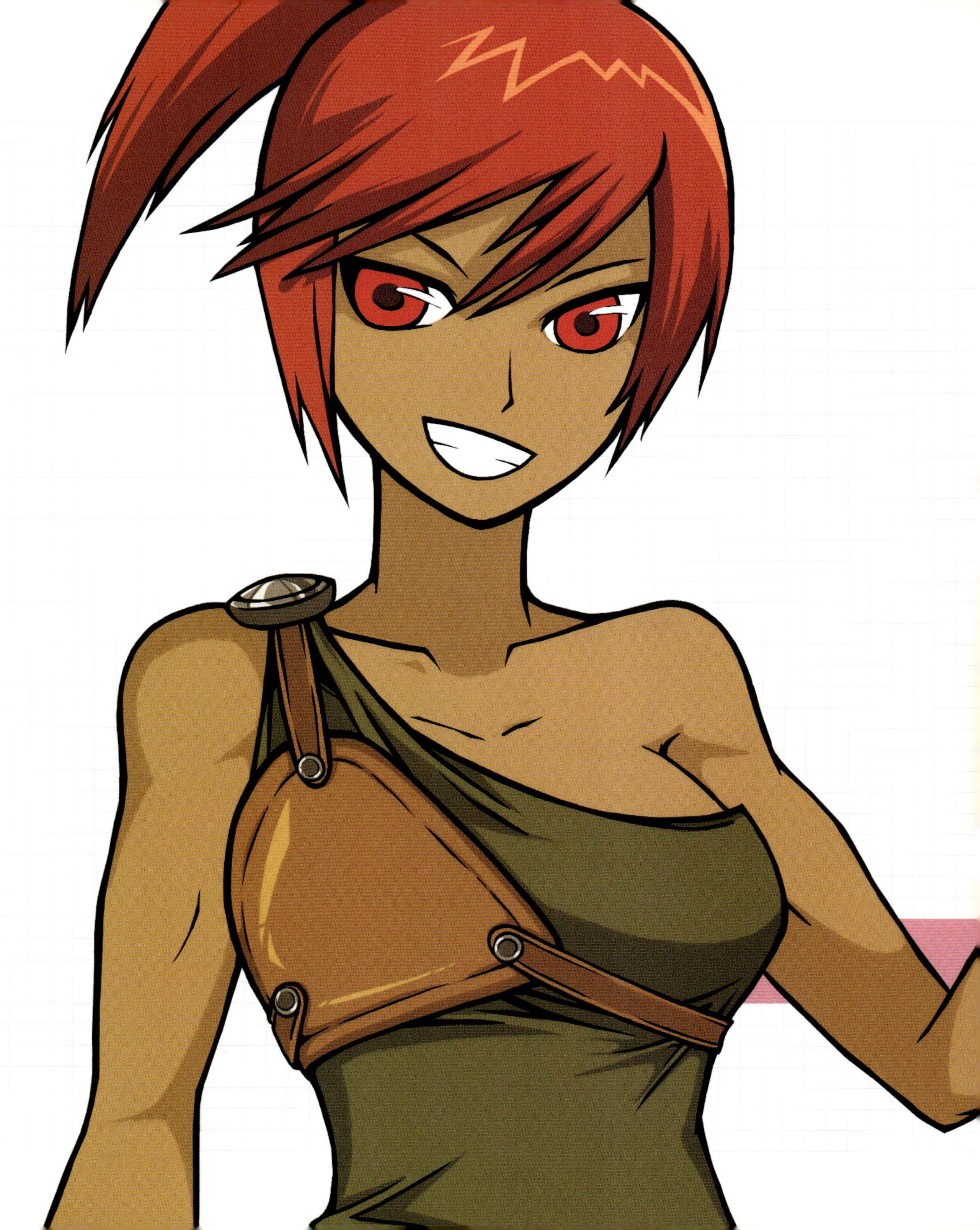

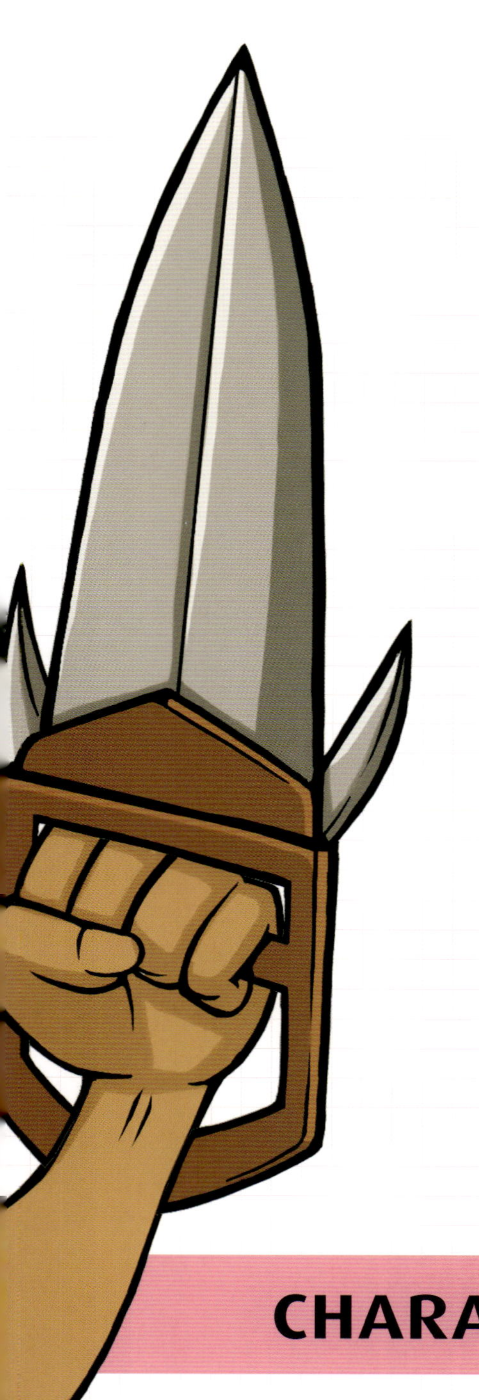

CHARACTERS

CONTEMPORARY 1

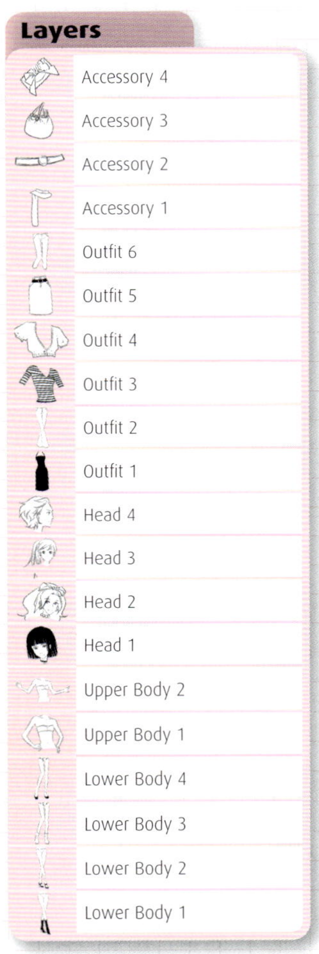

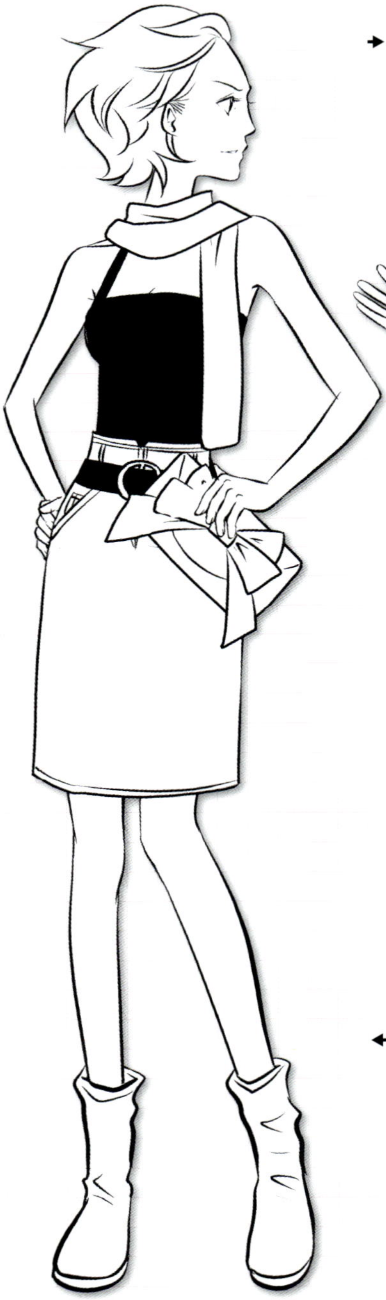

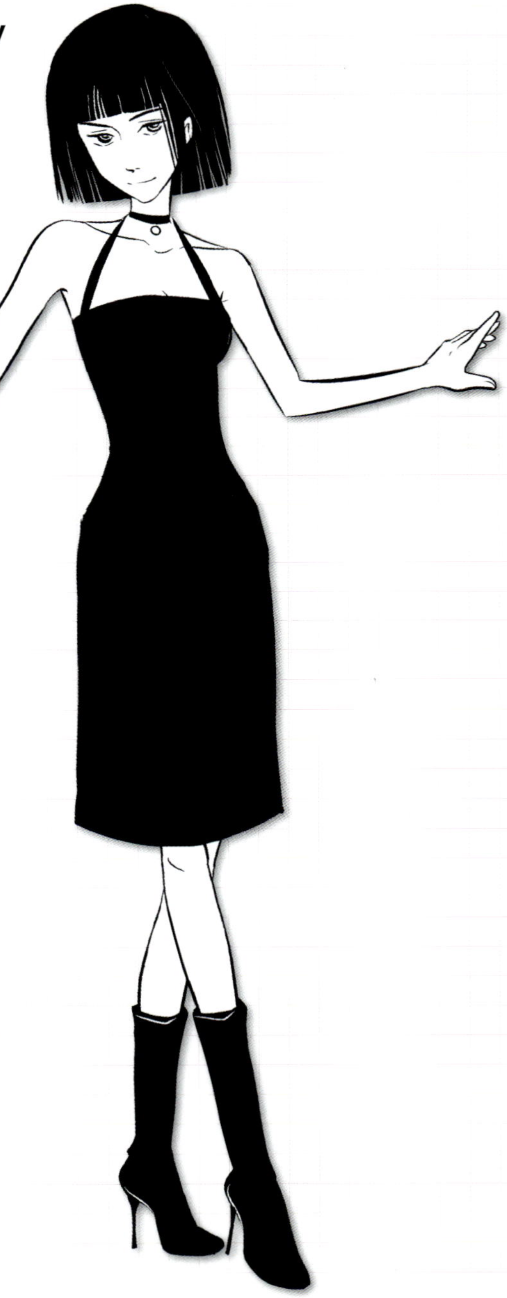

City Chic
This contemporary costume set has a wide variety of styles to alternate with, from elegant eveningwear to casual staples. Accessories could also be interchanged with other contemporary figures.

→ Cocktail Party
Head 1
Upper body 2
Lower body 1
Outfit 1

← Out to Lunch
Head 4
Upper body 1
Lower body 3
Outfit 1 (edited)
Outfit 5
Accessory 1
Accessory 4

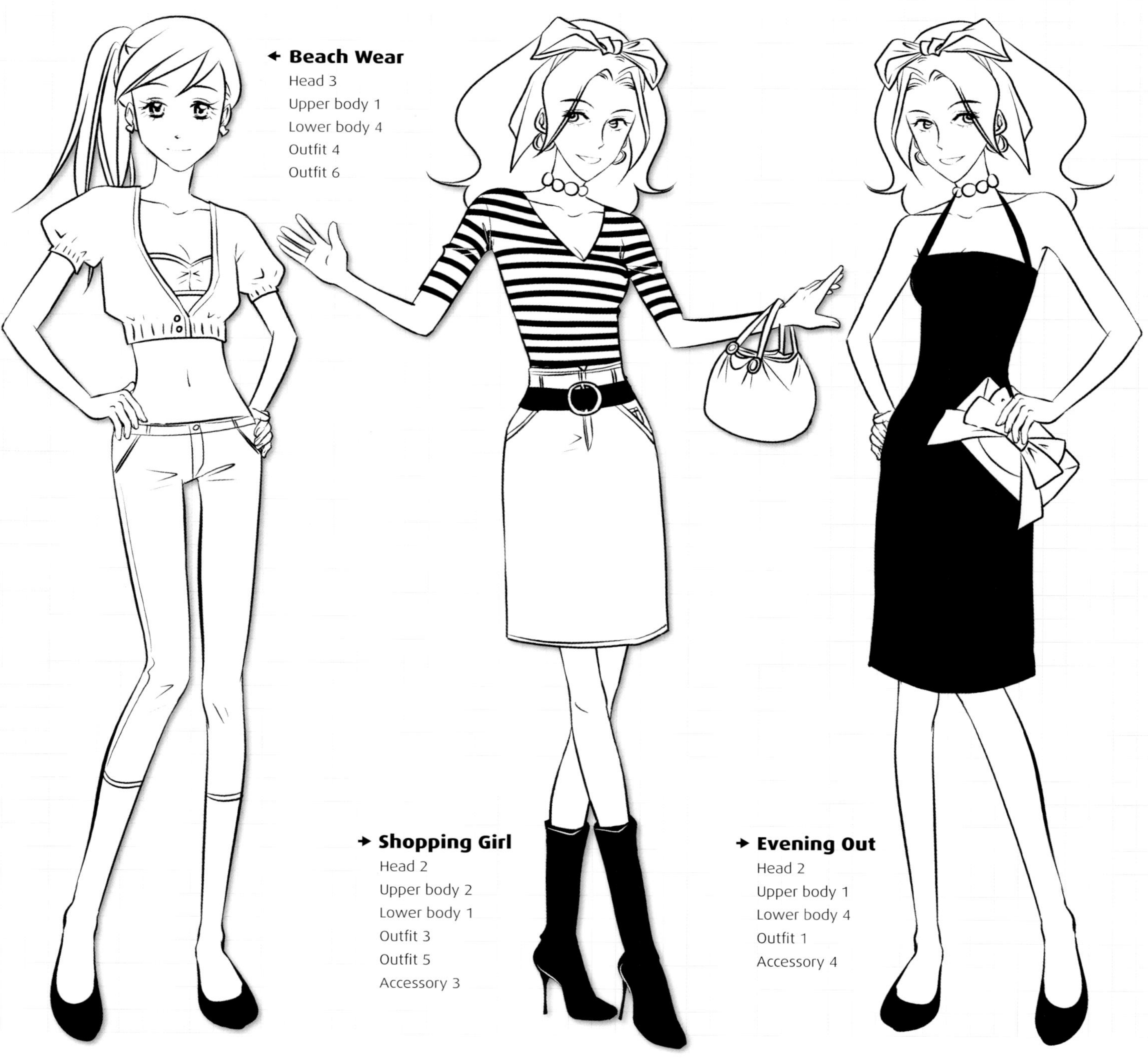

Beach Wear
Head 3
Upper body 1
Lower body 4
Outfit 4
Outfit 6

Shopping Girl
Head 2
Upper body 2
Lower body 1
Outfit 3
Outfit 5
Accessory 3

Evening Out
Head 2
Upper body 1
Lower body 4
Outfit 1
Accessory 4

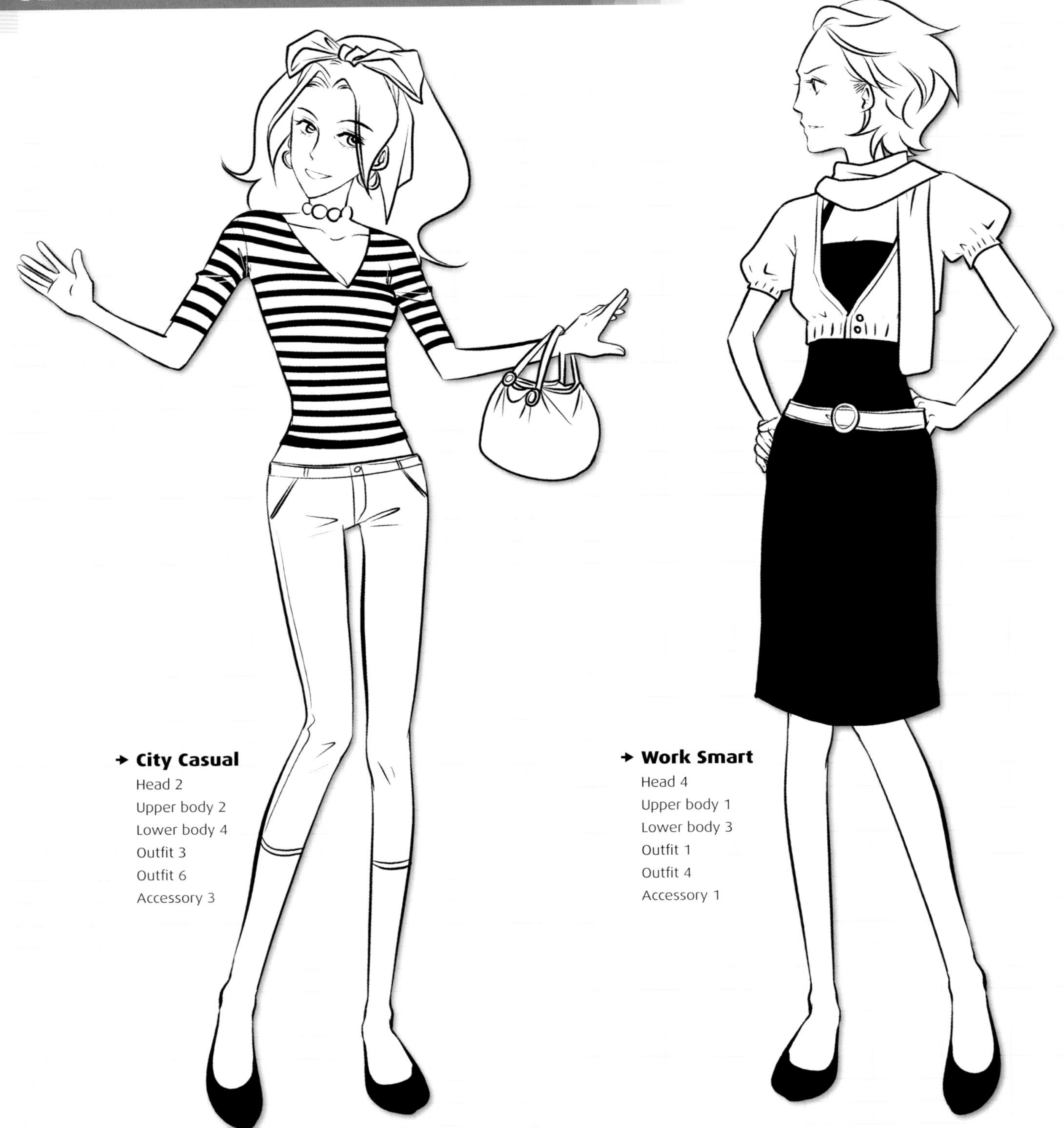

→ City Casual

Head 2
Upper body 2
Lower body 4
Outfit 3
Outfit 6
Accessory 3

→ Work Smart

Head 4
Upper body 1
Lower body 3
Outfit 1
Outfit 4
Accessory 1

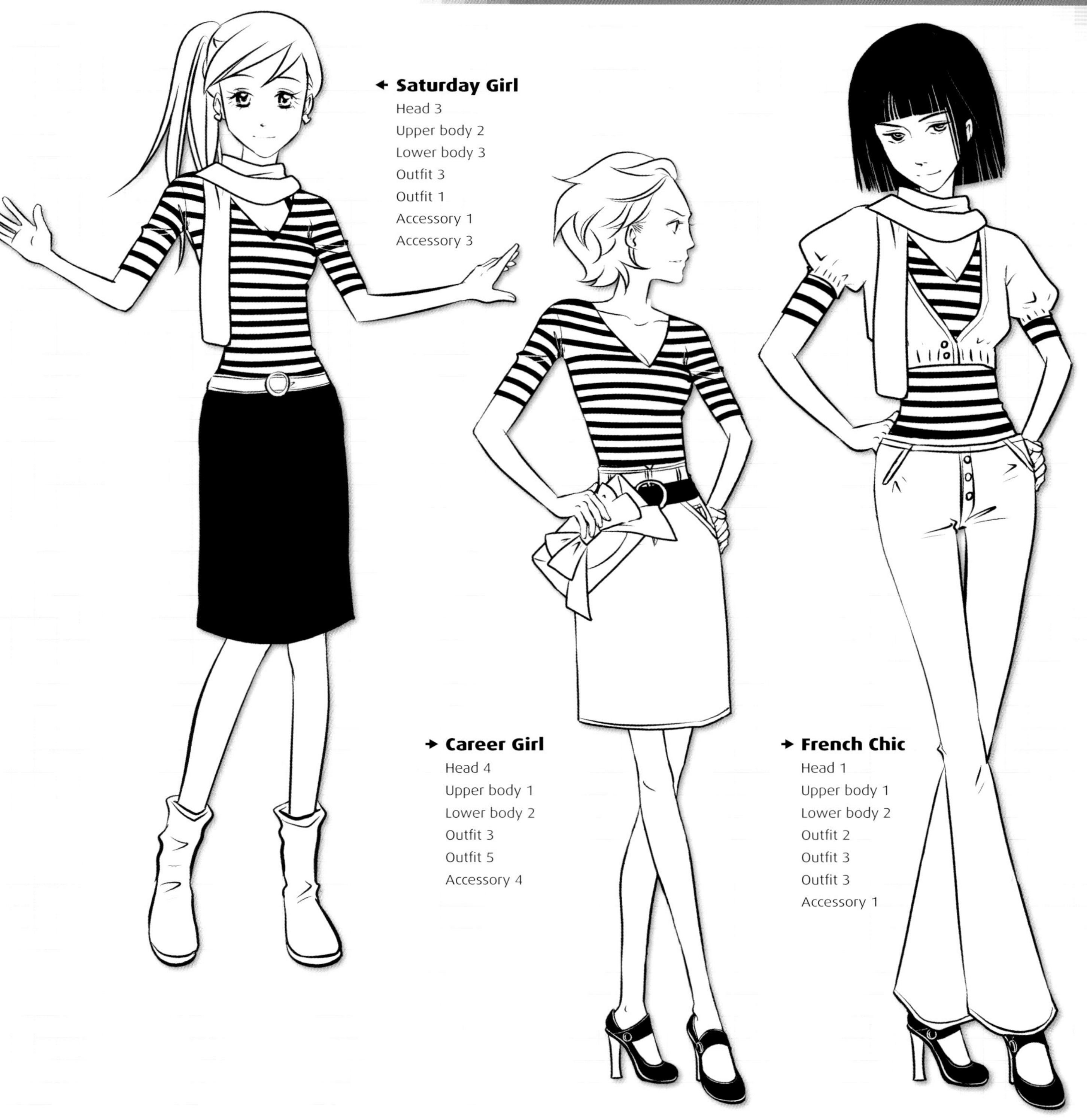

Saturday Girl
Head 3
Upper body 2
Lower body 3
Outfit 3
Outfit 1
Accessory 1
Accessory 3

Career Girl
Head 4
Upper body 1
Lower body 2
Outfit 3
Outfit 5
Accessory 4

French Chic
Head 1
Upper body 1
Lower body 2
Outfit 2
Outfit 3
Outfit 3
Accessory 1

CONTEMPORARY 2

Layers

- Accessory 4
- Accessory 3
- Accessory 2
- Accessory 1
- Outfit 6
- Outfit 5
- Outfit 4
- Outfit 3
- Outfit 2
- Outfit 1
- Head 4
- Head 3
- Head 2
- Head 1
- Upper Body 2
- Upper Body 1
- Lower Body 4
- Lower Body 3
- Lower Body 2
- Lower Body 1

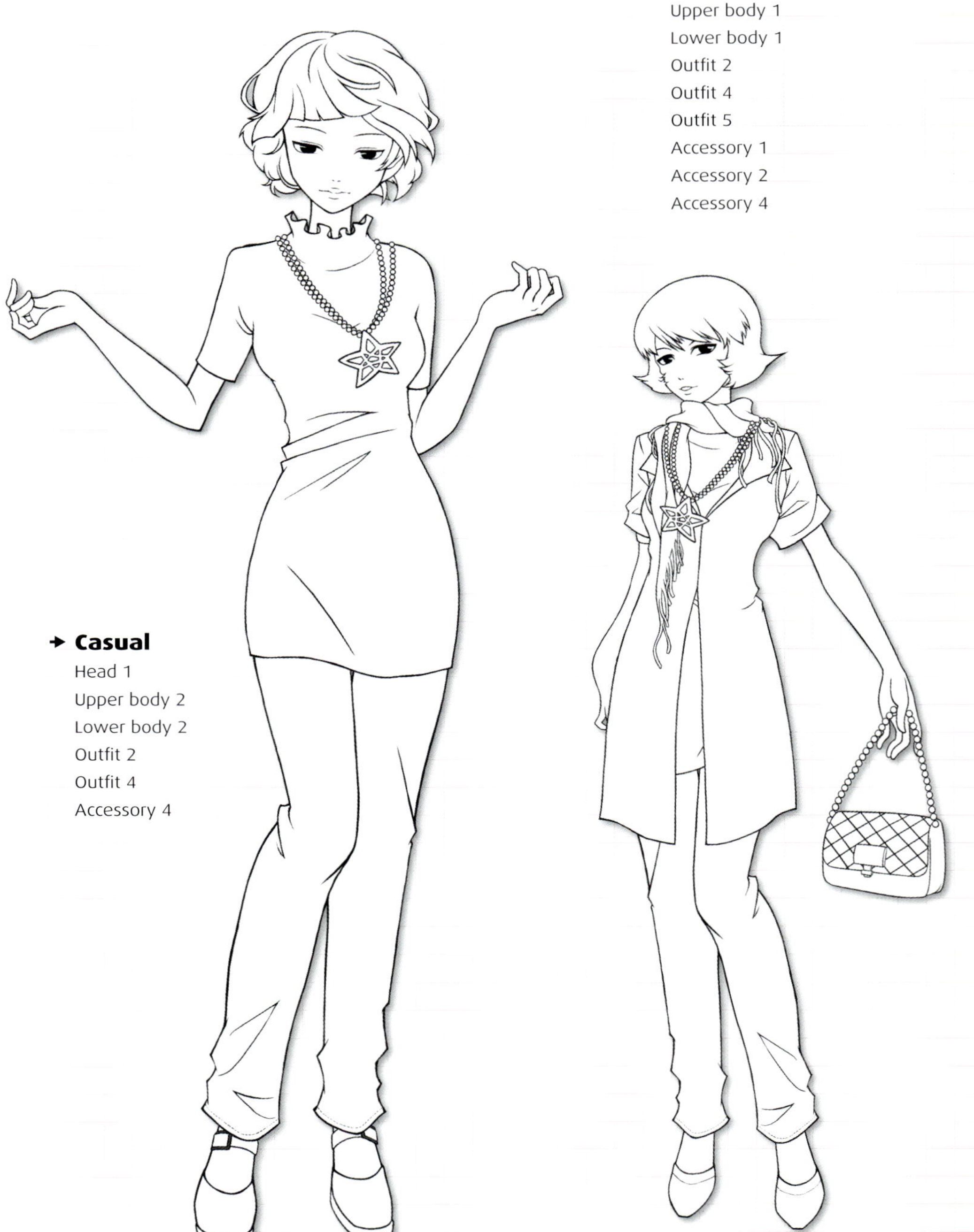

Art Student

Head 4
Upper body 1
Lower body 1
Outfit 2
Outfit 4
Outfit 5
Accessory 1
Accessory 2
Accessory 4

Casual

Head 1
Upper body 2
Lower body 2
Outfit 2
Outfit 4
Accessory 4

Fashionista

For the girl who loves to shop, this costume set is full of fun accessories and the interchangeable layers can be used to create many stylish looks.

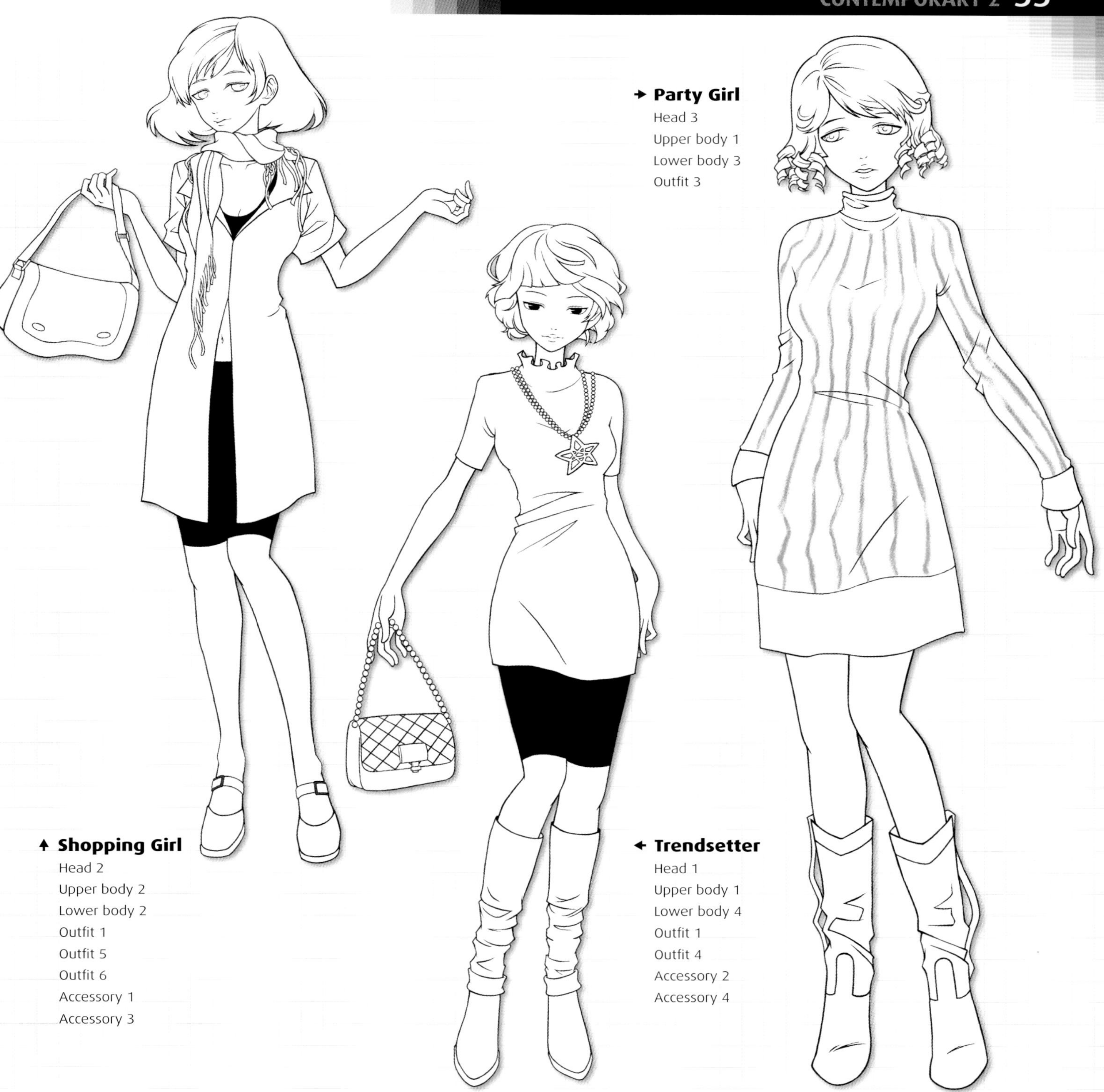

→ Party Girl

Head 3
Upper body 1
Lower body 3
Outfit 3

↑ Shopping Girl

Head 2
Upper body 2
Lower body 2
Outfit 1
Outfit 5
Outfit 6
Accessory 1
Accessory 3

← Trendsetter

Head 1
Upper body 1
Lower body 4
Outfit 1
Outfit 4
Accessory 2
Accessory 4

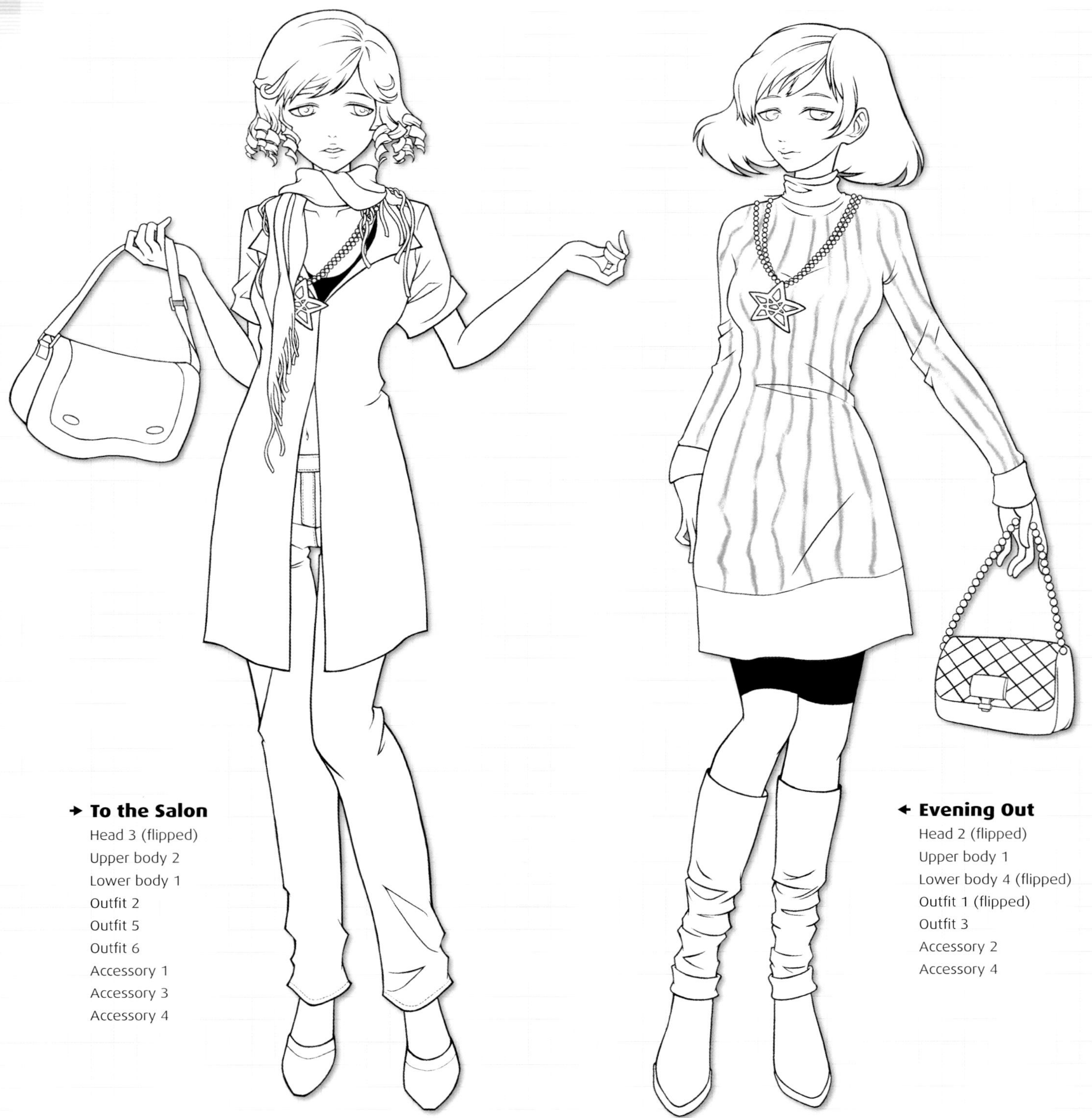

To the Salon

Head 3 (flipped)
Upper body 2
Lower body 1
Outfit 2
Outfit 5
Outfit 6
Accessory 1
Accessory 3
Accessory 4

Evening Out

Head 2 (flipped)
Upper body 1
Lower body 4 (flipped)
Outfit 1 (flipped)
Outfit 3
Accessory 2
Accessory 4

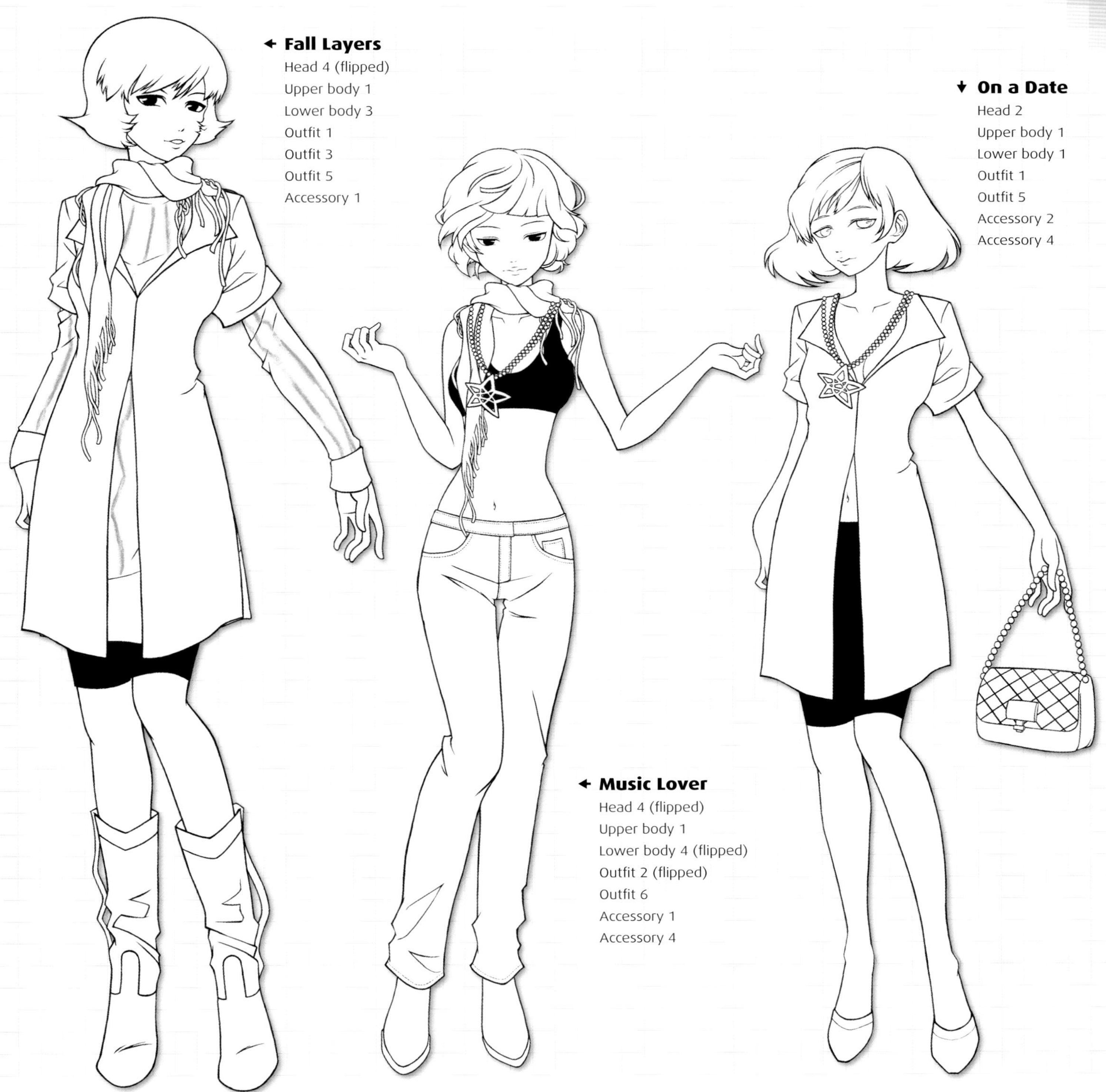

← Fall Layers
Head 4 (flipped)
Upper body 1
Lower body 3
Outfit 1
Outfit 3
Outfit 5
Accessory 1

↓ On a Date
Head 2
Upper body 1
Lower body 1
Outfit 1
Outfit 5
Accessory 2
Accessory 4

← Music Lover
Head 4 (flipped)
Upper body 1
Lower body 4 (flipped)
Outfit 2 (flipped)
Outfit 6
Accessory 1
Accessory 4

CONTEMPORARY 3

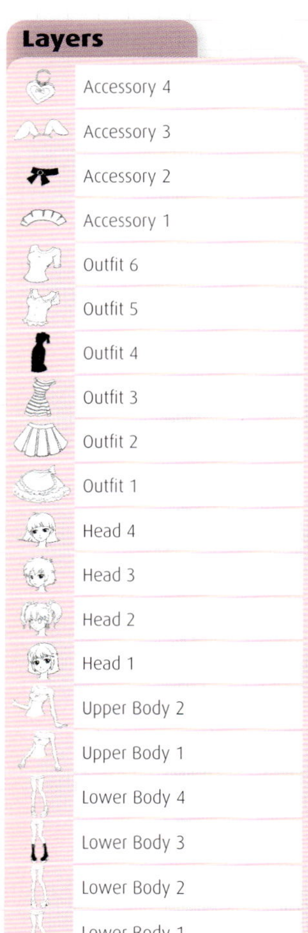

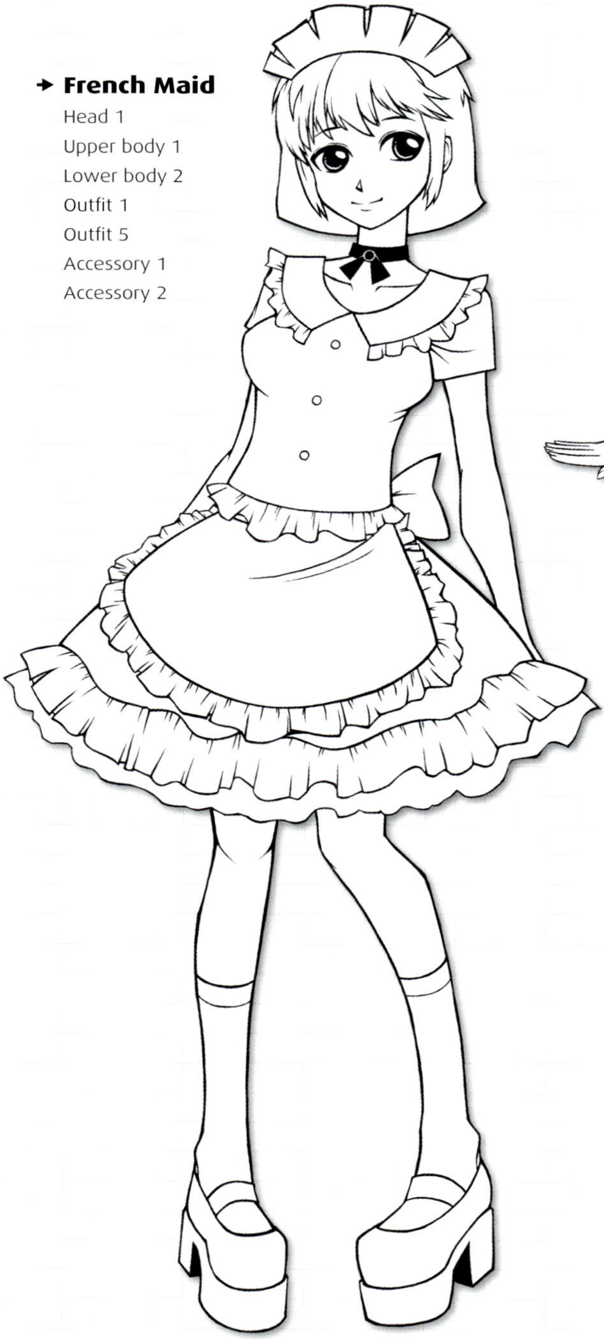

→ French Maid
Head 1
Upper body 1
Lower body 2
Outfit 1
Outfit 5
Accessory 1
Accessory 2

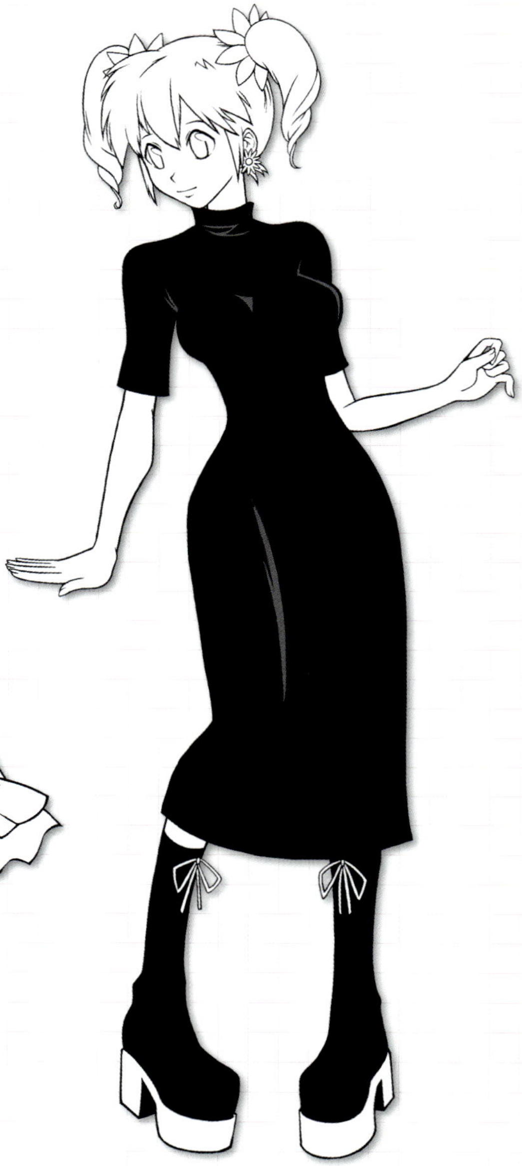

↑ Goth Chic
Head 2 (flipped)
Upper body 2
Lower body 3
Outfit 4

Fancy Dress

This costume set combines contemporary fashion with fancy dress. The layers can be used to create complete outfits such as the French Maid uniform, or can be mixed and matched to create more eclectic costumes.

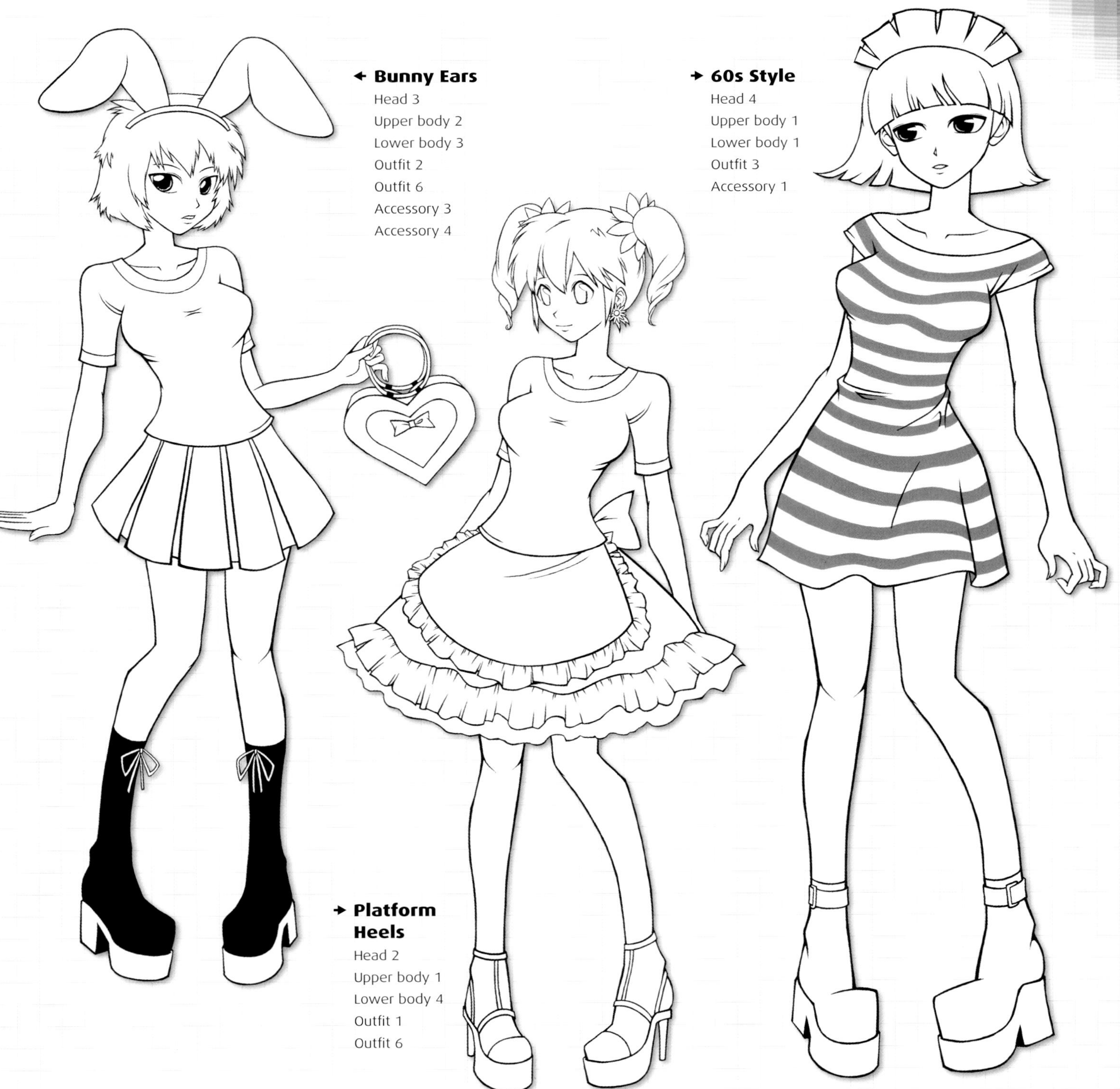

Bunny Ears
Head 3
Upper body 2
Lower body 3
Outfit 2
Outfit 6
Accessory 3
Accessory 4
60s Style
Head 4
Upper body 1
Lower body 1
Outfit 3
Accessory 1
Platform Heels
Head 2
Upper body 1
Lower body 4
Outfit 1
Outfit 6

SCI-FI 1

Layers

- Accessory 4
- Accessory 3
- Accessory 2
- Accessory 1
- Outfit 6
- Outfit 5
- Outfit 4
- Outfit 3
- Outfit 2
- Outfit 1
- Head 4
- Head 3
- Head 2
- Head 1
- Upper Body 2
- Upper Body 1
- Lower Body 4
- Lower Body 3
- Lower Body 2
- Lower Body 1

Ram
Head 1
Upper 1
Lower 1
Outfit 3
Outfit 4
Accessory 2

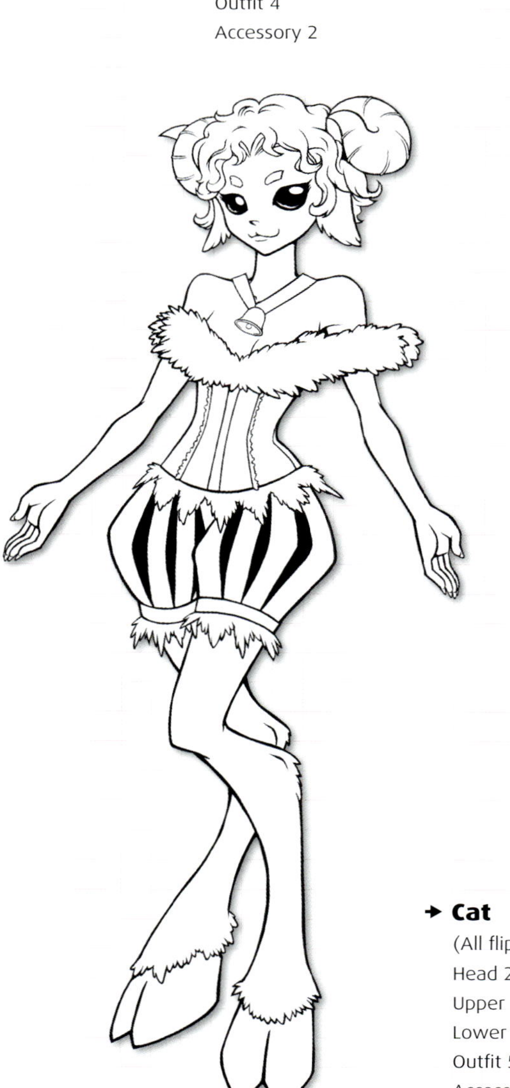

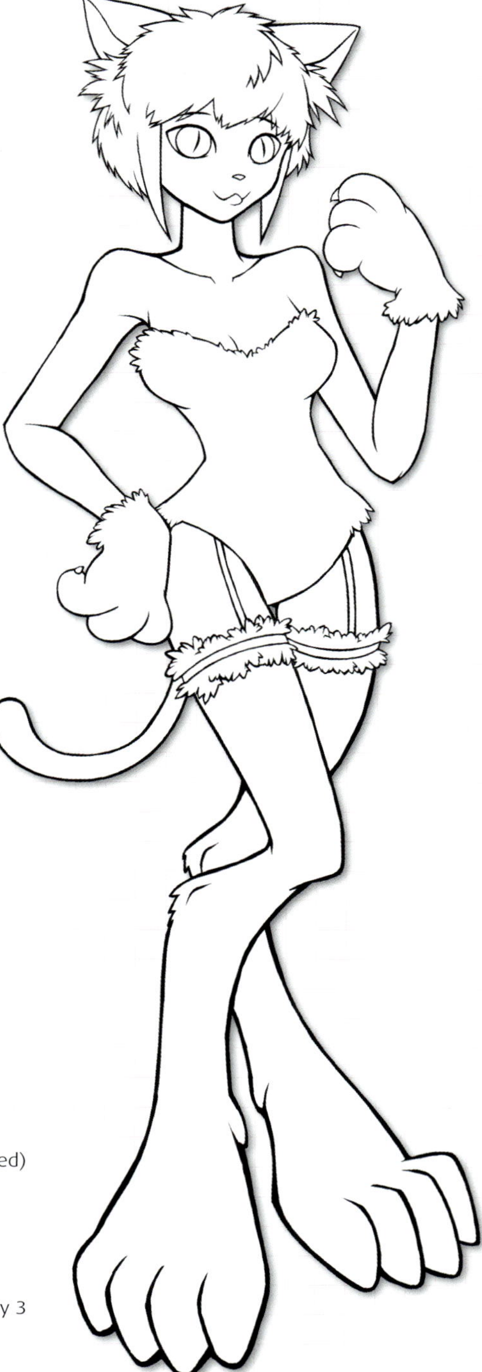

Cat
(All flipped)
Head 2
Upper 1
Lower 2
Outfit 5
Accessory 3

Fantasy

The fantasy set includes witches, elfs, and animals. The "cat" layers can be used to create a complete manga feline, or alternatively they can be mixed with other parts to create some truly fantastical creatures.

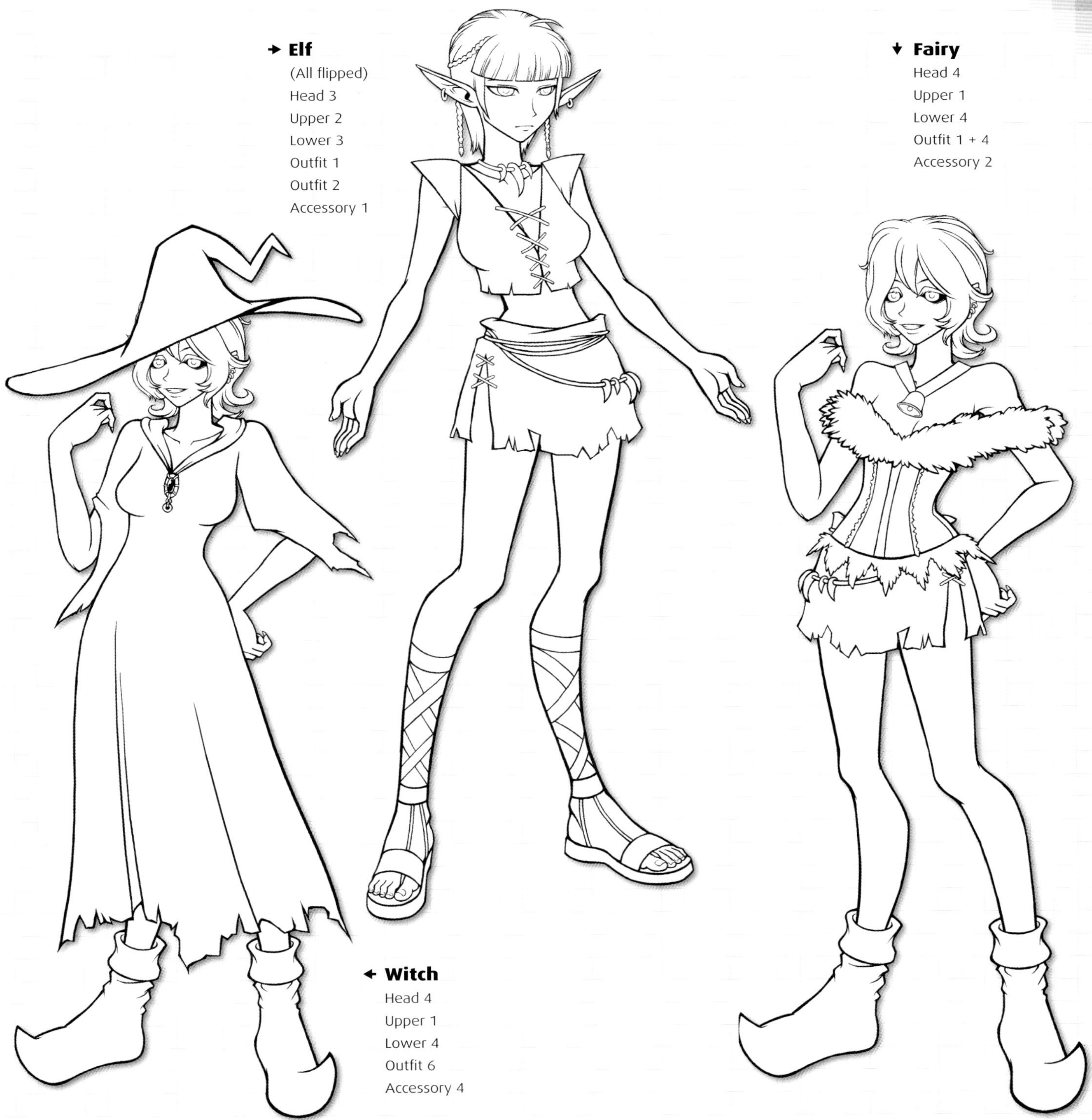
→ Elf
(All flipped)
Head 3
Upper 2
Lower 3
Outfit 1
Outfit 2
Accessory 1
↓ Fairy
Head 4
Upper 1
Lower 4
Outfit 1 + 4
Accessory 2
← Witch
Head 4
Upper 1
Lower 4
Outfit 6
Accessory 4

SCI-FI 2

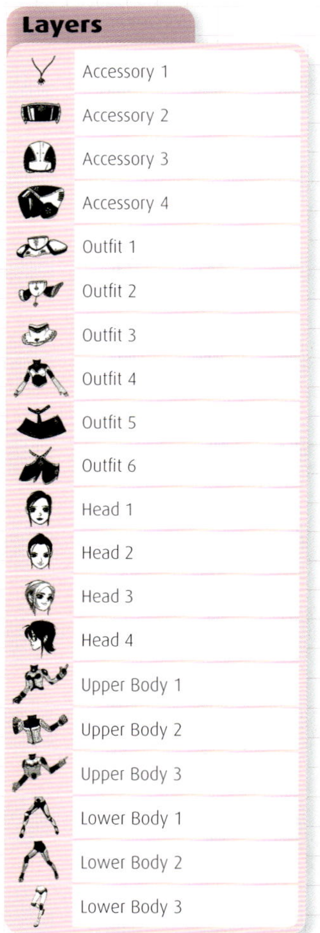

Space Age

The Space Age females come with armor for accessories. The faces may look friendly, but a weapon borrowed from one of the Warriors would not look out of place in any one of these gloved hands.

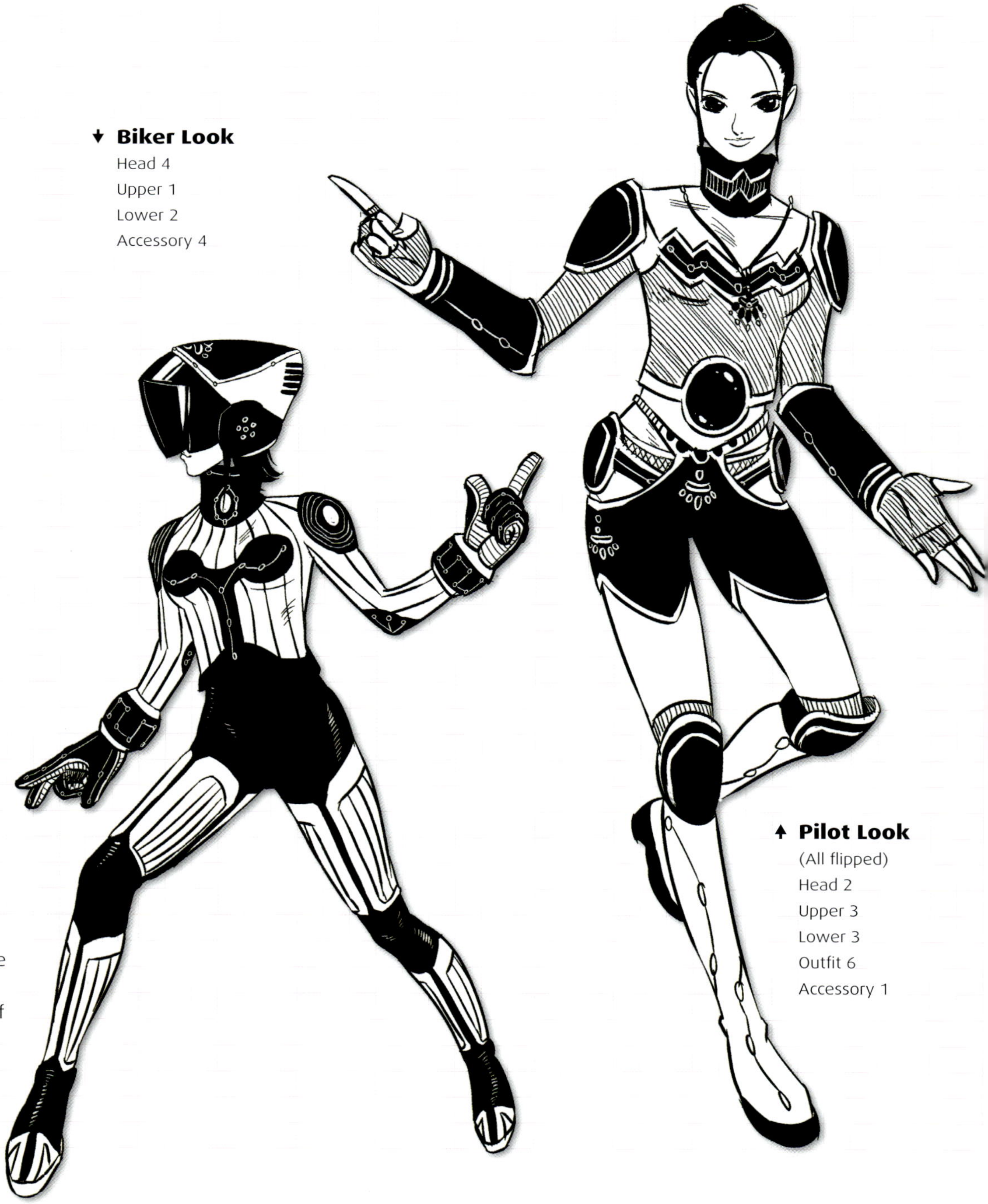

↓ Biker Look

Head 4
Upper 1
Lower 2
Accessory 4

↑ Pilot Look

(All flipped)
Head 2
Upper 3
Lower 3
Outfit 6
Accessory 1

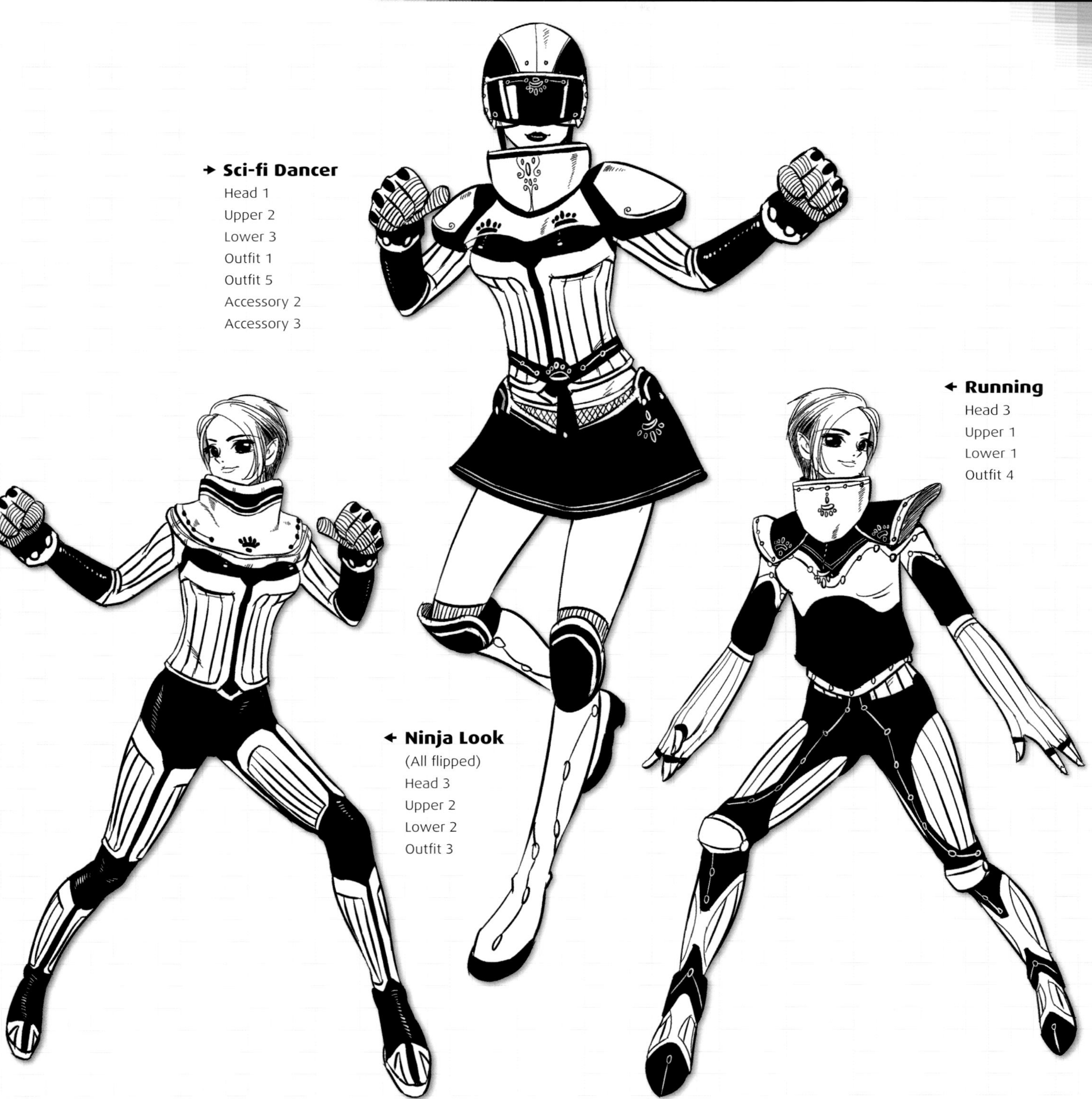
→ Sci-fi Dancer
Head 1
Upper 2
Lower 3
Outfit 1
Outfit 5
Accessory 2
Accessory 3
← Running
Head 3
Upper 1
Lower 1
Outfit 4
← Ninja Look
(All flipped)
Head 3
Upper 2
Lower 2
Outfit 3

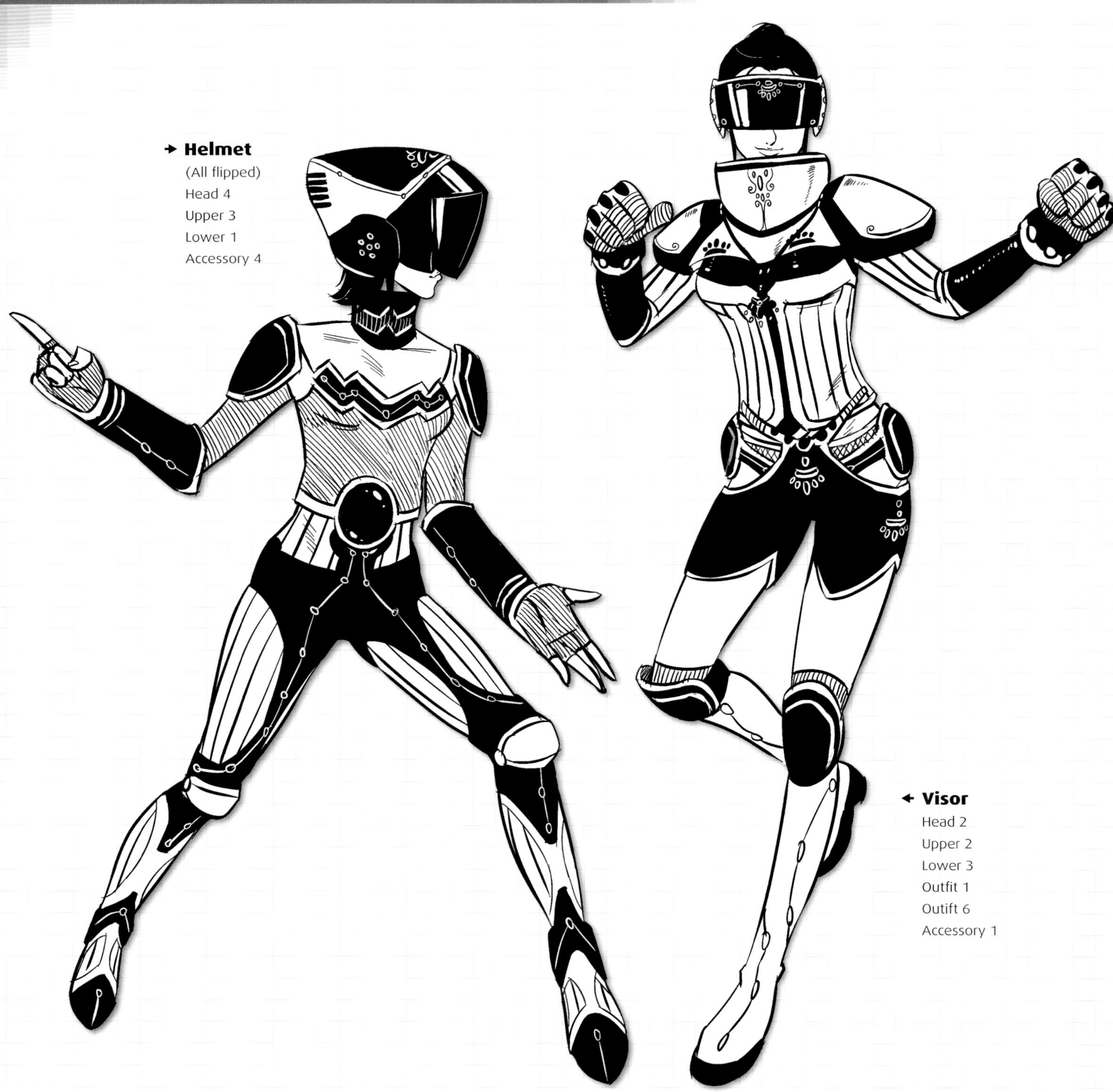
Helmet
(All flipped)
Head 4
Upper 3
Lower 1
Accessory 4
Visor
Head 2
Upper 2
Lower 3
Outfit 1
Outfit 6
Accessory 1

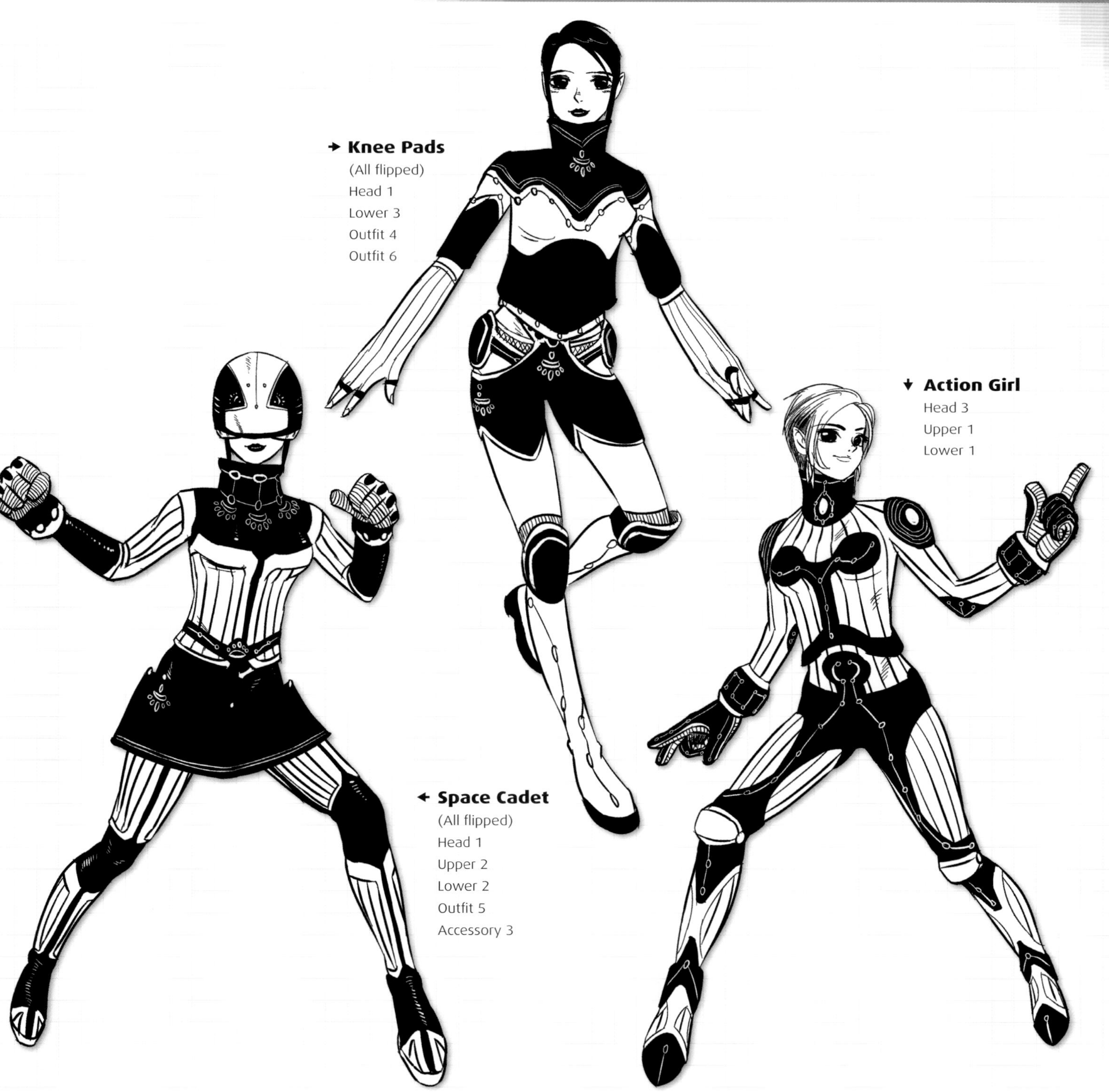
Knee Pads
(All flipped)
Head 1
Lower 3
Outfit 4
Outfit 6
Action Girl
Head 3
Upper 1
Lower 1
Space Cadet
(All flipped)
Head 1
Upper 2
Lower 2
Outfit 5
Accessory 3

SCI-FI 3

Layers

Layers
Accessory 4
Accessory 3
Accessory 2
Accessory 1
Outfit 6
Outfit 5
Outfit 4
Outfit 3
Outfit 2
Outfit 1
Head 4
Head 3
Head 2
Head 1
Upper Body 2
Upper Body 1
Lower Body 4
Lower Body 3
Lower Body 2
Lower Body 1

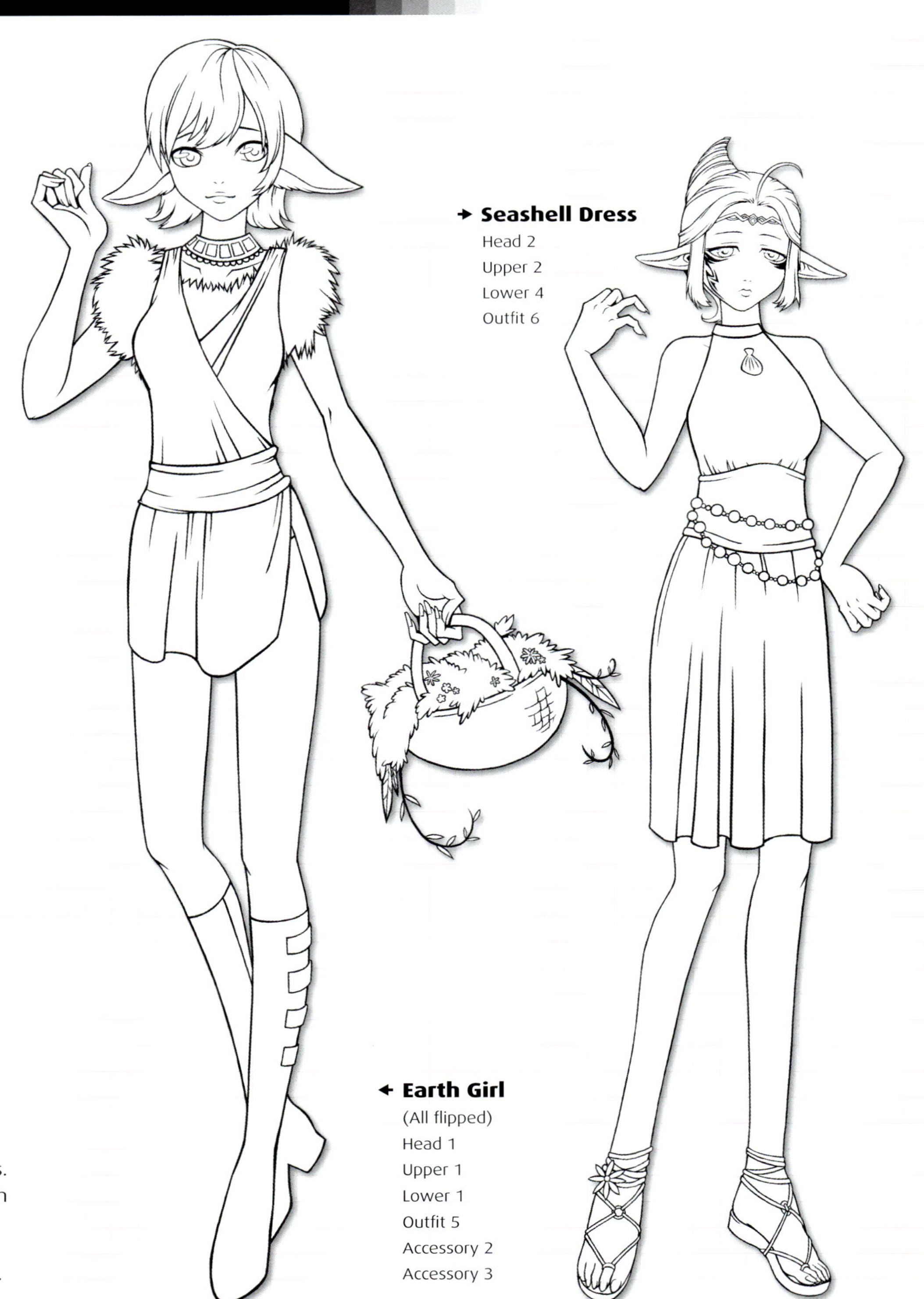

→ Seashell Dress
Head 2
Upper 2
Lower 4
Outfit 6

← Earth Girl
(All flipped)
Head 1
Upper 1
Lower 1
Outfit 5
Accessory 2
Accessory 3

Mythical

You can experiment with the order of the layers for this Sci-fi costume set and create many different looks. Outfit 4 can sit above or underneath other layers, and the skirts can be moved and manipulated to create different dresses and combinations.

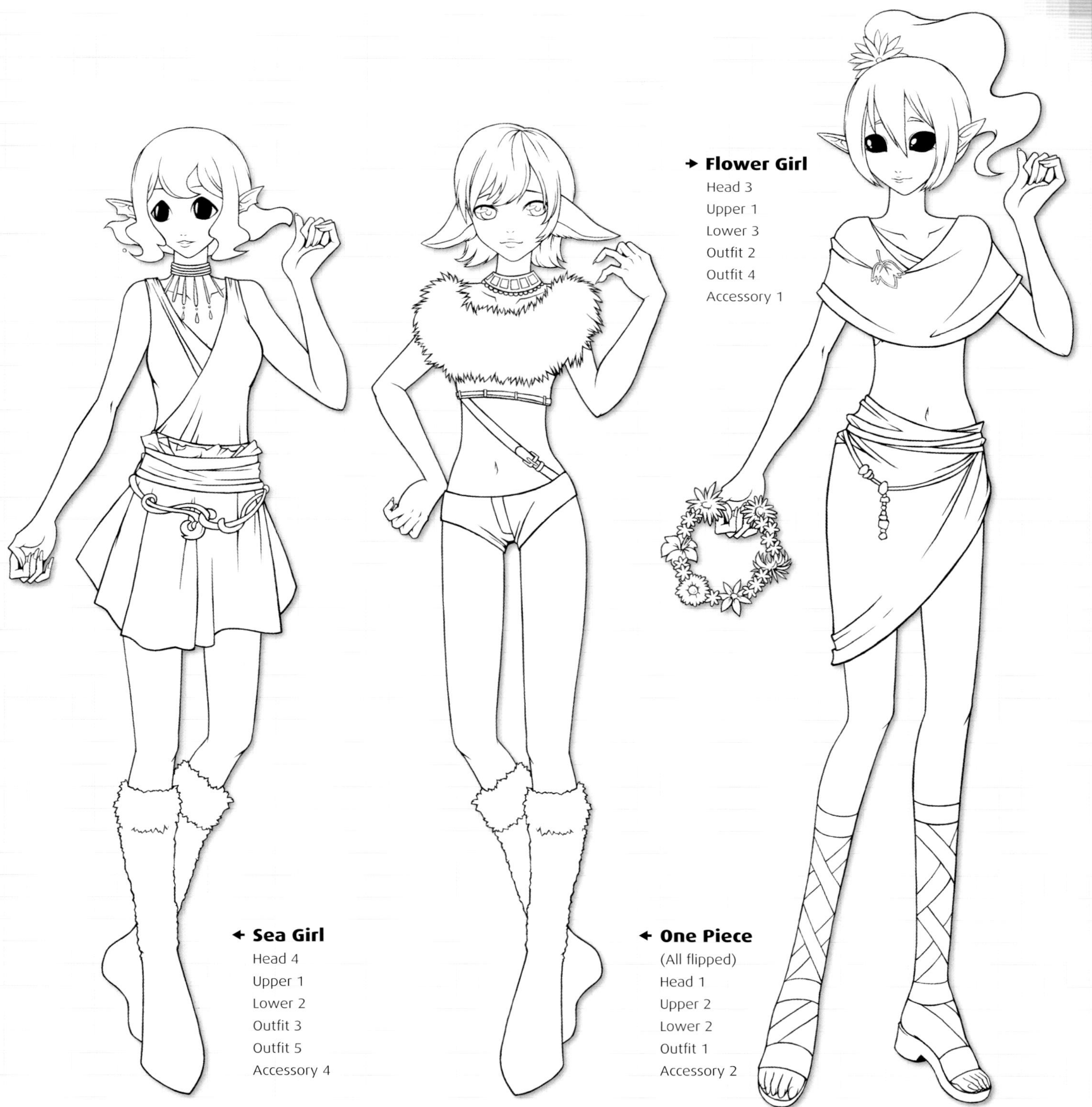

Flower Girl
Head 3
Upper 1
Lower 3
Outfit 2
Outfit 4
Accessory 1

Sea Girl
Head 4
Upper 1
Lower 2
Outfit 3
Outfit 5
Accessory 4

One Piece
(All flipped)
Head 1
Upper 2
Lower 2
Outfit 1
Accessory 2

TRADITIONAL ASIAN 1

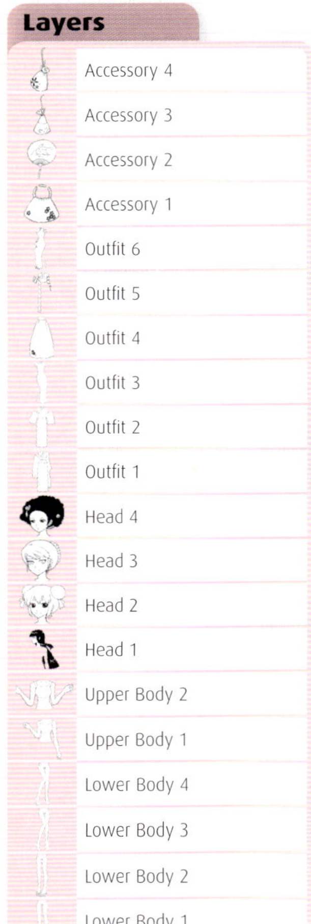

Kimono
Head 1
Upper body 1
Lower body 1
Outfit 1
Accessory 3

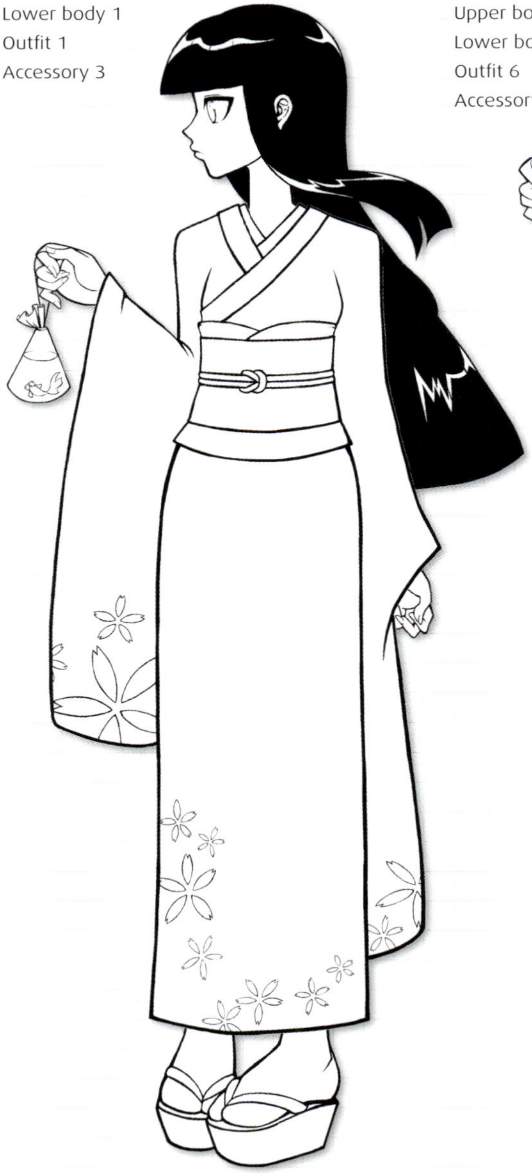

Chinese Cheongsam
Head 4 (flipped)
Upper body 1
Lower body 4
Outfit 6
Accessory 1

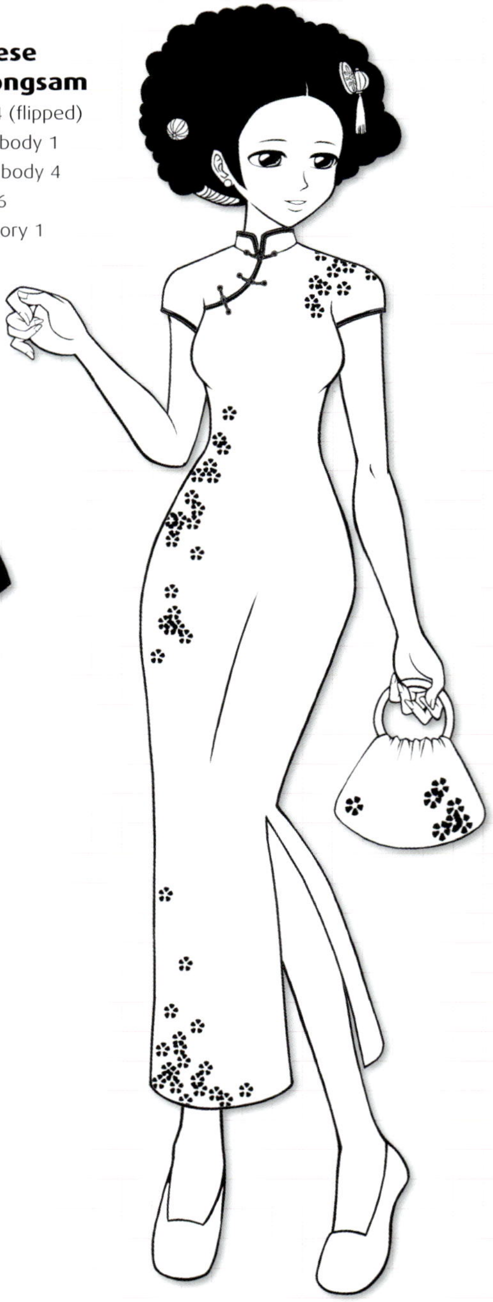

Traditional Dress

These characters are all wearing traditional clothes, whether a Chinese cheongsam or Japanese kimono. However, they needn't be from the past. Contemporary accessories can transform any of these figures into a fashionable female.

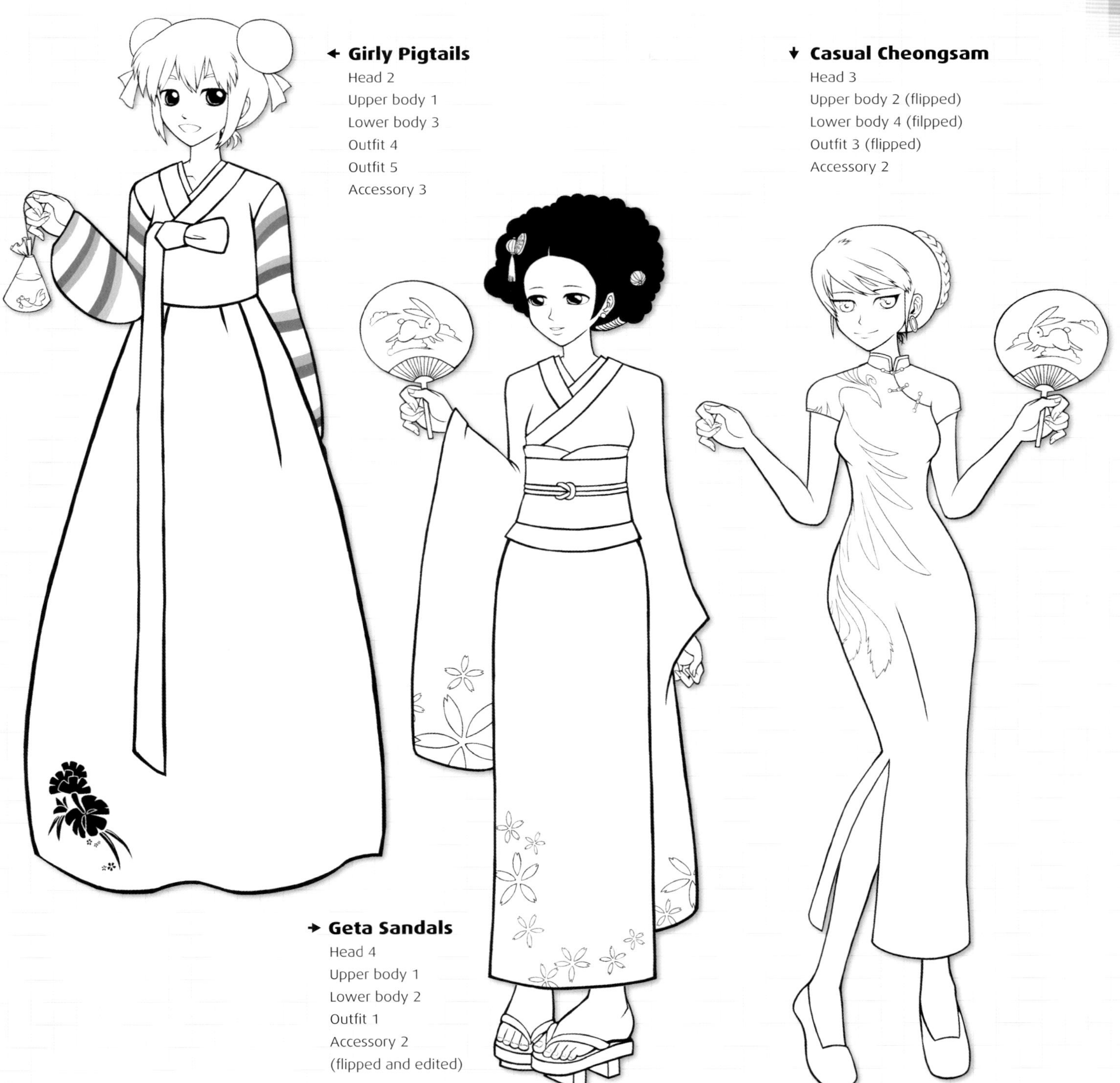

Girly Pigtails
Head 2
Upper body 1
Lower body 3
Outfit 4
Outfit 5
Accessory 3

Casual Cheongsam
Head 3
Upper body 2 (flipped)
Lower body 4 (filpped)
Outfit 3 (flipped)
Accessory 2

Geta Sandals
Head 4
Upper body 1
Lower body 2
Outfit 1
Accessory 2
(flipped and edited)

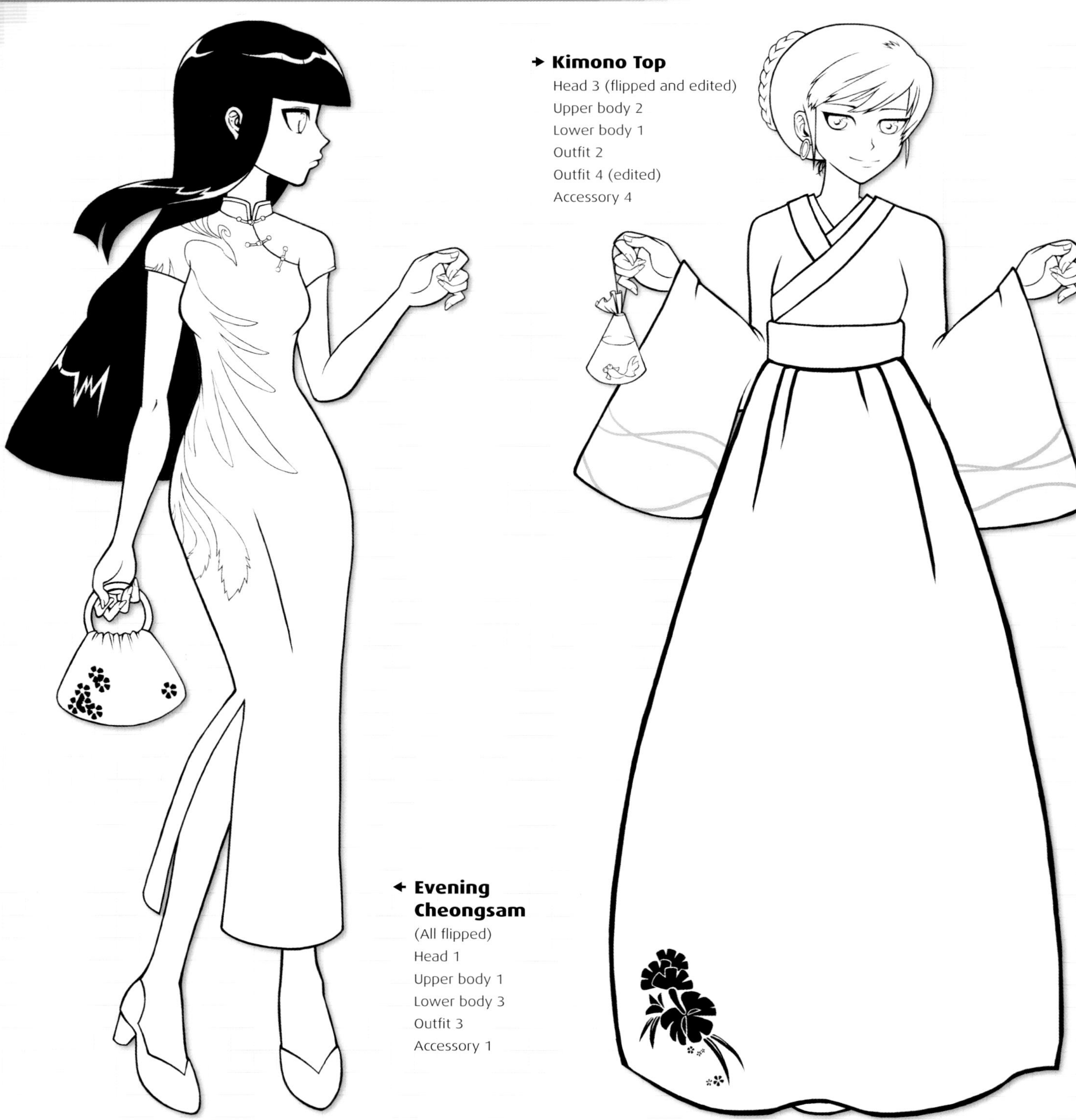

→ Kimono Top

Head 3 (flipped and edited)
Upper body 2
Lower body 1
Outfit 2
Outfit 4 (edited)
Accessory 4

← Evening Cheongsam

(All flipped)
Head 1
Upper body 1
Lower body 3
Outfit 3
Accessory 1

Short Sleeve Kimono
(All flipped)
Head 2
Upper body 2
Lower body 1
Outfit 2
Accessory 3

Cooling Fan
Head 4
Upper body 1
Lower body 3
Outfit 4
Accessory 2 (flipped and edited)

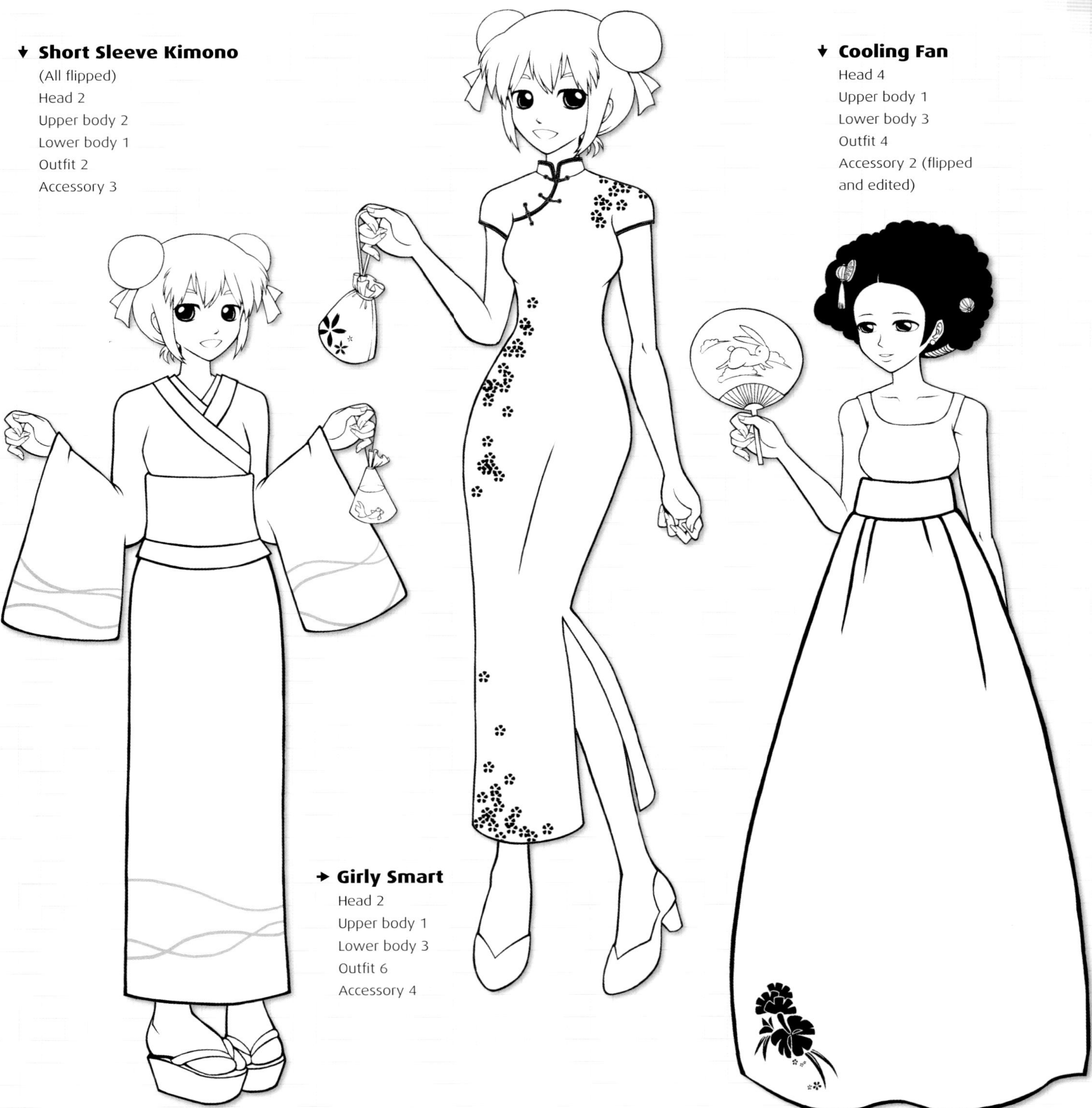

Girly Smart
Head 2
Upper body 1
Lower body 3
Outfit 6
Accessory 4

TRADITIONAL ASIAN 2

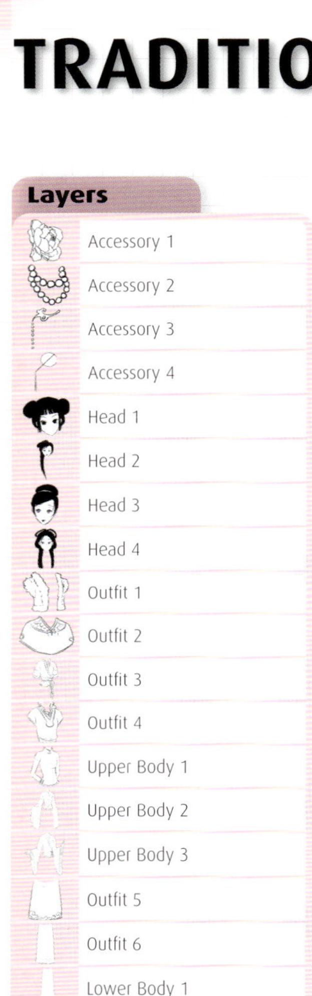

↓ Layered Look

Head 1
Upper body 1
Lower body 1
Outfit 1 + 3 + 5
Accessory 1

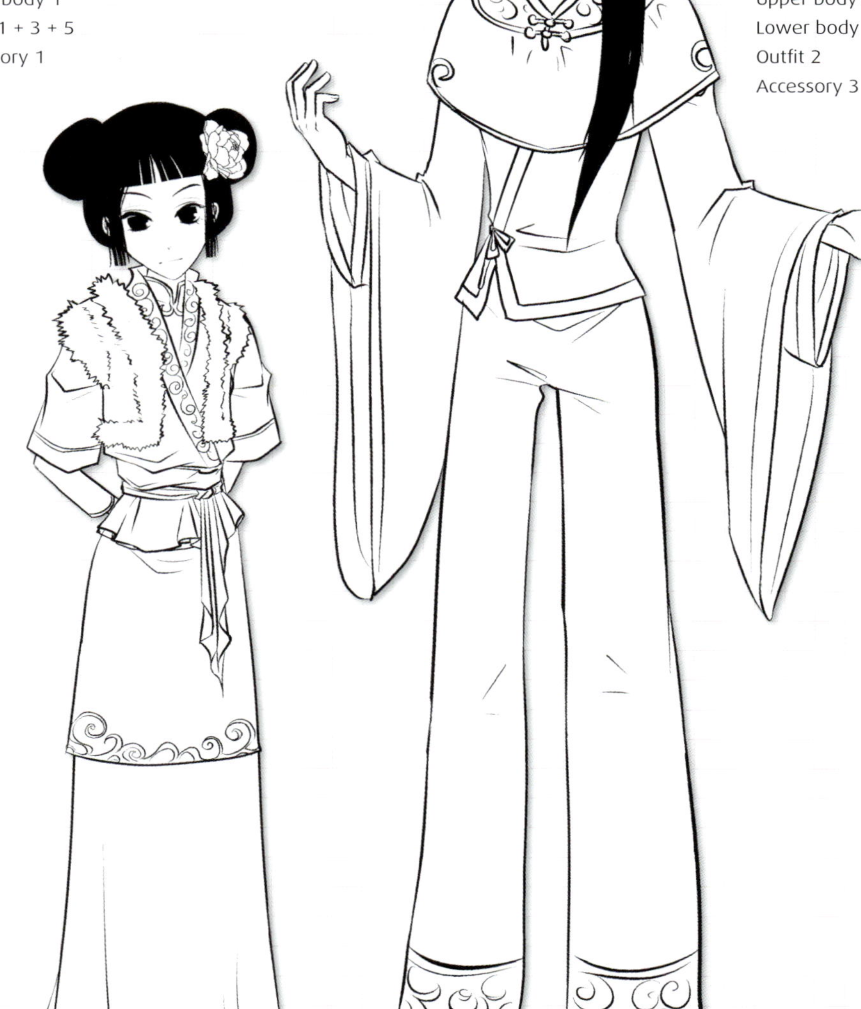

← Large Sleeves

(All flipped)
Head 2
Upper body 3
Lower body 2
Outfit 2
Accessory 3

Traditional Elegance

Many of the pieces that make up the traditional outfits for these figures can be used at the same time, creating a layered effect. This means there are even more opportunities to mix and match clothes and make lots of different characters.

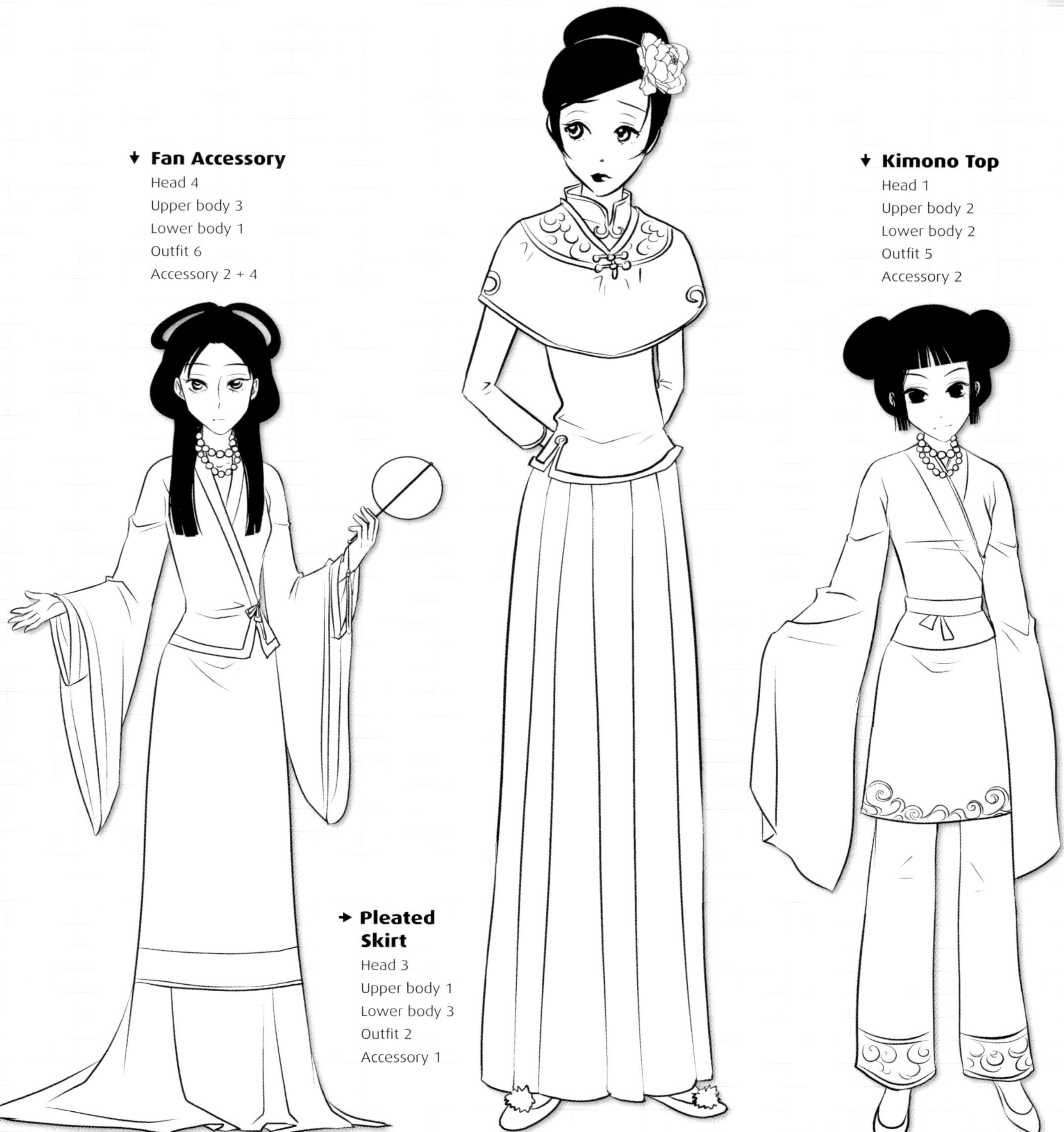

Fan Accessory
Head 4
Upper body 3
Lower body 1
Outfit 6
Accessory 2 + 4

Kimono Top
Head 1
Upper body 2
Lower body 2
Outfit 5
Accessory 2

Pleated Skirt
Head 3
Upper body 1
Lower body 3
Outfit 2
Accessory 1

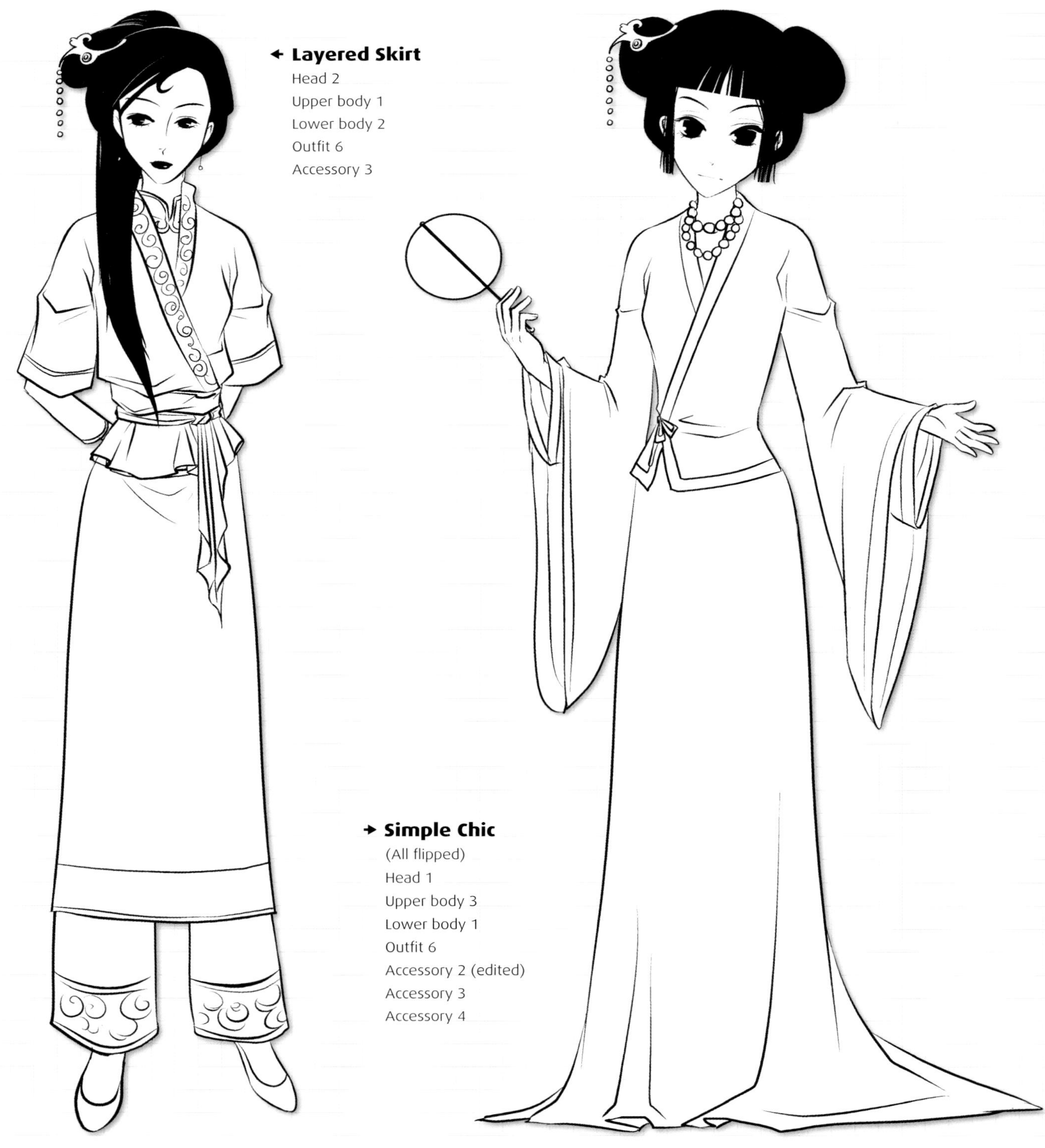

Layered Skirt

Head 2
Upper body 1
Lower body 2
Outfit 6
Accessory 3

Simple Chic

(All flipped)
Head 1
Upper body 3
Lower body 1
Outfit 6
Accessory 2 (edited)
Accessory 3
Accessory 4

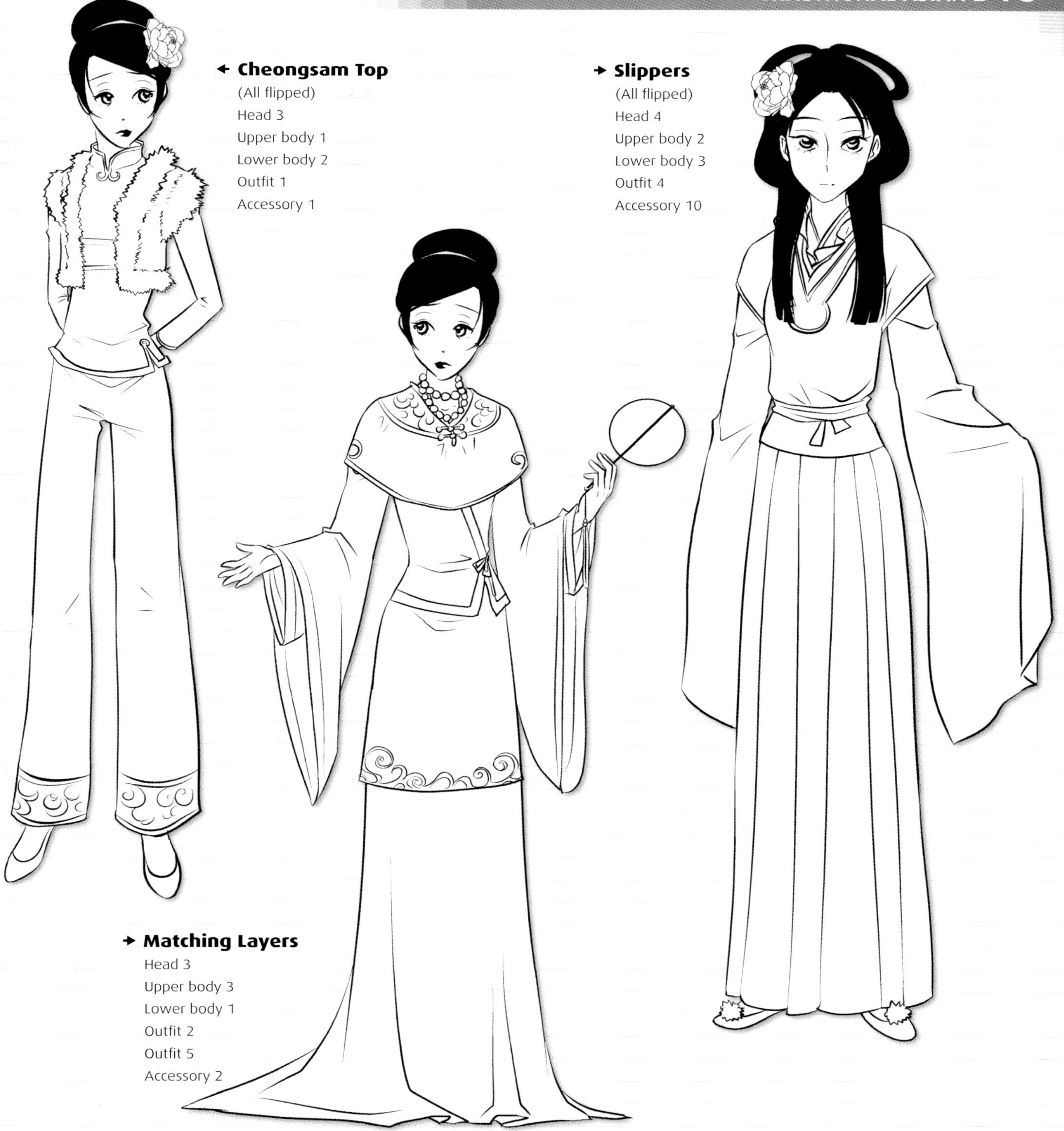

Cheongsam Top
(All flipped)
Head 3
Upper body 1
Lower body 2
Outfit 1
Accessory 1

Slippers
(All flipped)
Head 4
Upper body 2
Lower body 3
Outfit 4
Accessory 10

Matching Layers
Head 3
Upper body 3
Lower body 1
Outfit 2
Outfit 5
Accessory 2

TRADITIONAL ASIAN 3

Layers

- Accessory 1
- Accessory 2
- Accessory 3
- Accessory 4
- Head 1
- Head 2
- Head 3
- Head 4
- Outfit 1
- Outfit 2
- Outfit 3
- Outfit 4
- Upper Body 1
- Upper Body 2
- Outfit 5
- Outfit 6
- Lower Body 1
- Lower Body 2
- Lower Body 3
- Lower Body 4

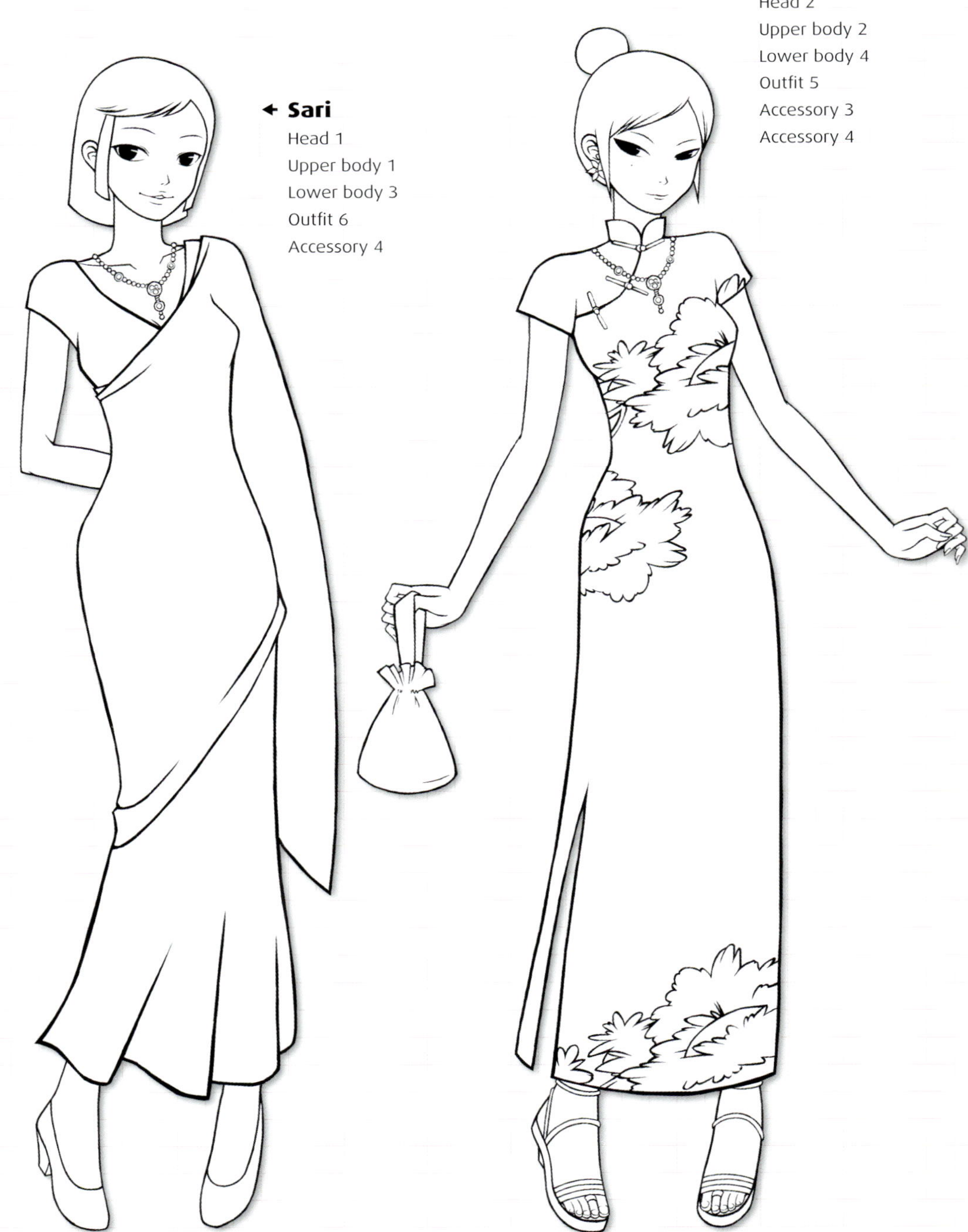

Traditional Casual

The simplicity of the clothes in this set are great for adding your own patterns to when coloring. Outfits can be dressed up with jewelry and heels, or dressed down with sandals.

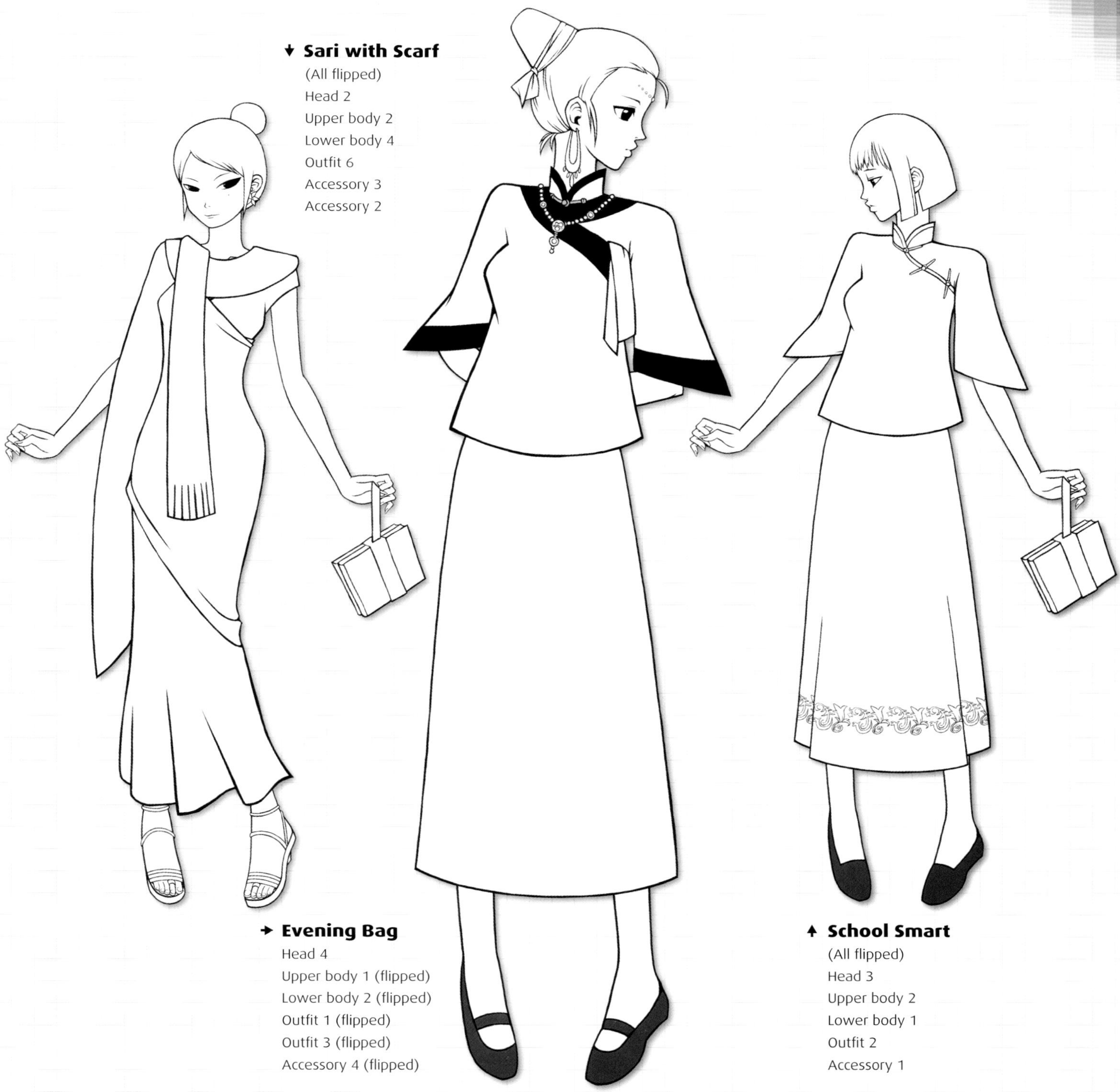

↓ Sari with Scarf
(All flipped)
Head 2
Upper body 2
Lower body 4
Outfit 6
Accessory 3
Accessory 2

→ Evening Bag
Head 4
Upper body 1 (flipped)
Lower body 2 (flipped)
Outfit 1 (flipped)
Outfit 3 (flipped)
Accessory 4 (flipped)

↑ School Smart
(All flipped)
Head 3
Upper body 2
Lower body 1
Outfit 2
Accessory 1

TRADITIONAL EUROPEAN 1

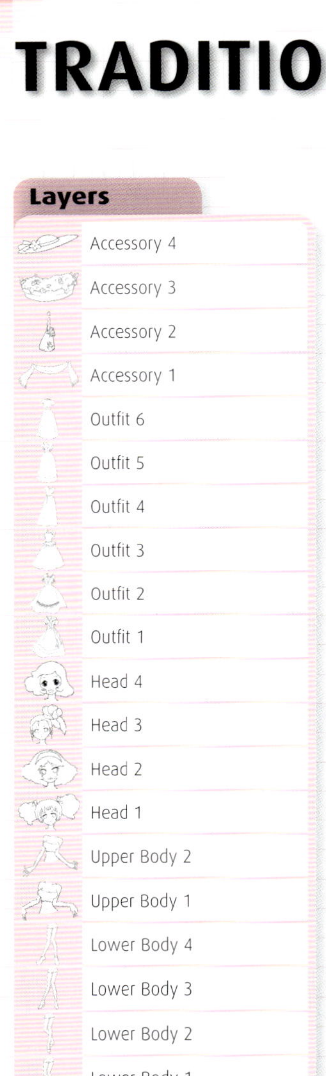

↓ Flower Girl

Head 1
Upper body 1
Lower body 3
Outfit 6
Accessory 1

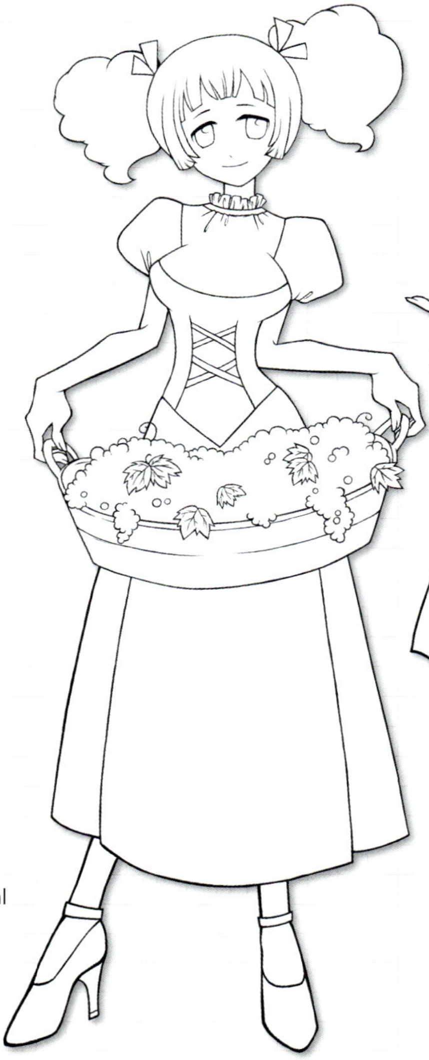

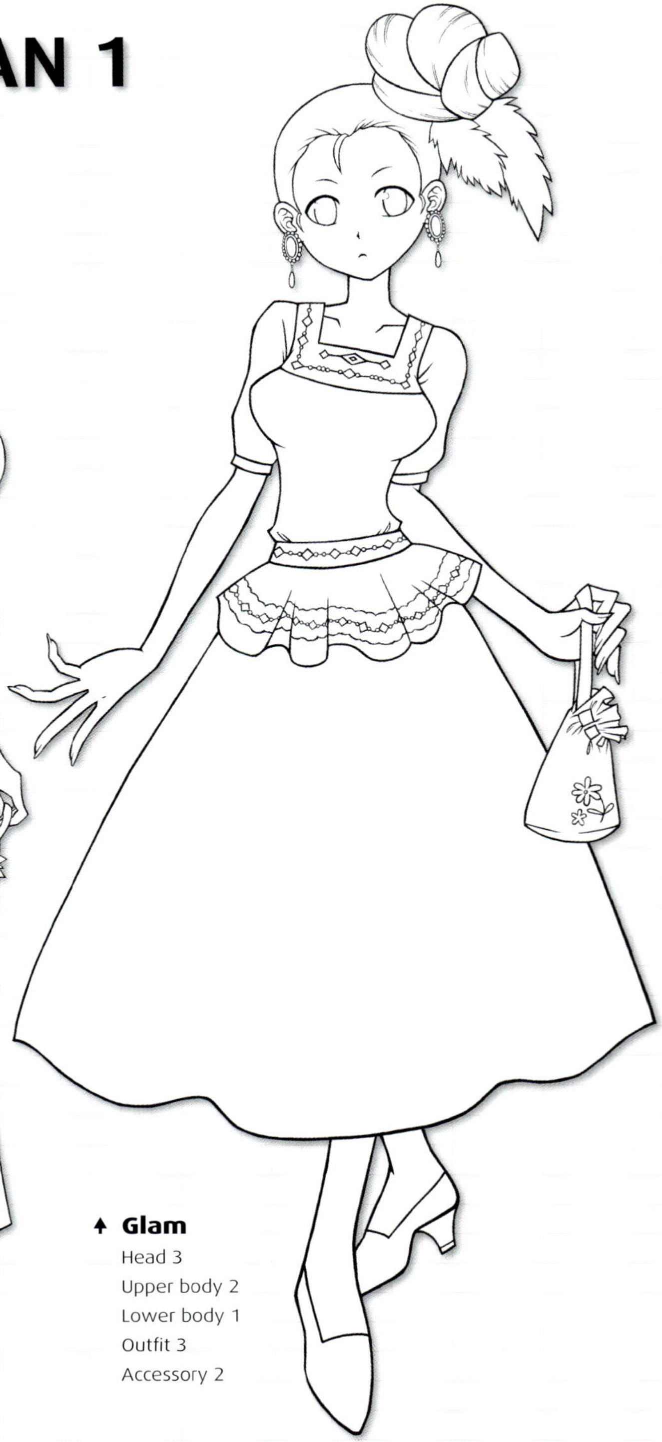

↑ Glam

Head 3
Upper body 2
Lower body 1
Outfit 3
Accessory 2

Maidens

There are lots of full, floaty dresses for these traditional maidens, who would look perfect in the Traditional European Town background. The clutched-hand poses make it easy to add accessories to these figures.

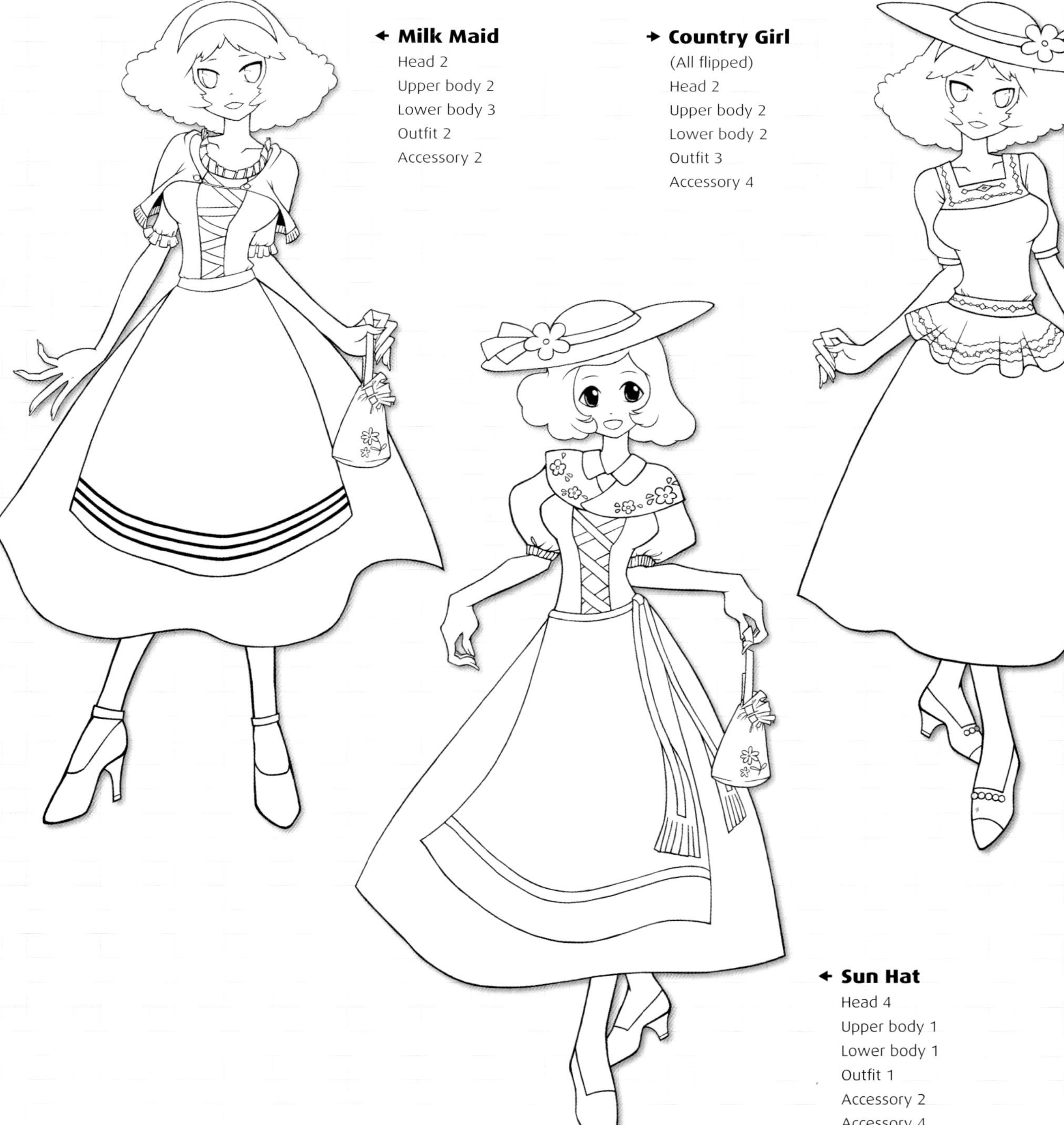

← Milk Maid
Head 2
Upper body 2
Lower body 3
Outfit 2
Accessory 2

→ Country Girl
(All flipped)
Head 2
Upper body 2
Lower body 2
Outfit 3
Accessory 4

← Sun Hat
Head 4
Upper body 1
Lower body 1
Outfit 1
Accessory 2
Accessory 4

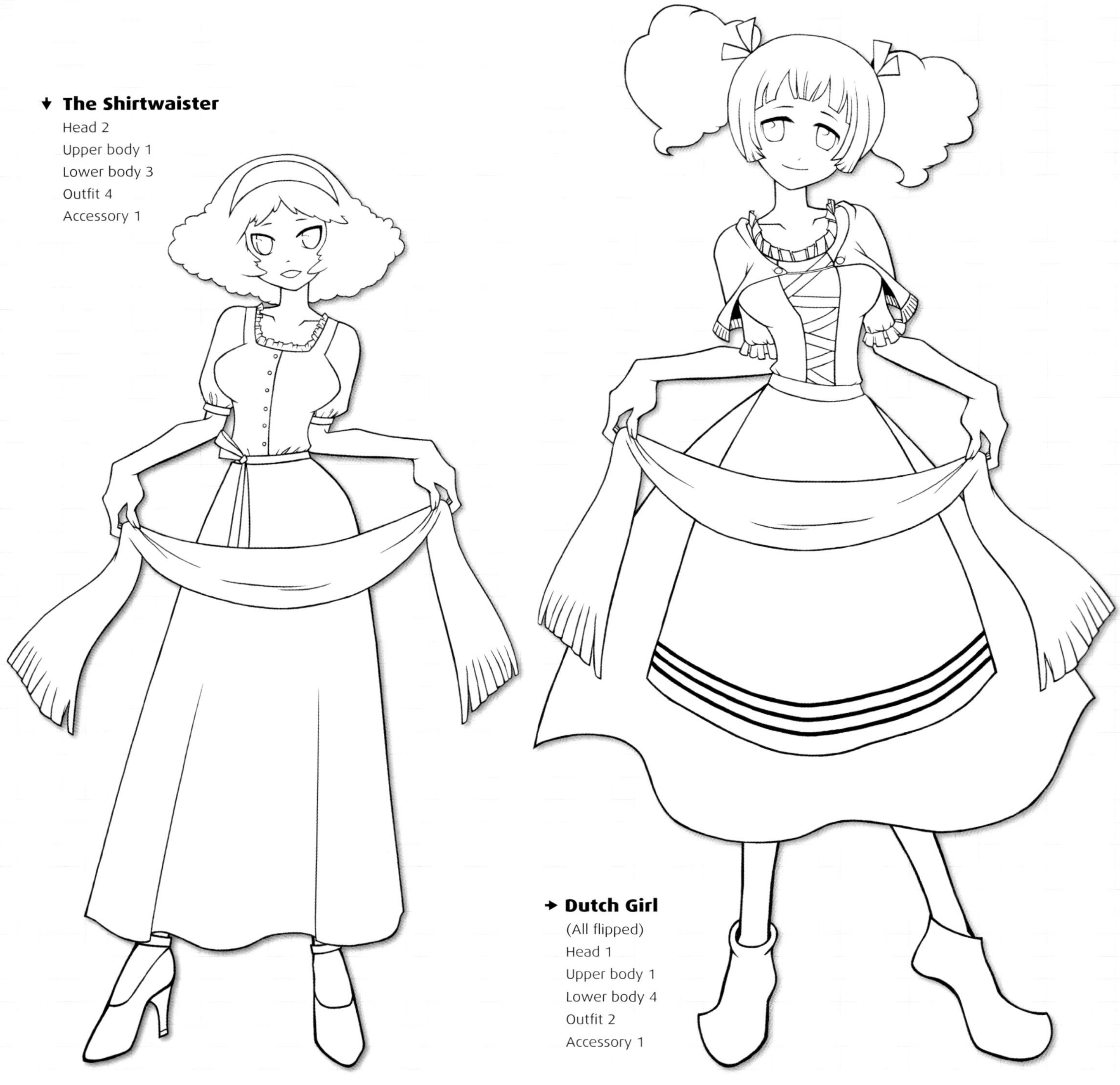

The Shirtwaister

Head 2
Upper body 1
Lower body 3
Outfit 4
Accessory 1

Dutch Girl

(All flipped)
Head 1
Upper body 1
Lower body 4
Outfit 2
Accessory 1

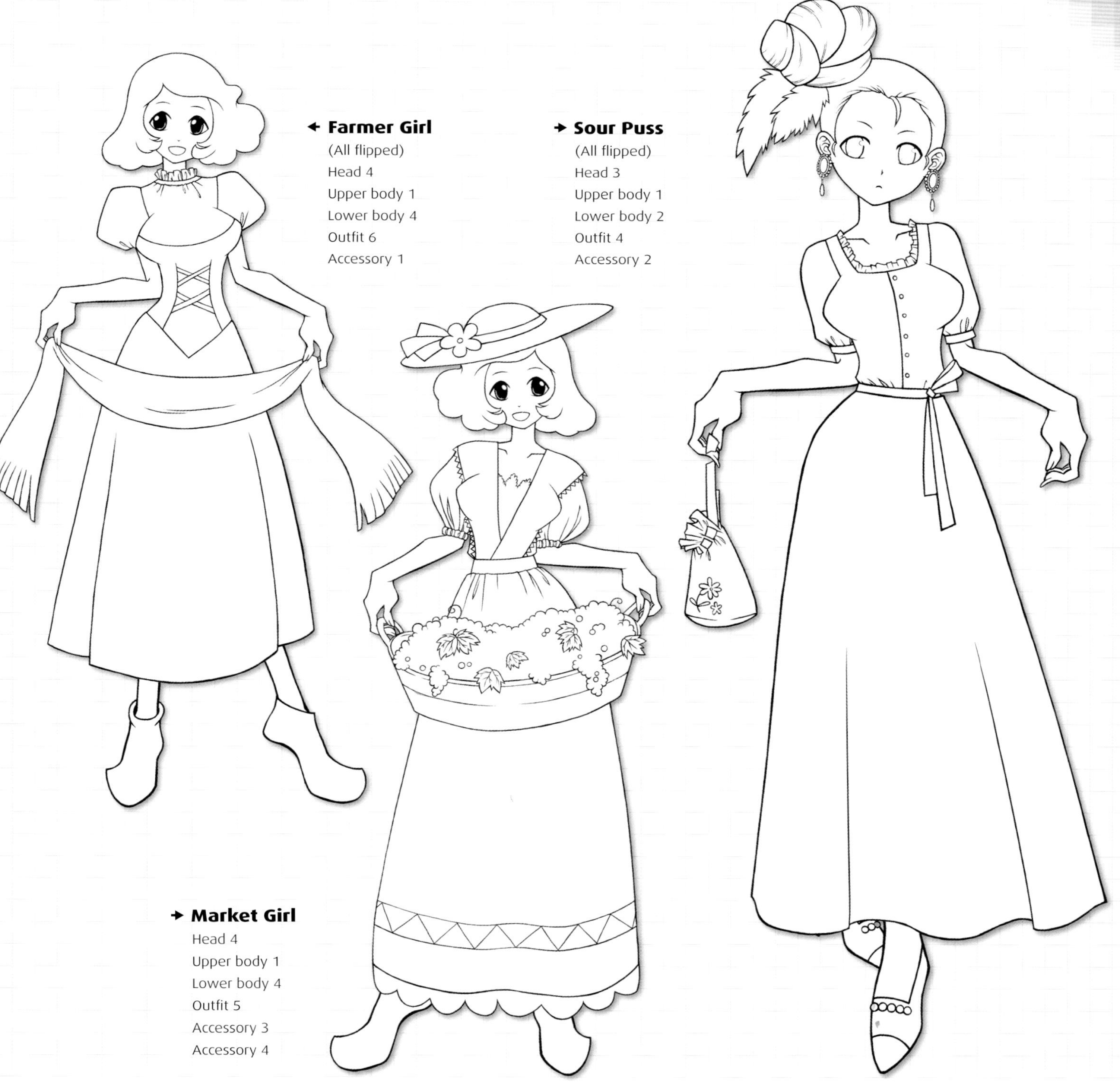

← Farmer Girl
(All flipped)
Head 4
Upper body 1
Lower body 4
Outfit 6
Accessory 1

→ Sour Puss
(All flipped)
Head 3
Upper body 1
Lower body 2
Outfit 4
Accessory 2

→ Market Girl
Head 4
Upper body 1
Lower body 4
Outfit 5
Accessory 3
Accessory 4

TRADITIONAL EUROPEAN 2

Layers

- Accessory 4
- Accessory 3
- Accessory 2
- Accessory 1
- Outfit 6
- Outfit 5
- Outfit 4
- Outfit 3
- Outfit 2
- Outfit 1
- Head 4
- Head 3
- Head 2
- Head 1
- Upper Body 2
- Upper Body 1
- Lower Body 4
- Lower Body 3
- Lower Body 2
- Lower Body 1

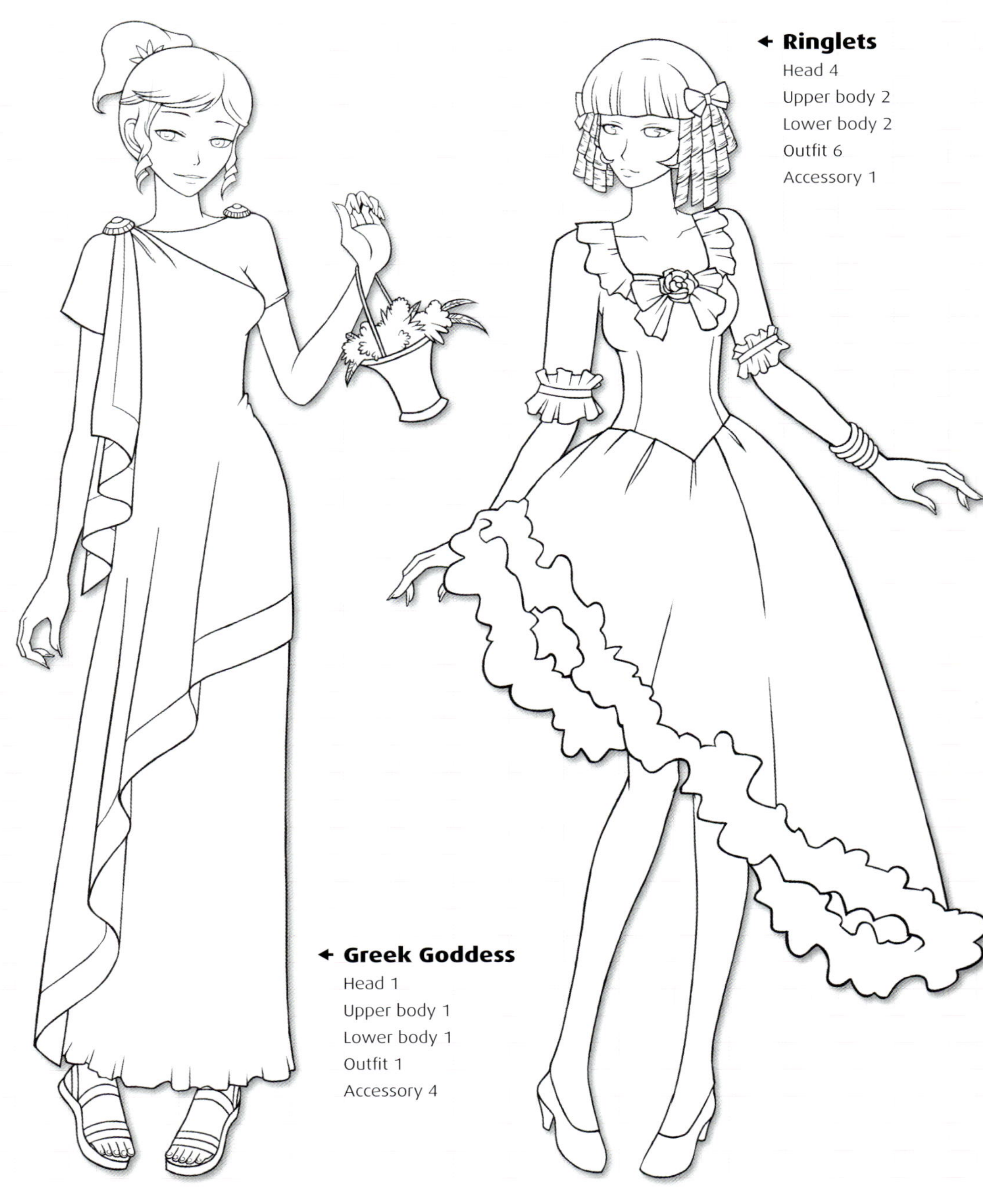

Ringlets
Head 4
Upper body 2
Lower body 2
Outfit 6
Accessory 1

Greek Goddess
Head 1
Upper body 1
Lower body 1
Outfit 1
Accessory 4

Princesses

Here the traditional fairy-tale princess gets a manga makeover. Choose from six different dresses and pair them with the accessories of your choice to create your own manga princess.

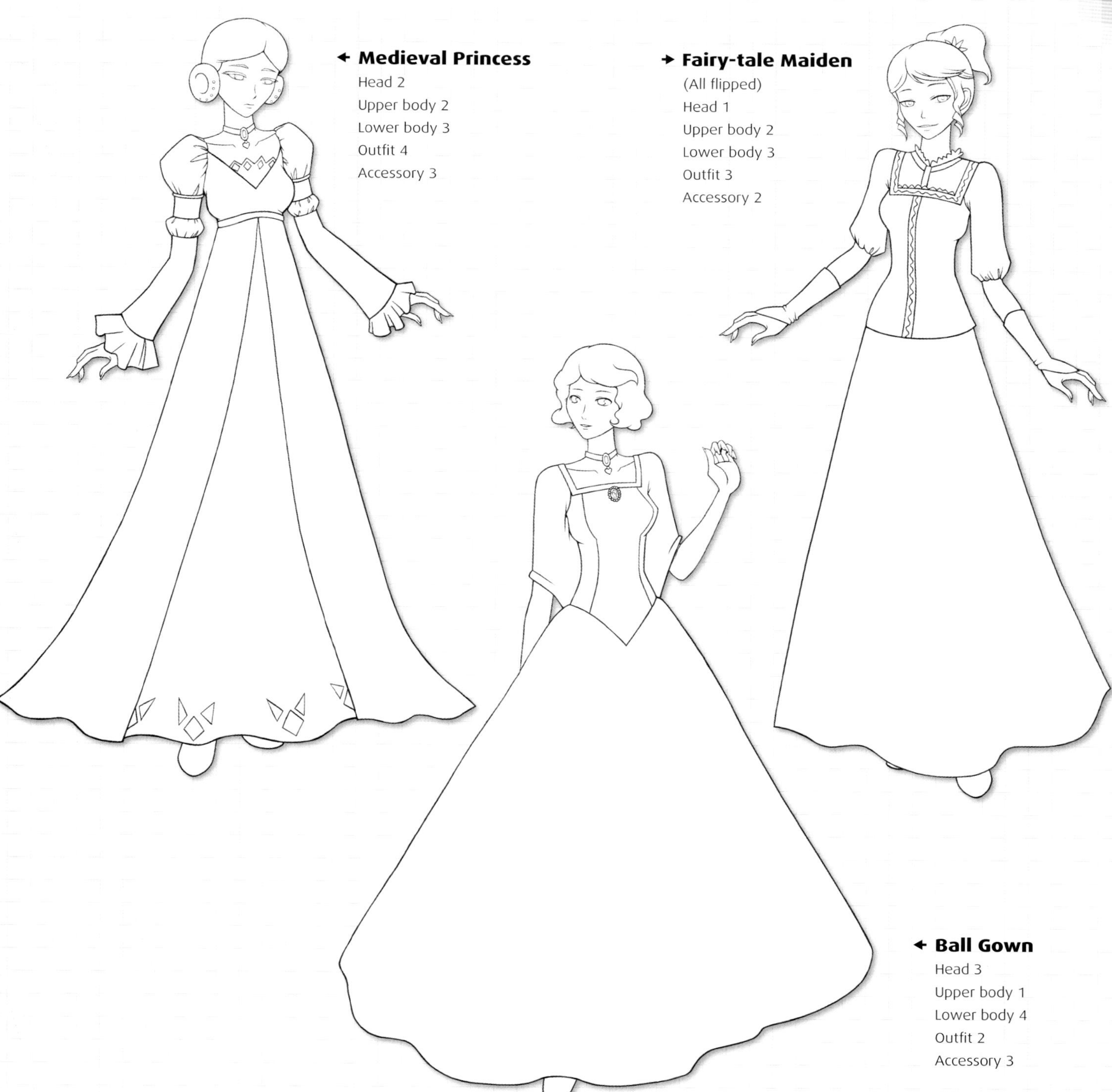

← Medieval Princess
Head 2
Upper body 2
Lower body 3
Outfit 4
Accessory 3
→ Fairy-tale Maiden
(All flipped)
Head 1
Upper body 2
Lower body 3
Outfit 3
Accessory 2
← Ball Gown
Head 3
Upper body 1
Lower body 4
Outfit 2
Accessory 3

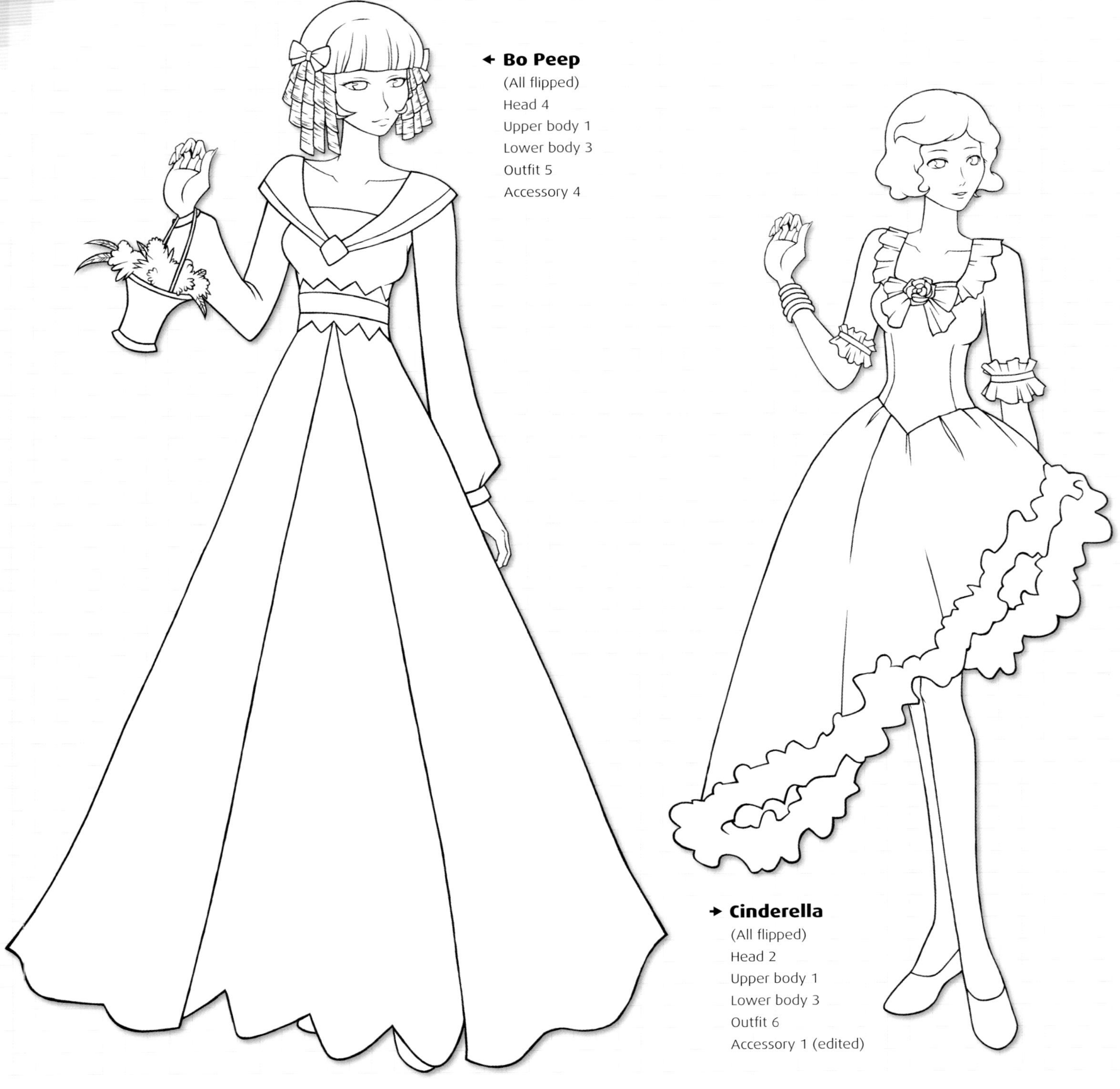
Bo Peep
(All flipped)
Head 4
Upper body 1
Lower body 3
Outfit 5
Accessory 4
Cinderella
(All flipped)
Head 2
Upper body 1
Lower body 3
Outfit 6
Accessory 1 (edited)

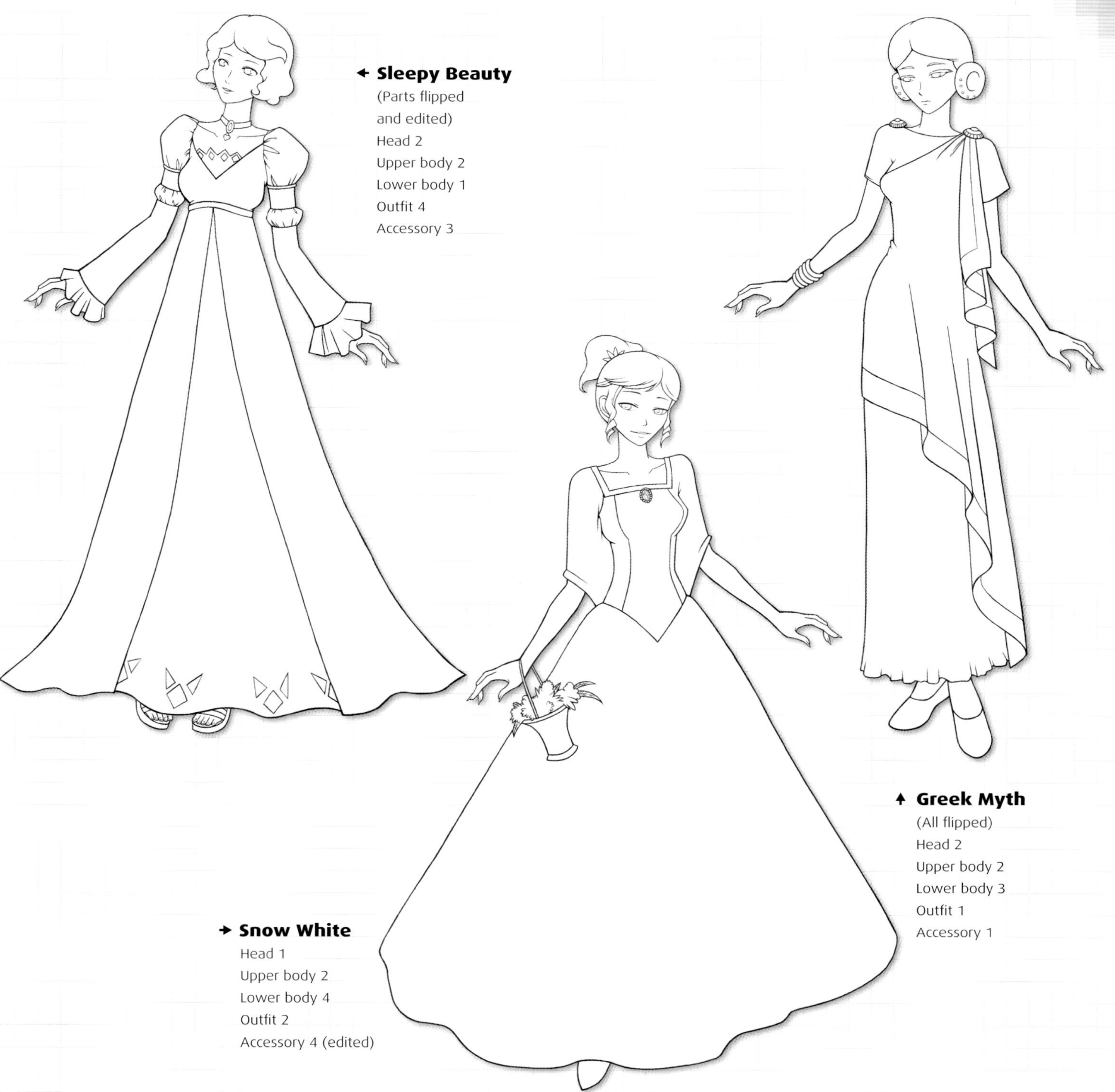

← Sleepy Beauty
(Parts flipped and edited)
Head 2
Upper body 2
Lower body 1
Outfit 4
Accessory 3

→ Snow White
Head 1
Upper body 2
Lower body 4
Outfit 2
Accessory 4 (edited)

↑ Greek Myth
(All flipped)
Head 2
Upper body 2
Lower body 3
Outfit 1
Accessory 1

TRADITIONAL EUROPEAN 3

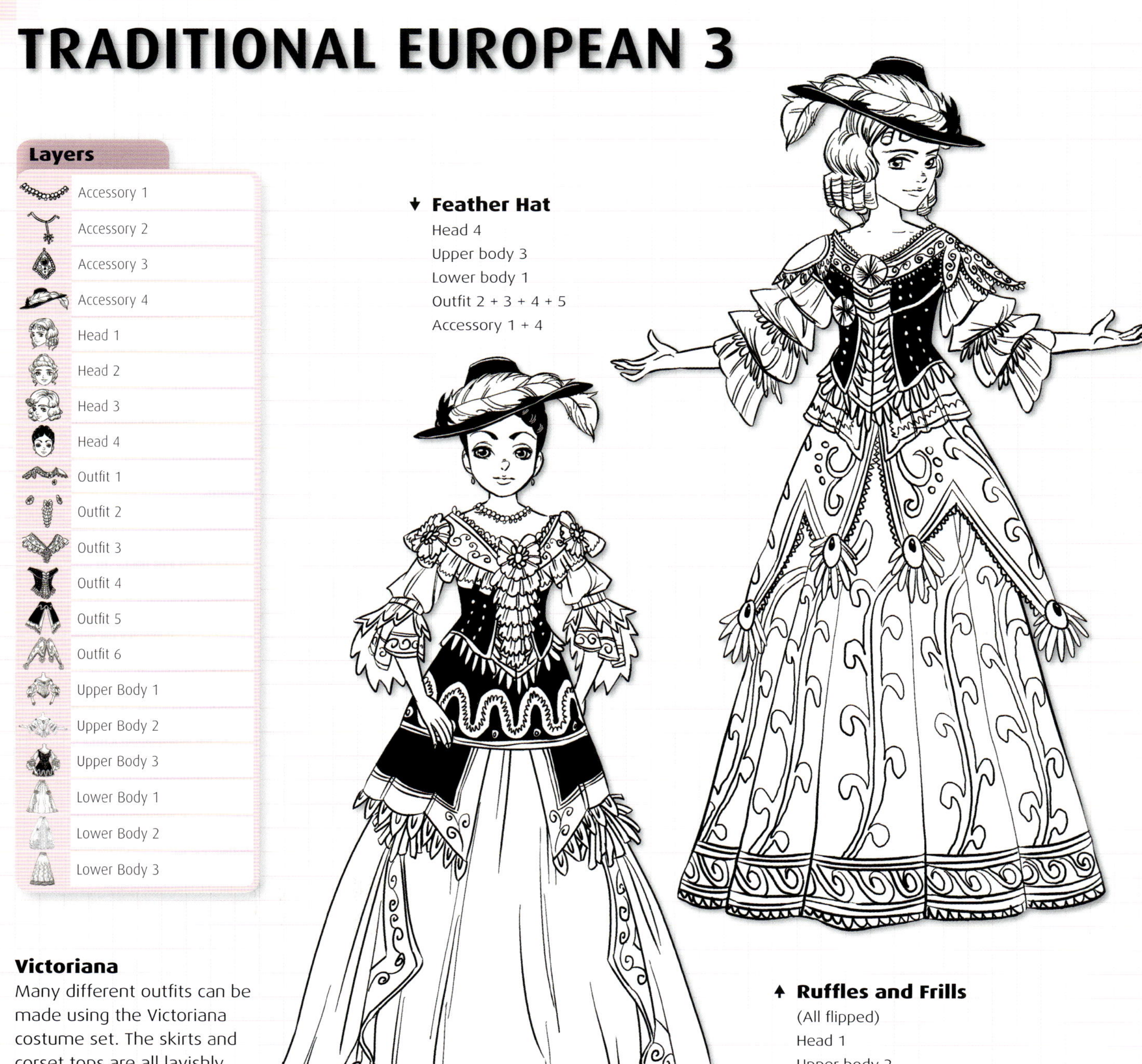

↓ Feather Hat
Head 4
Upper body 3
Lower body 1
Outfit 2 + 3 + 4 + 5
Accessory 1 + 4

↑ Ruffles and Frills
(All flipped)
Head 1
Upper body 2
Lower body 3
Outfit 1 + 4 + 6
Accessory 4

Victoriana

Many different outfits can be made using the Victoriana costume set. The skirts and corset tops are all lavishly decorated and can be accessorized with delicate trims and elaborate jewelry.

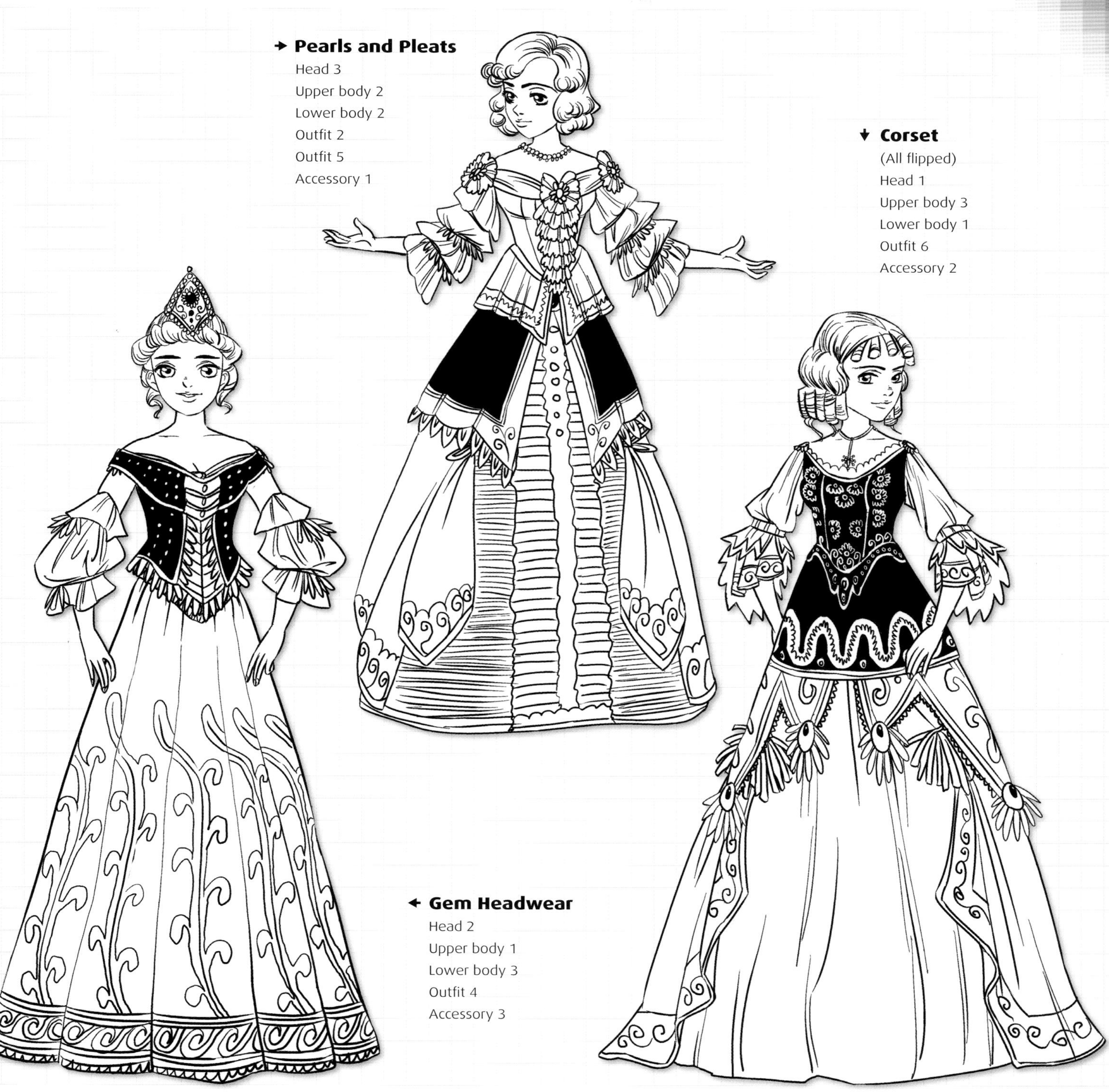

→ Pearls and Pleats
Head 3
Upper body 2
Lower body 2
Outfit 2
Outfit 5
Accessory 1

↓ Corset
(All flipped)
Head 1
Upper body 3
Lower body 1
Outfit 6
Accessory 2

← Gem Headwear
Head 2
Upper body 1
Lower body 3
Outfit 4
Accessory 3

WARRIOR 1

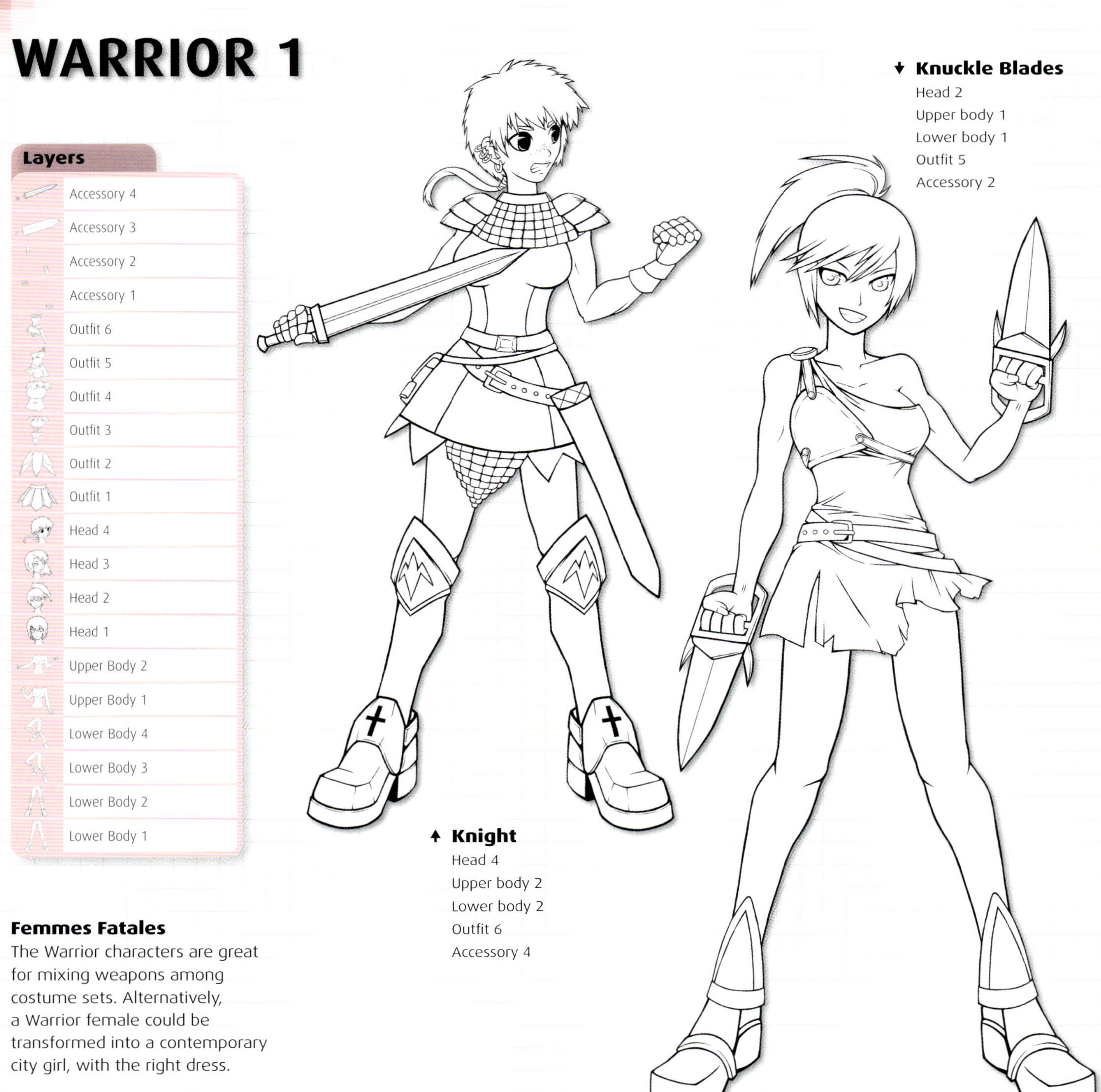

Femmes Fatales

The Warrior characters are great for mixing weapons among costume sets. Alternatively, a Warrior female could be transformed into a contemporary city girl, with the right dress.

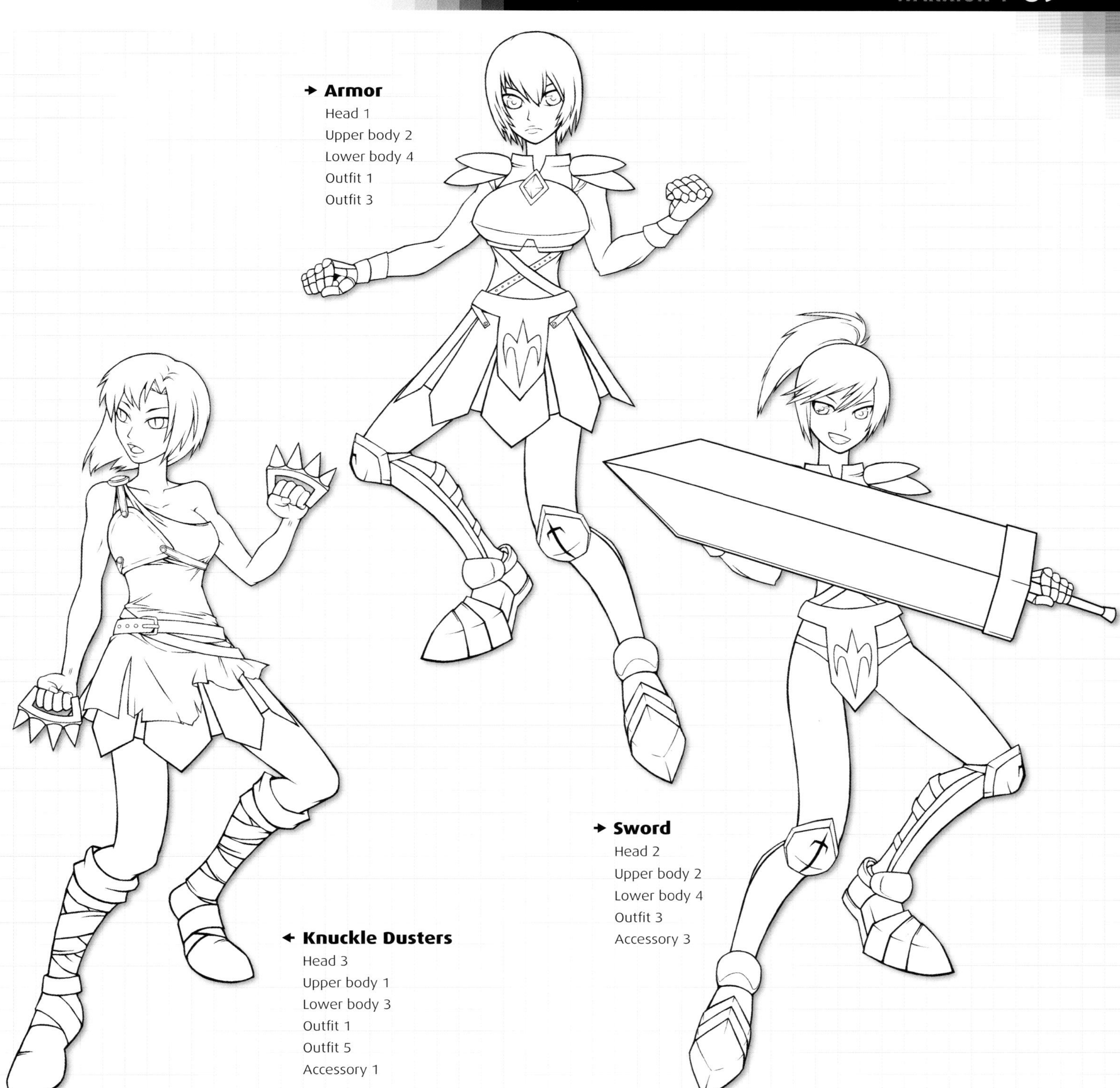
➔ Armor
Head 1
Upper body 2
Lower body 4
Outfit 1
Outfit 3
➔ Sword
Head 2
Upper body 2
Lower body 4
Outfit 3
Accessory 3
← Knuckle Dusters
Head 3
Upper body 1
Lower body 3
Outfit 1
Outfit 5
Accessory 1

WARRIOR 2

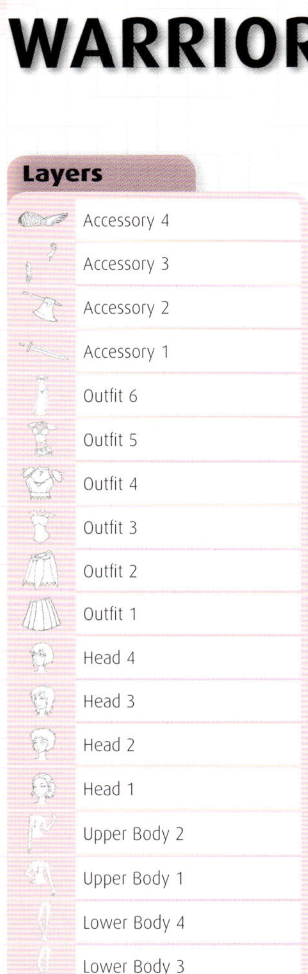

→ Armored Dress

Head 2 (flipped)
Upper body 2
Lower body 2
Outfit 6
Accessory 3

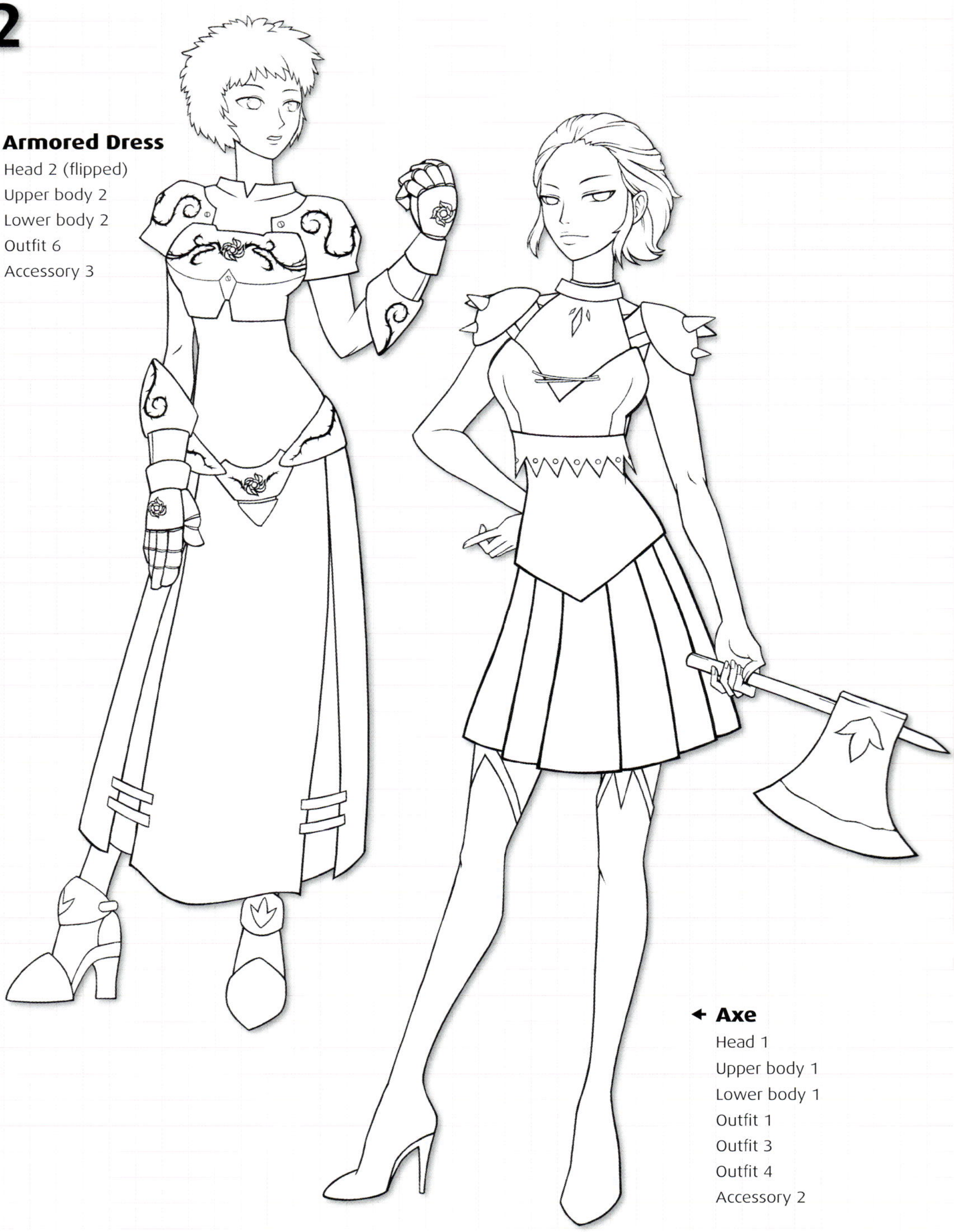

Medieval Warriors

These Warriors are straight out of the Middle Ages. Among their armored accessories are a sword and an axe. Choose from a variety of looks to create your own knightess of the Round Table.

← Axe

Head 1
Upper body 1
Lower body 1
Outfit 1
Outfit 3
Outfit 4
Accessory 2

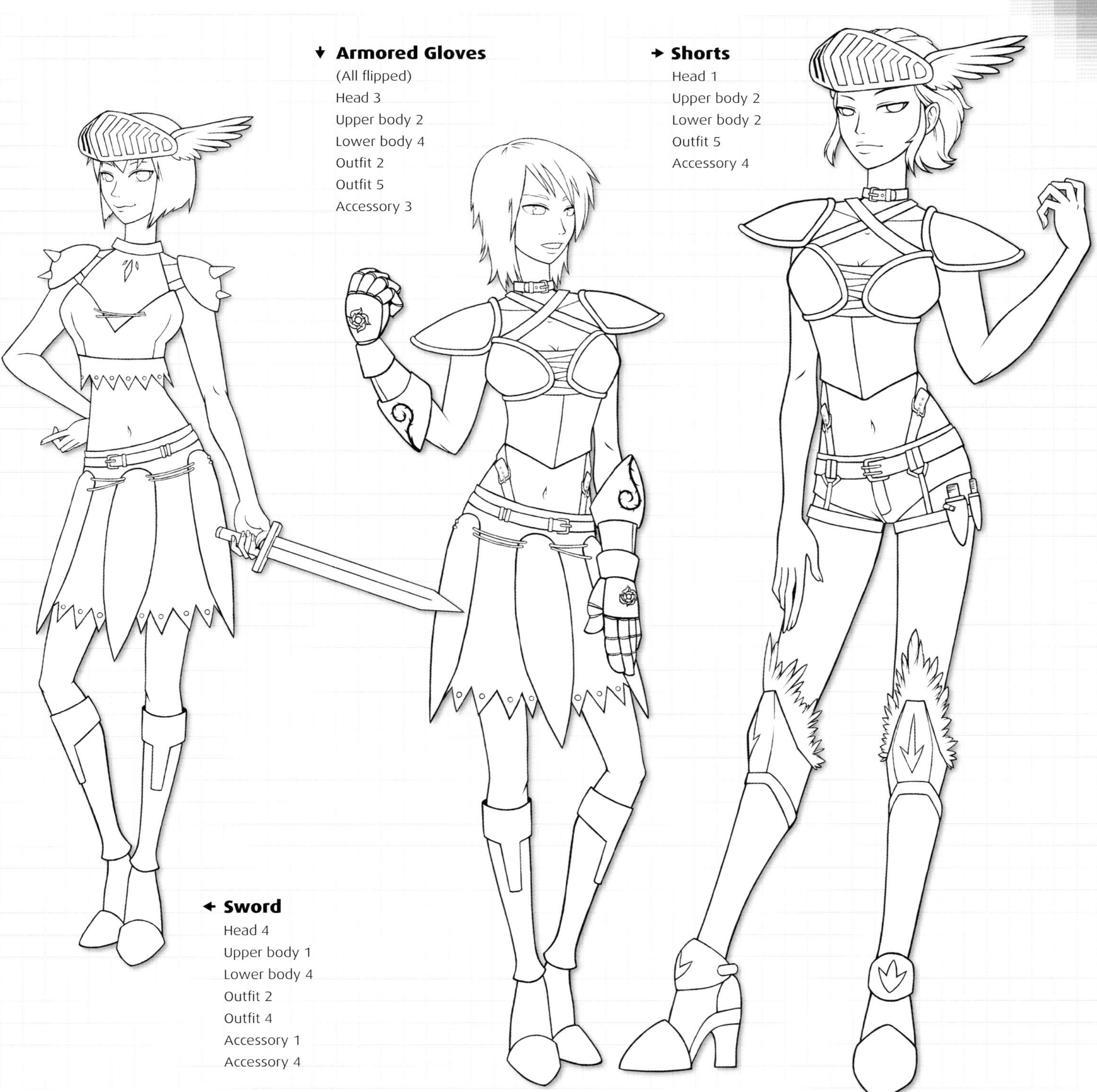

↓ Armored Gloves
(All flipped)
Head 3
Upper body 2
Lower body 4
Outfit 2
Outfit 5
Accessory 3
→ Shorts
Head 1
Upper body 2
Lower body 2
Outfit 5
Accessory 4
← Sword
Head 4
Upper body 1
Lower body 4
Outfit 2
Outfit 4
Accessory 1
Accessory 4

WARRIOR 3

Layers

- Accessory 1
- Accessory 2
- Accessory 3
- Accessory 4
- Outfit 1
- Outfit 2
- Outfit 3
- Outfit 4
- Outfit 5
- Outfit 6
- Head 1
- Head 2
- Head 3
- Head 4
- Upper Body 1
- Upper Body 2
- Upper Body 3
- Lower Body 1
- Lower Body 2
- Lower Body 3

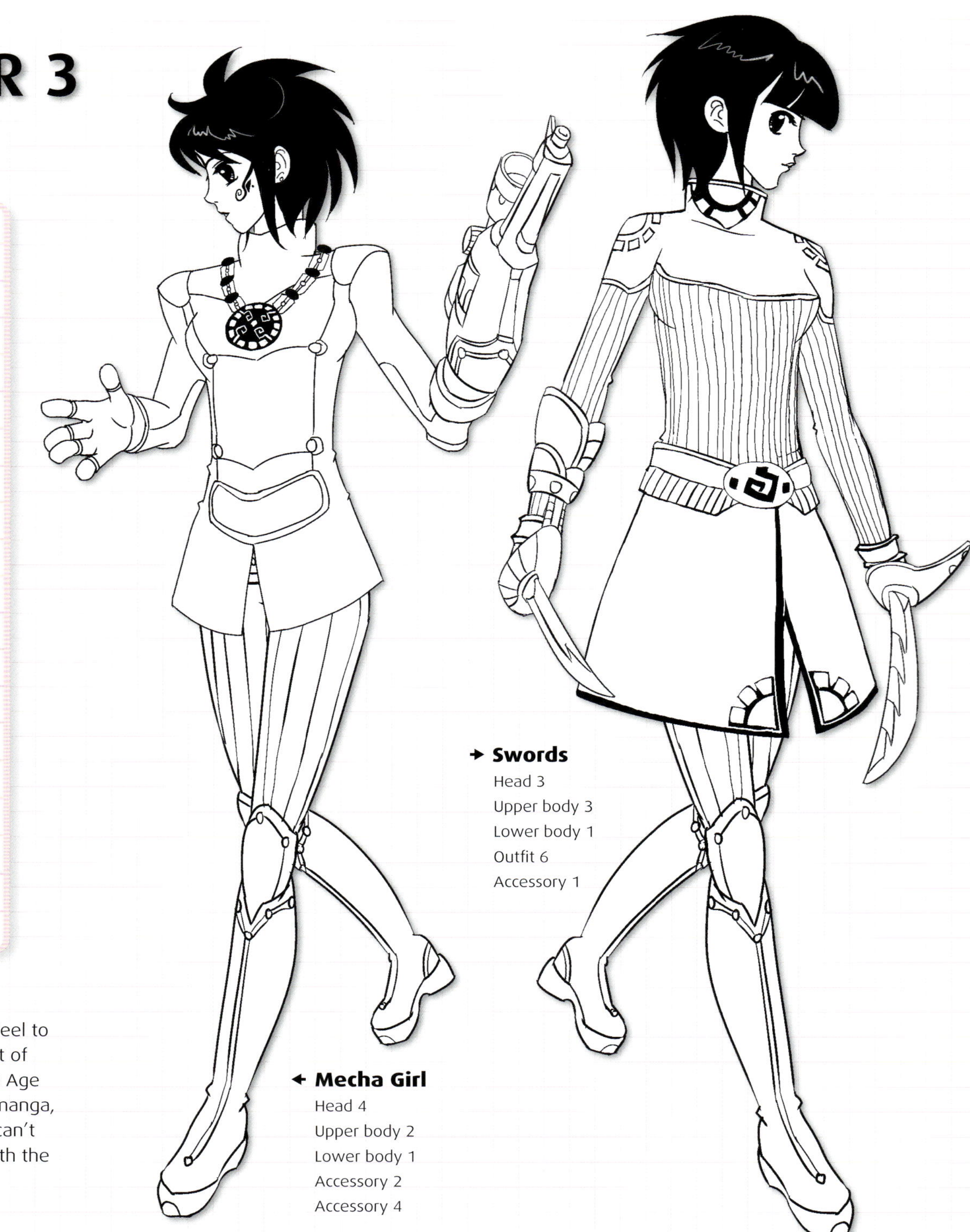

Swords
Head 3
Upper body 3
Lower body 1
Outfit 6
Accessory 1

Mecha Girl
Head 4
Upper body 2
Lower body 1
Accessory 2
Accessory 4

Futuristic Fighters

These Warriors have a Sci-fi feel to them. They wouldn't look out of place battling with the Space Age gals. But, when it comes to manga, there's no reason why they can't travel back in time to war with the Medieval knightesses.

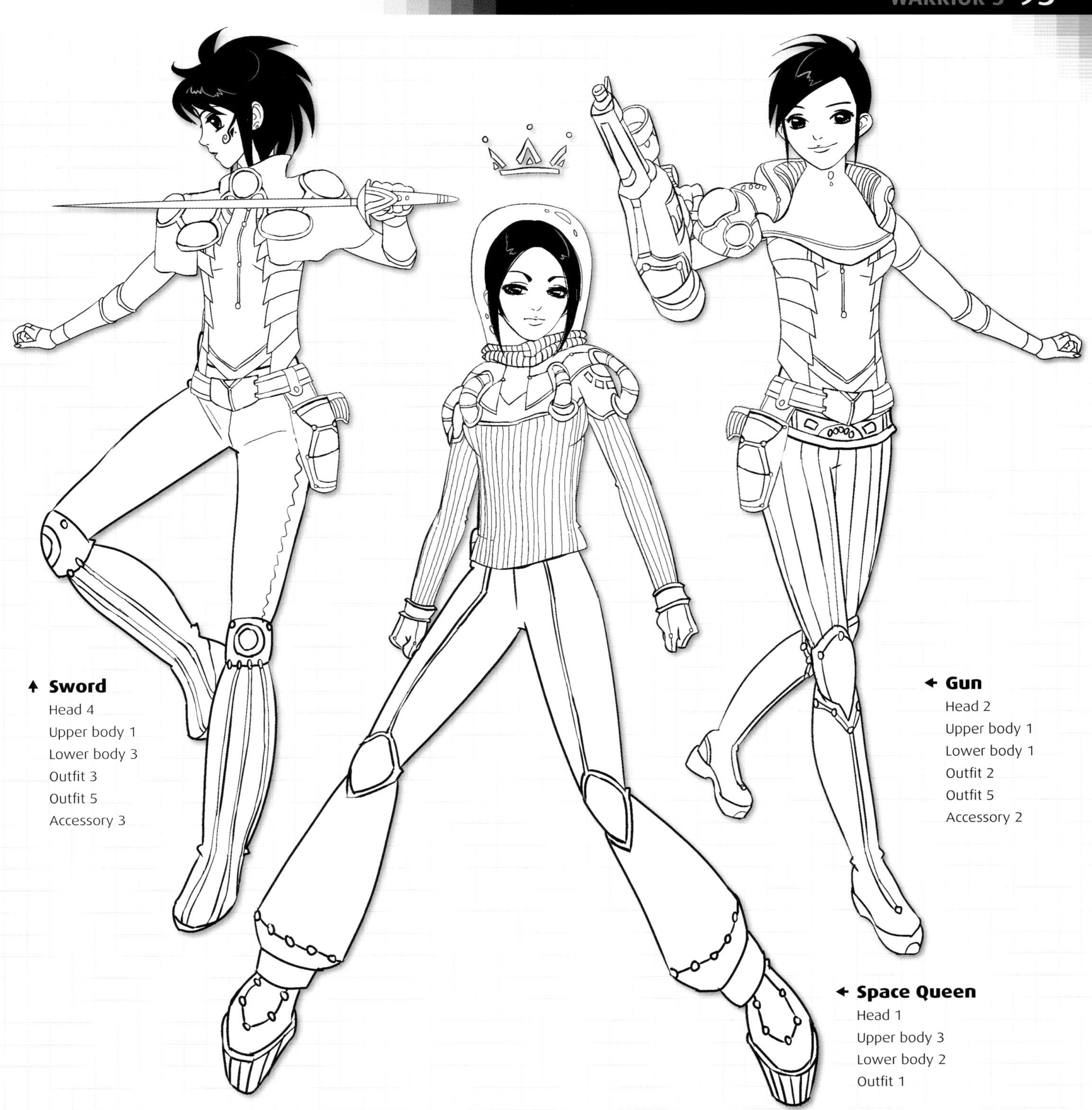

↑ Sword
Head 4
Upper body 1
Lower body 3
Outfit 3
Outfit 5
Accessory 3

← Gun
Head 2
Upper body 1
Lower body 1
Outfit 2
Outfit 5
Accessory 2

← Space Queen
Head 1
Upper body 3
Lower body 2
Outfit 1

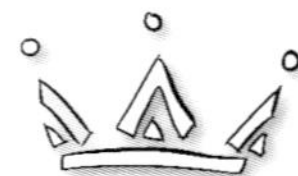

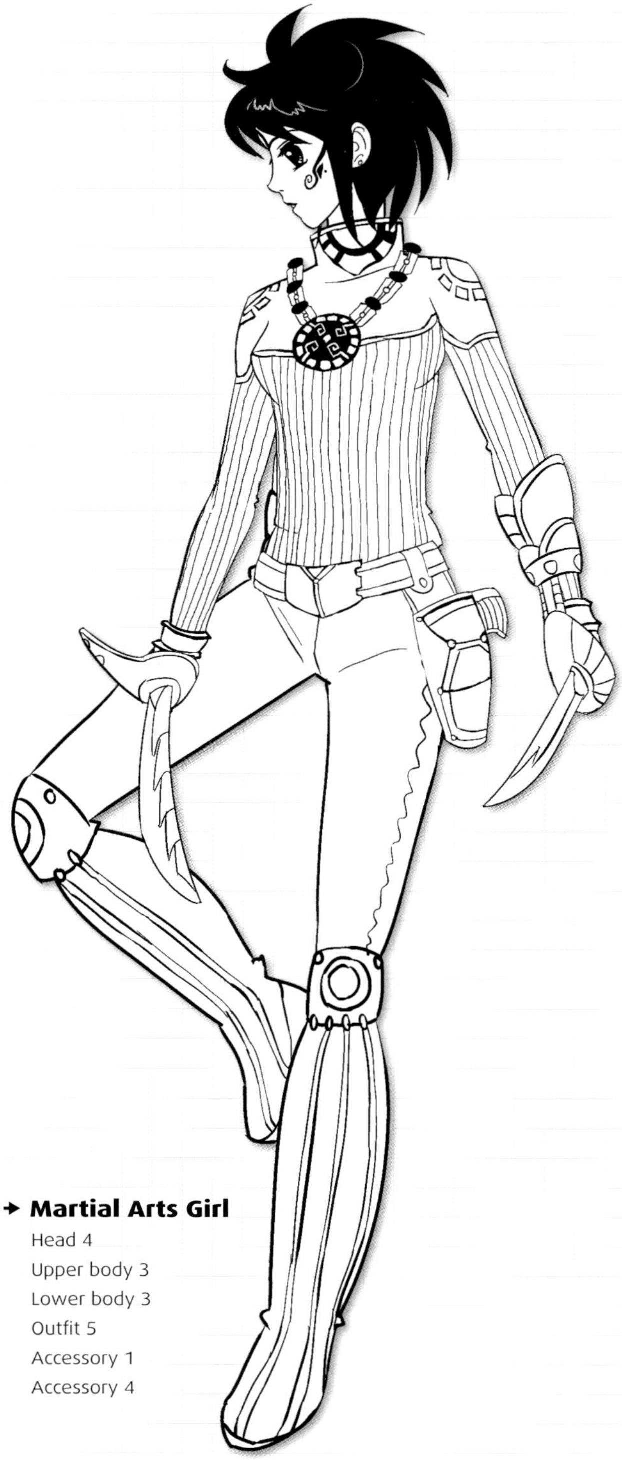

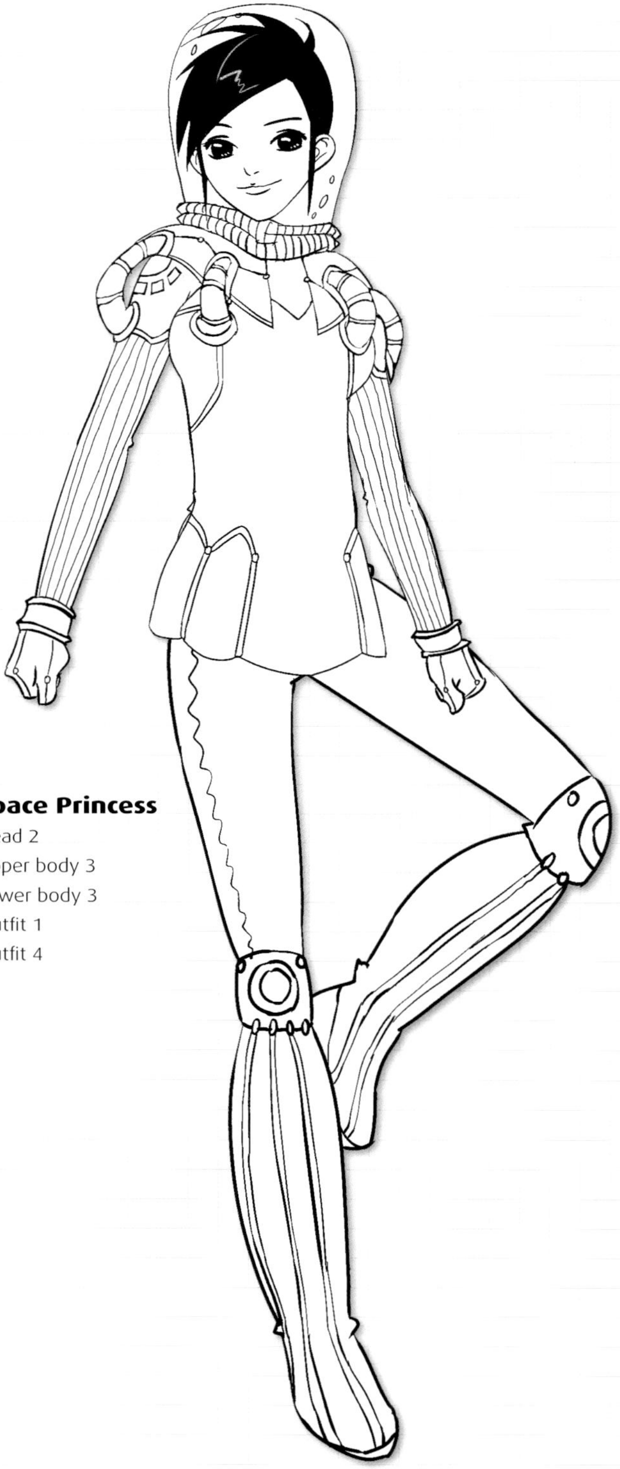

→ Space Princess

Head 2
Upper body 3
Lower body 3
Outfit 1
Outfit 4

→ Martial Arts Girl

Head 4
Upper body 3
Lower body 3
Outfit 5
Accessory 1
Accessory 4

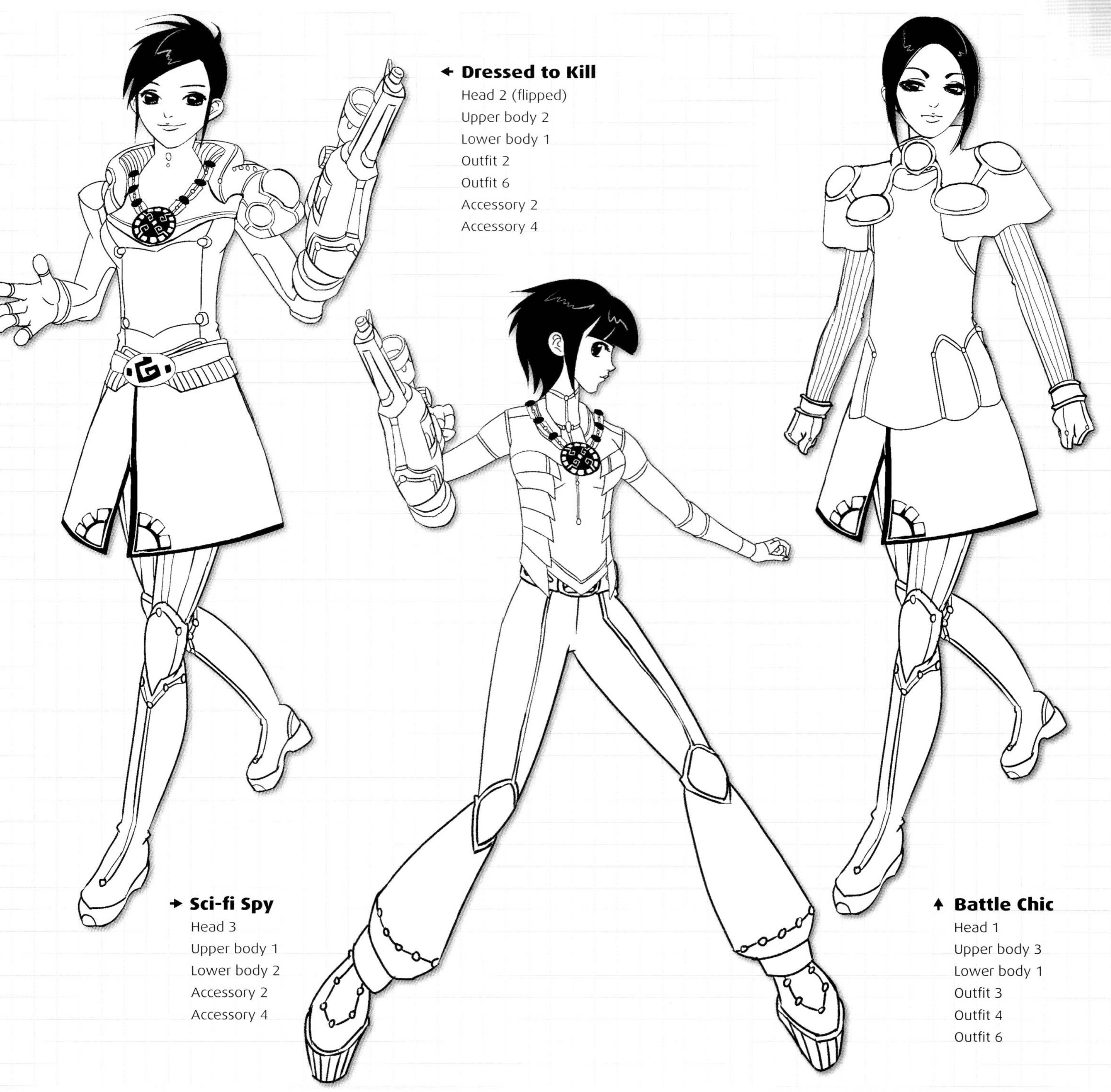

← Dressed to Kill
Head 2 (flipped)
Upper body 2
Lower body 1
Outfit 2
Outfit 6
Accessory 2
Accessory 4

→ Sci-fi Spy
Head 3
Upper body 1
Lower body 2
Accessory 2
Accessory 4

↑ Battle Chic
Head 1
Upper body 3
Lower body 1
Outfit 3
Outfit 4
Outfit 6

CHILD 1

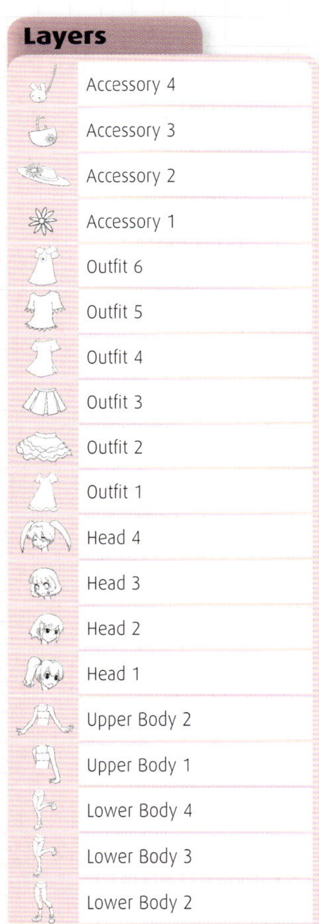

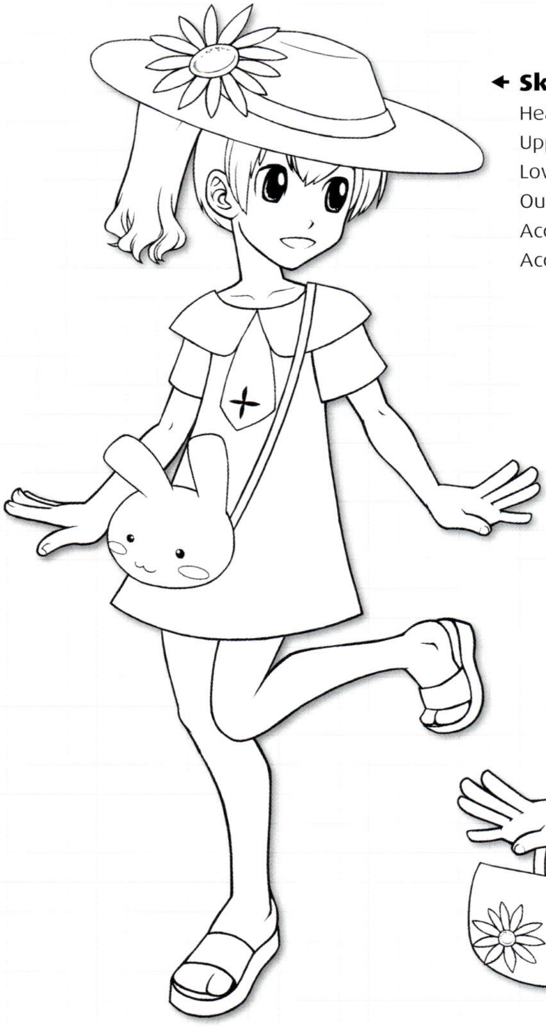

Skipping Girl

Head 1
Upper body 2
Lower body 3
Outfit 6
Accessory 2
Accessory 4

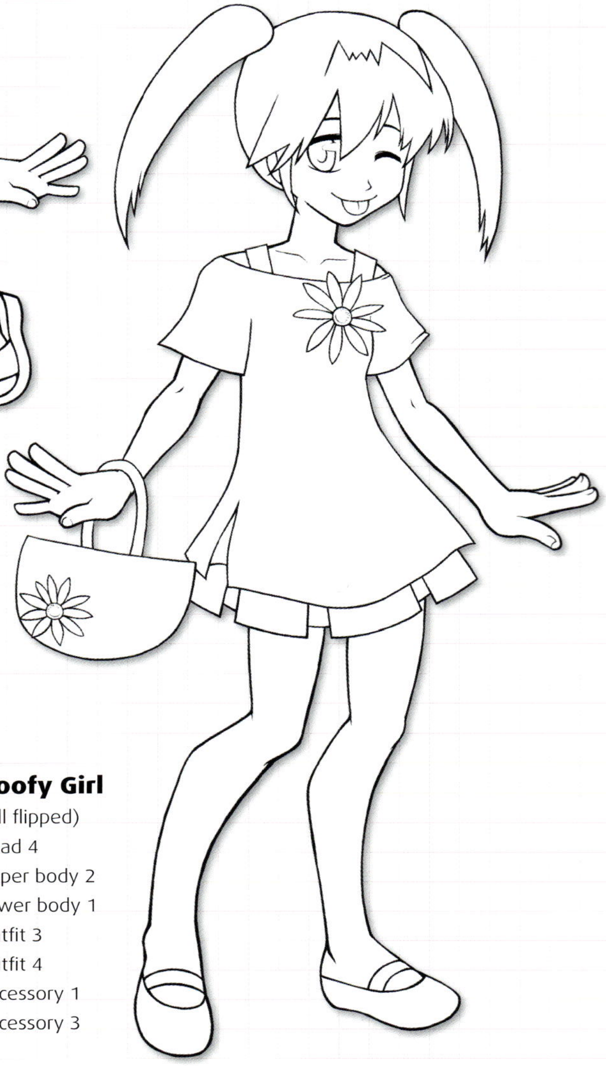

Goofy Girl

(All flipped)
Head 4
Upper body 2
Lower body 1
Outfit 3
Outfit 4
Accessory 1
Accessory 3

School Days

These schoolgirls make a lot of faces! Choose from a range of their cheeky expressions to pair with these cute outifts. Many of the Child and Kawaii sets are also of a similar size so be sure to experiment and mix and match. Remember if the costumes don't fit exactly on other characters you can always edit them!

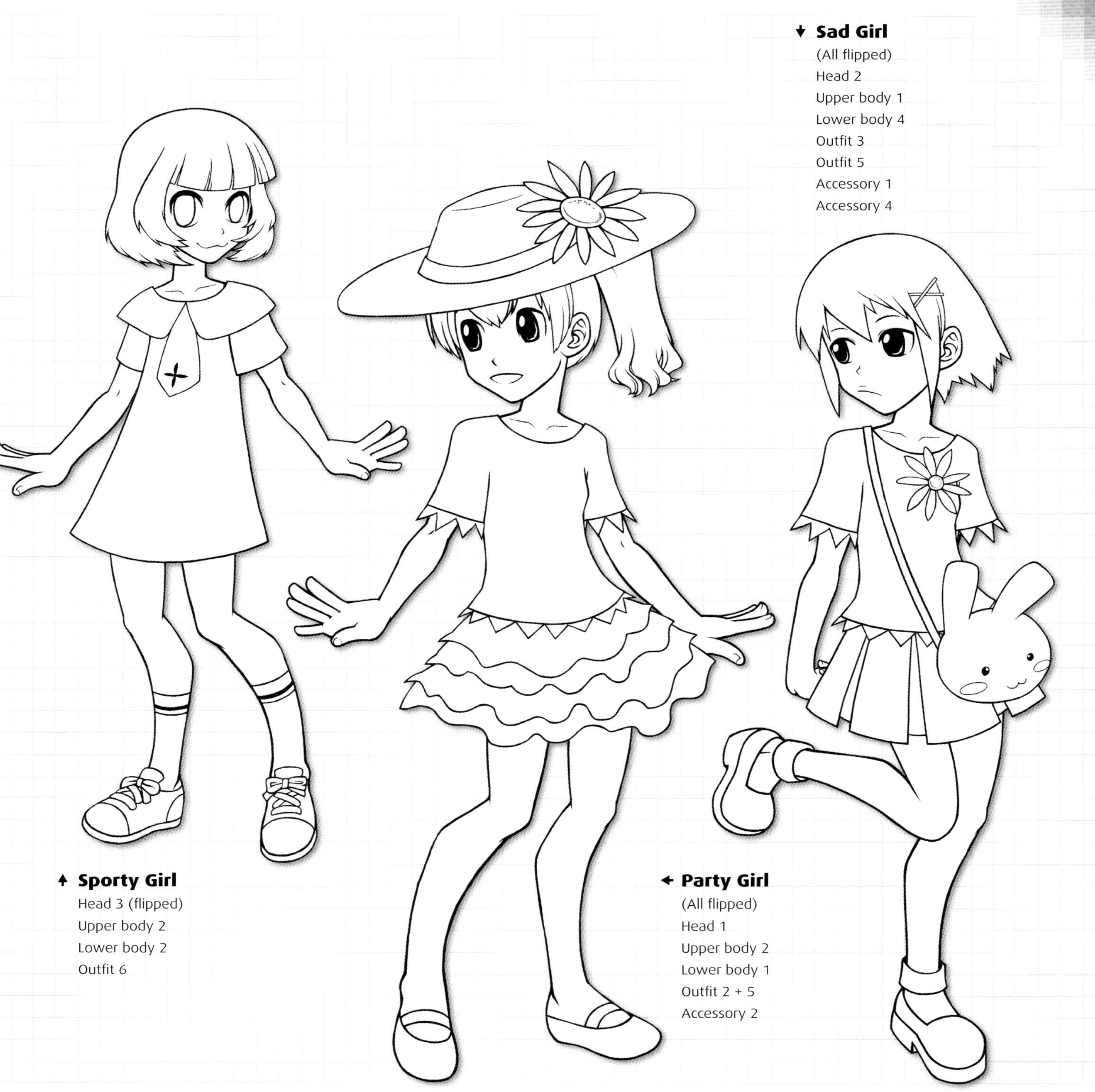

Sad Girl
(All flipped)
Head 2
Upper body 1
Lower body 4
Outfit 3
Outfit 5
Accessory 1
Accessory 4

Sporty Girl
Head 3 (flipped)
Upper body 2
Lower body 2
Outfit 6

Party Girl
(All flipped)
Head 1
Upper body 2
Lower body 1
Outfit 2 + 5
Accessory 2

CHILD 2

Layers

- Accessory 4
- Accessory 3
- Accessory 2
- Accessory 1
- Outfit 6
- Outfit 5
- Outfit 4
- Outfit 3
- Outfit 2
- Outfit 1
- Head 4
- Head 3
- Head 2
- Head 1
- Upper Body 2
- Upper Body 1
- Lower Body 4
- Lower Body 3
- Lower Body 2
- Lower Body 1

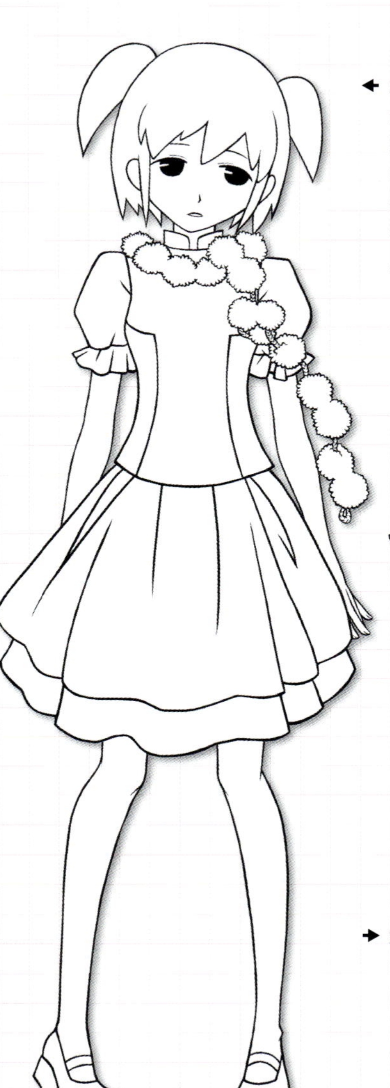

Sad Face
Head 2
Upper body 2
Lower body 2
Outfit 2
Outfit 3
Accessory 4

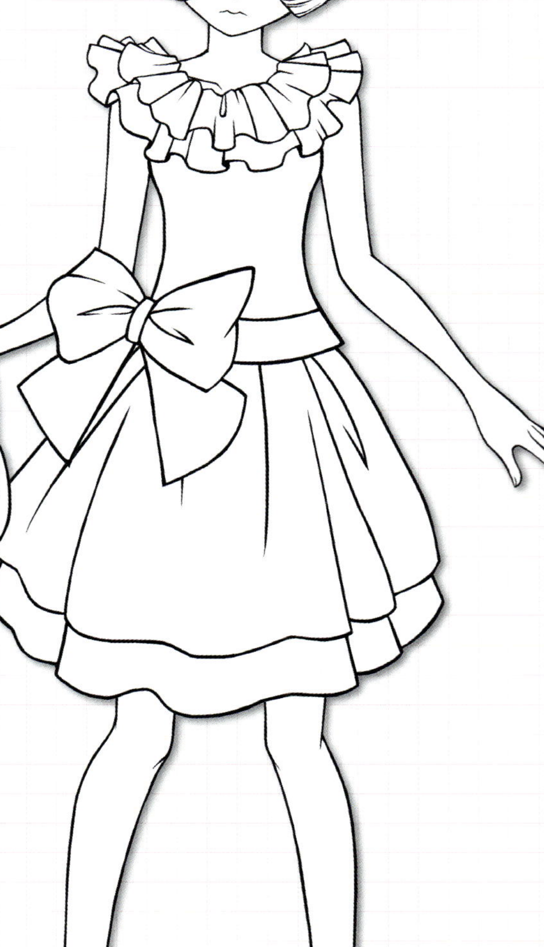

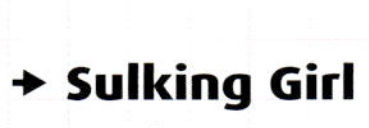

Sulking Girl
Head 1
Upper body 1
Lower body 1
Outfit 2
Outfit 4
Accessory 1
Accessory 3

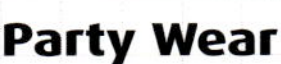

Party Wear

Although these girls are dressed for a party, they don't look very happy about going! Maybe they need some encouragement from some of the more cheerful Child sets. Mix and match these skirts and tops to make different outfits.

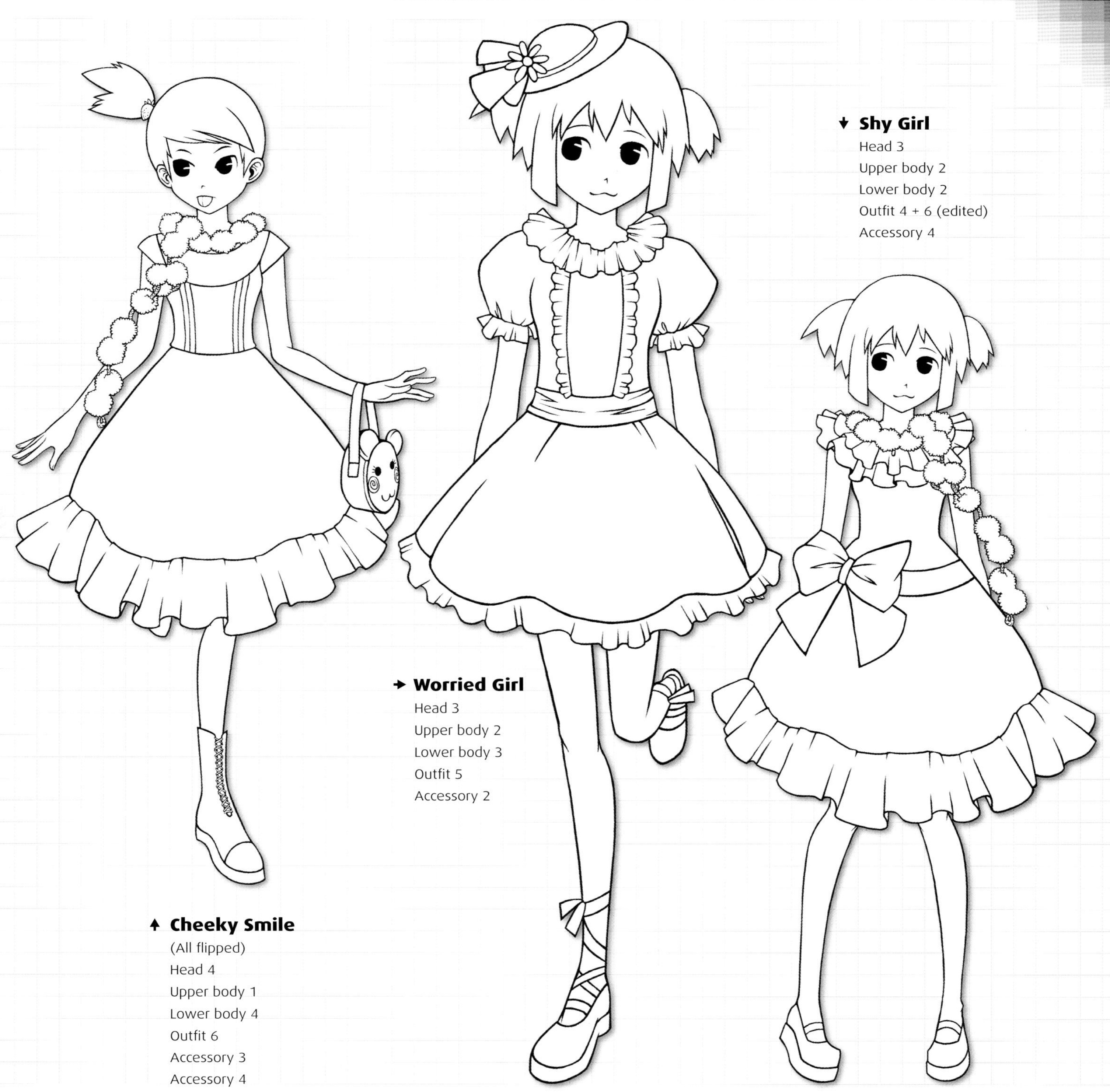

Shy Girl
Head 3
Upper body 2
Lower body 2
Outfit 4 + 6 (edited)
Accessory 4

Worried Girl
Head 3
Upper body 2
Lower body 3
Outfit 5
Accessory 2

Cheeky Smile
(All flipped)
Head 4
Upper body 1
Lower body 4
Outfit 6
Accessory 3
Accessory 4

CHILD 3

Layers

	Accessory 4
	Accessory 1
	Accessory 2
	Accessory 3
	Head 1
	Head 2
	Head 3
	Head 4
	Outfit 1
	Outfit 2
	Outfit 3
	Outfit 4
	Outfit 5
	Outfit 6
	Upper Body 1
	Upper Body 2
	Upper Body 3
	Lower Body 1
	Lower Body 2
	Lower Body 3

Teen Fashionista

These girls are on the way to being contemporary fashionistas. You can make many different looks using the outfits in this set. The upper-body and lower-body silhouettes are already clothed, meaning there are additional variations on outfits that can be made.

↓ Peace Sign

(All flipped)
Head 4
Upper body 2
Lower body 1
Outfit 4
Outfit 6
Accessory 3

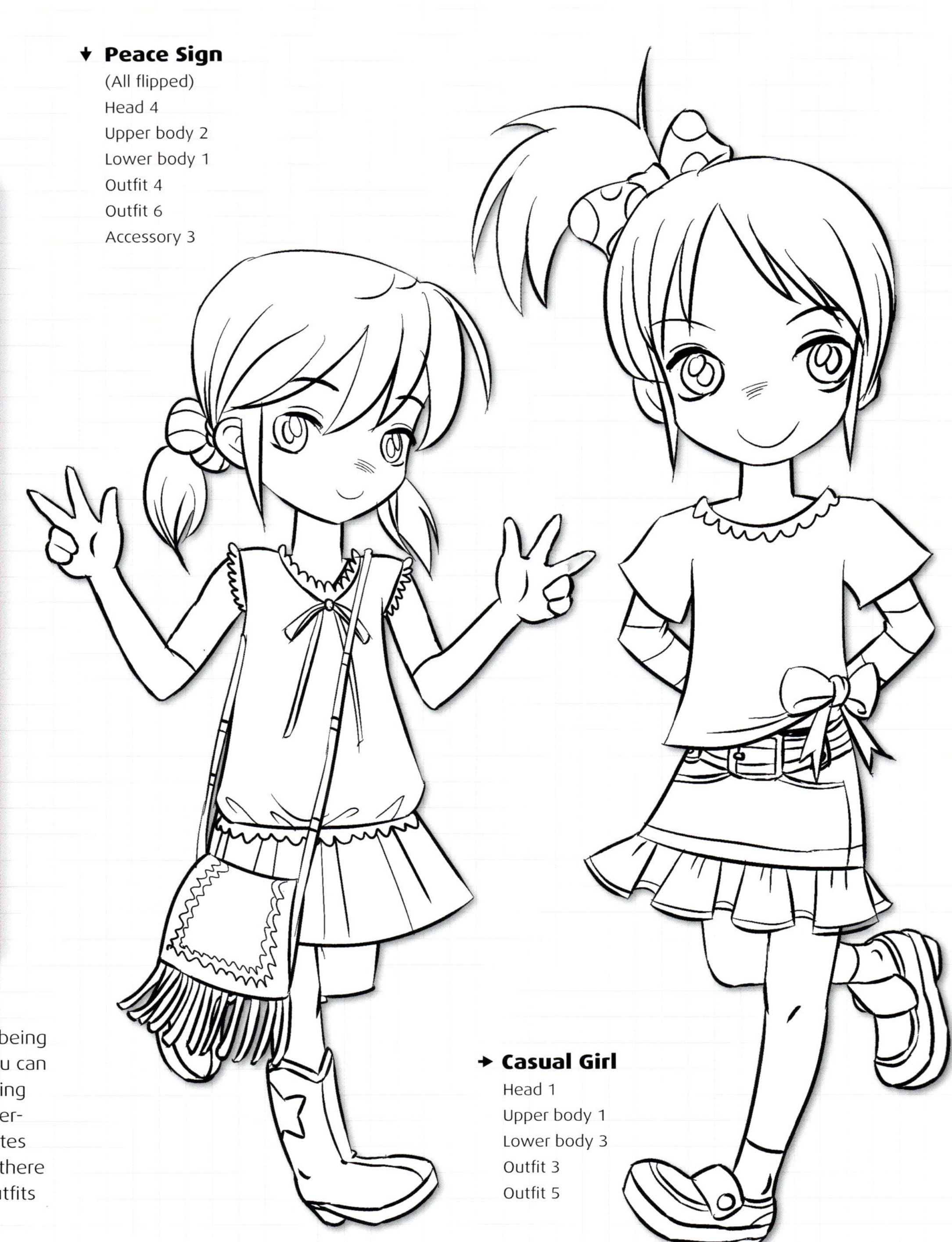

→ Casual Girl

Head 1
Upper body 1
Lower body 3
Outfit 3
Outfit 5

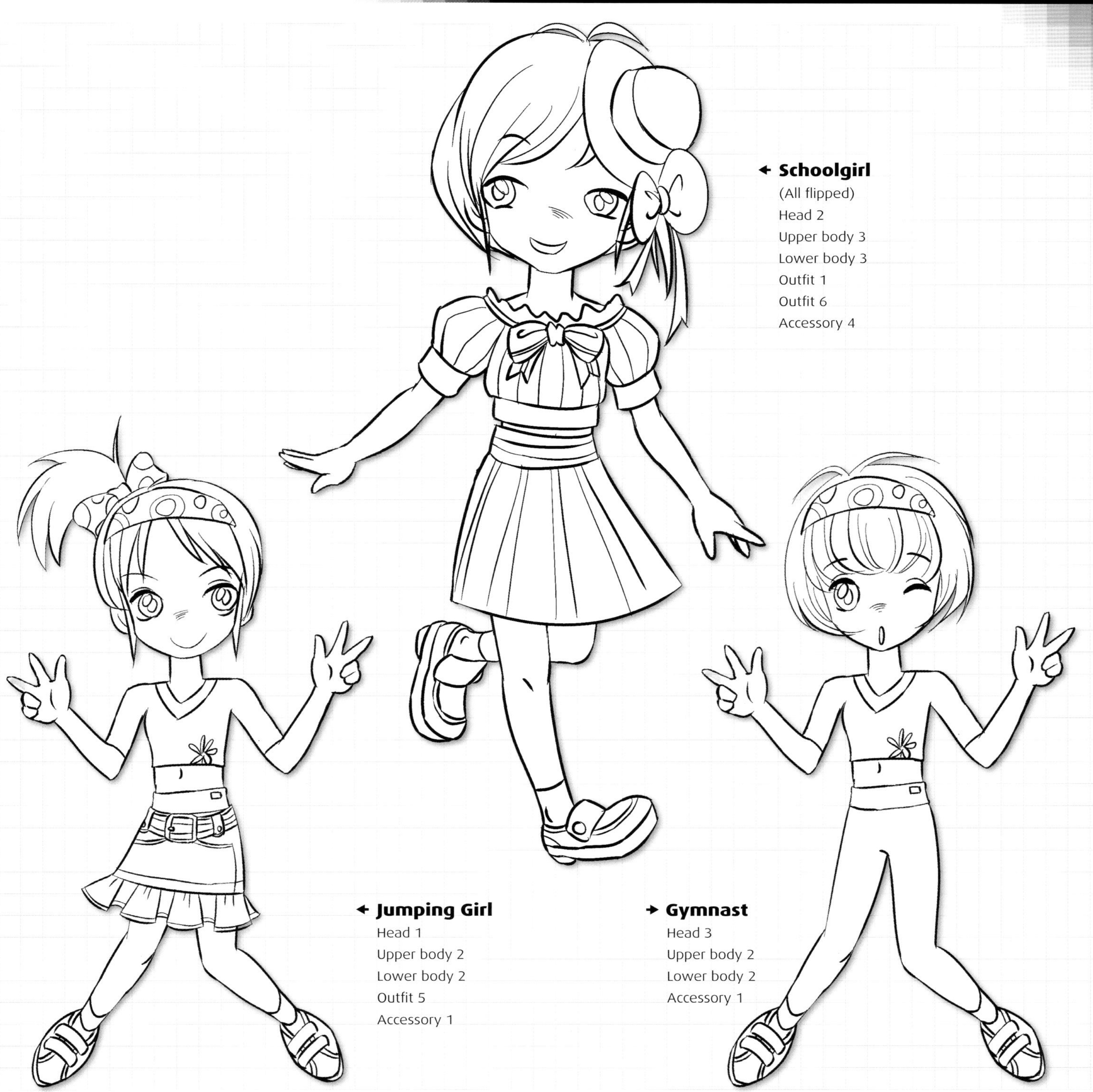

Schoolgirl
(All flipped)
Head 2
Upper body 3
Lower body 3
Outfit 1
Outfit 6
Accessory 4

Jumping Girl
Head 1
Upper body 2
Lower body 2
Outfit 5
Accessory 1

Gymnast
Head 3
Upper body 2
Lower body 2
Accessory 1

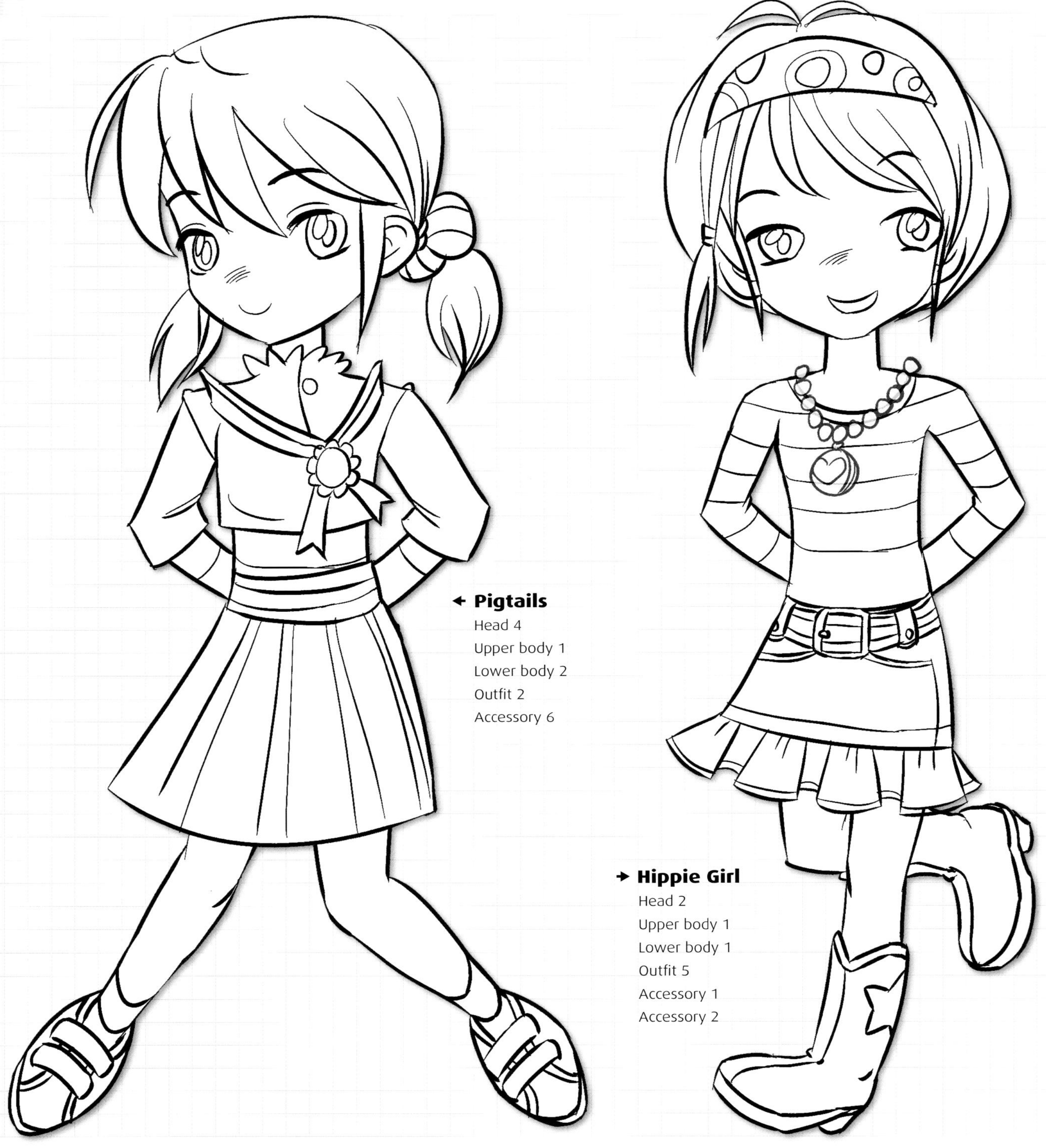

Pigtails

Head 4
Upper body 1
Lower body 2
Outfit 2
Accessory 6

Hippie Girl

Head 2
Upper body 1
Lower body 1
Outfit 5
Accessory 1
Accessory 2

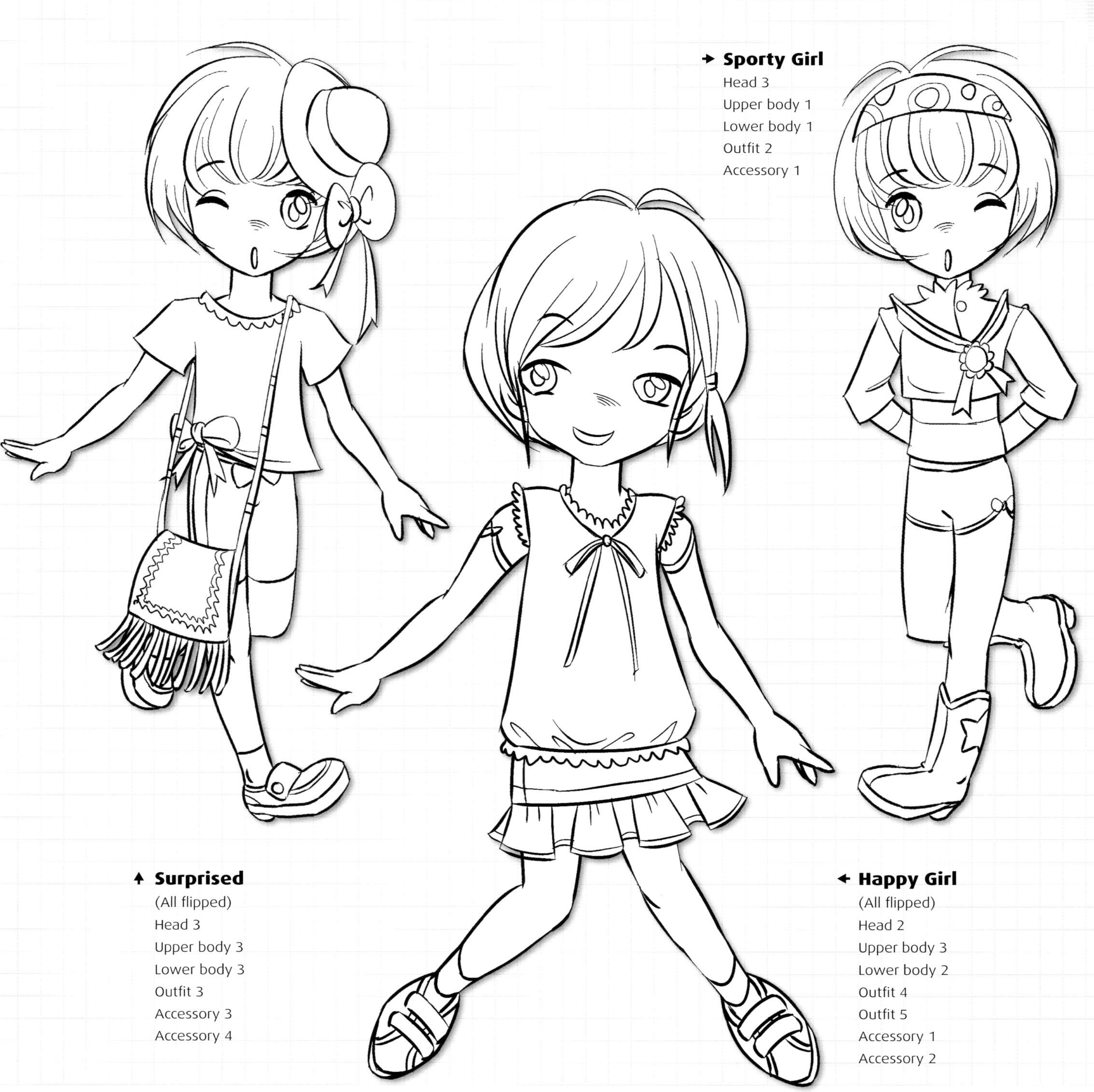

→ **Sporty Girl**
Head 3
Upper body 1
Lower body 1
Outfit 2
Accessory 1

↑ **Surprised**
(All flipped)
Head 3
Upper body 3
Lower body 3
Outfit 3
Accessory 3
Accessory 4

← **Happy Girl**
(All flipped)
Head 2
Upper body 3
Lower body 2
Outfit 4
Outfit 5
Accessory 1
Accessory 2

KAWAII 1

Layers

- Accessory 4
- Accessory 3
- Accessory 2
- Accessory 1
- Outfit 6
- Outfit 5
- Outfit 4
- Outfit 3
- Outfit 2
- Outfit 1
- Head 4
- Head 3
- Head 2
- Head 1
- Upper Body 2
- Upper Body 1
- Lower Body 4
- Lower Body 3
- Lower Body 2
- Lower Body 1

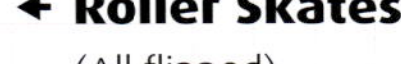

← Roller Skates
(All flipped)
Head 2
Upper body 1
Lower body 3
Outfit 1
Outfit 4
Accessory 1

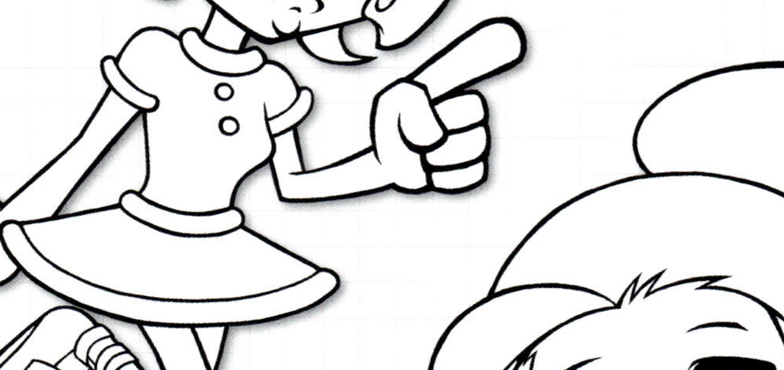

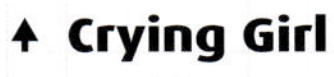

↑ Crying Girl
Head 3
Upper body 2
Lower body 4
Outfit 2 + 6
Accessory 4

Retro

Kawaii is the Japanese word for "cute." With the cute Retro characters, the skirts and tops can be alternated to make many different outfits. Versatile accessories like the star can also be used with many other costume sets.

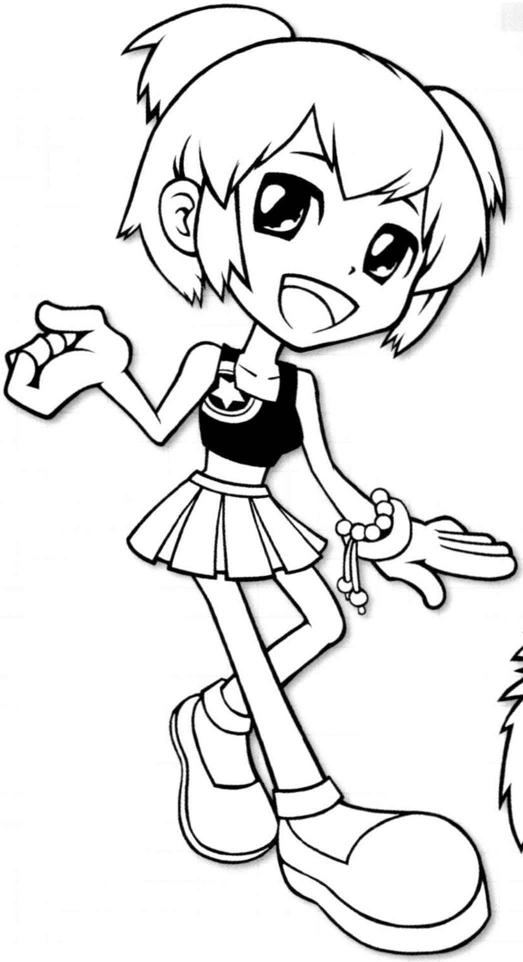

← **Happy Girl**
(All flipped)
Head 1
Upper body 2
Lower body 2
Outfit 3
Outfit 6
Accessory 3

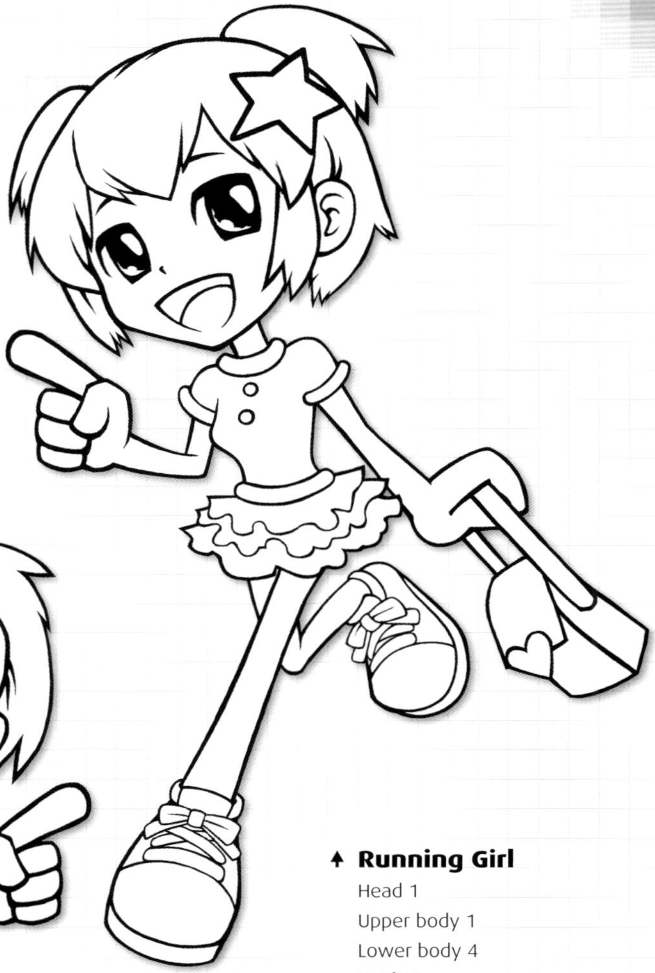

↑ **Running Girl**
Head 1
Upper body 1
Lower body 4
Outfit 2
Outfit 4
Accessory 1
Accessory 2

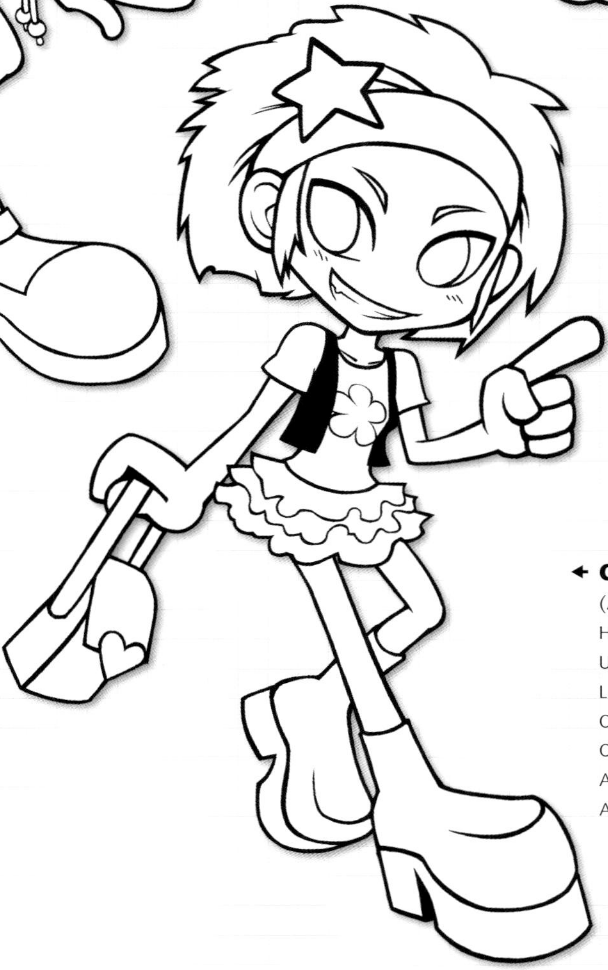

← **Cheeky Girl**
(All flipped)
Head 4
Upper body 1
Lower body 1
Outfit 2
Outfit 5
Accessory 1
Accessory 2

KAWAII 2

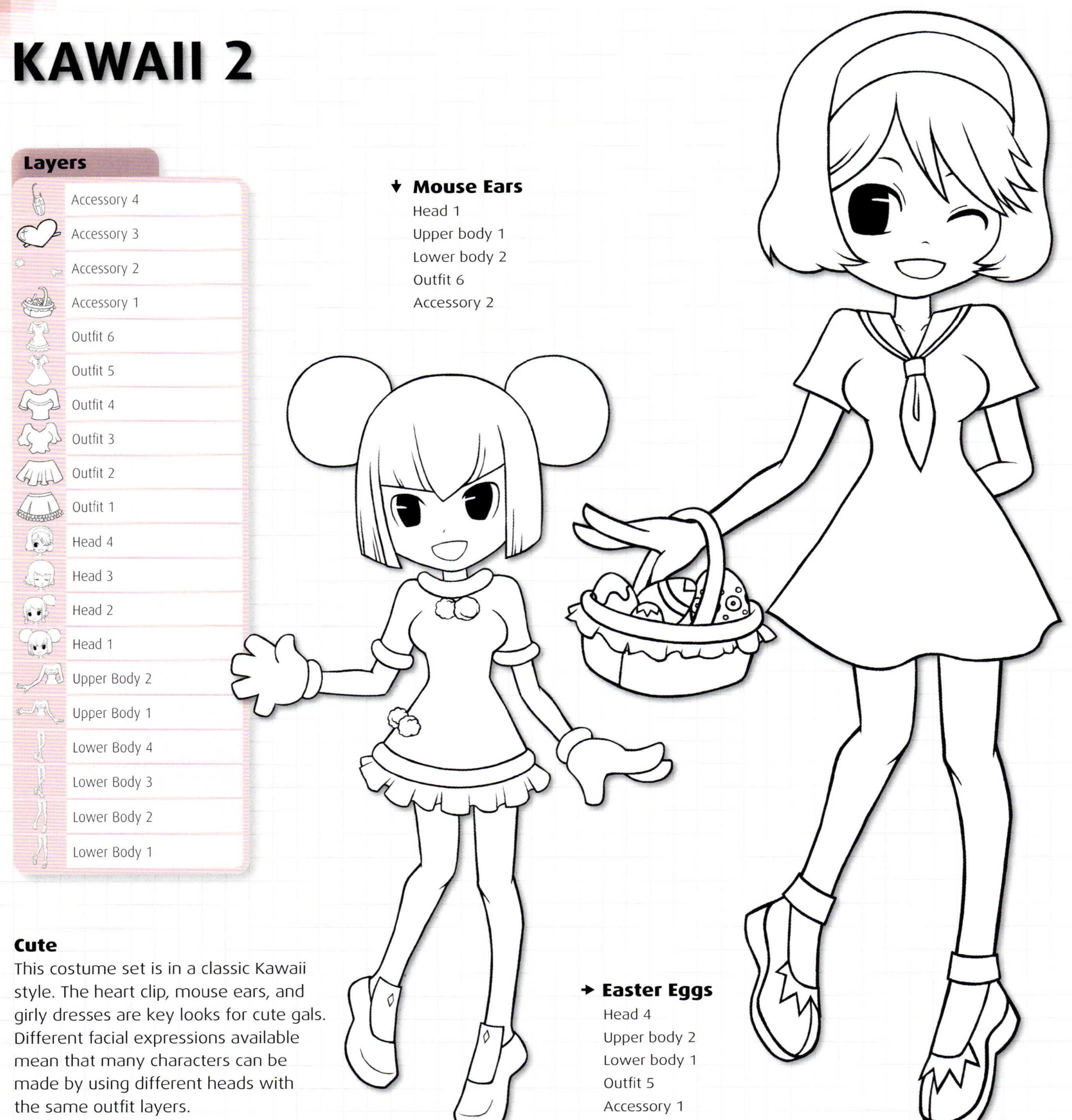

Cute

This costume set is in a classic Kawaii style. The heart clip, mouse ears, and girly dresses are key looks for cute gals. Different facial expressions available mean that many characters can be made by using different heads with the same outfit layers.

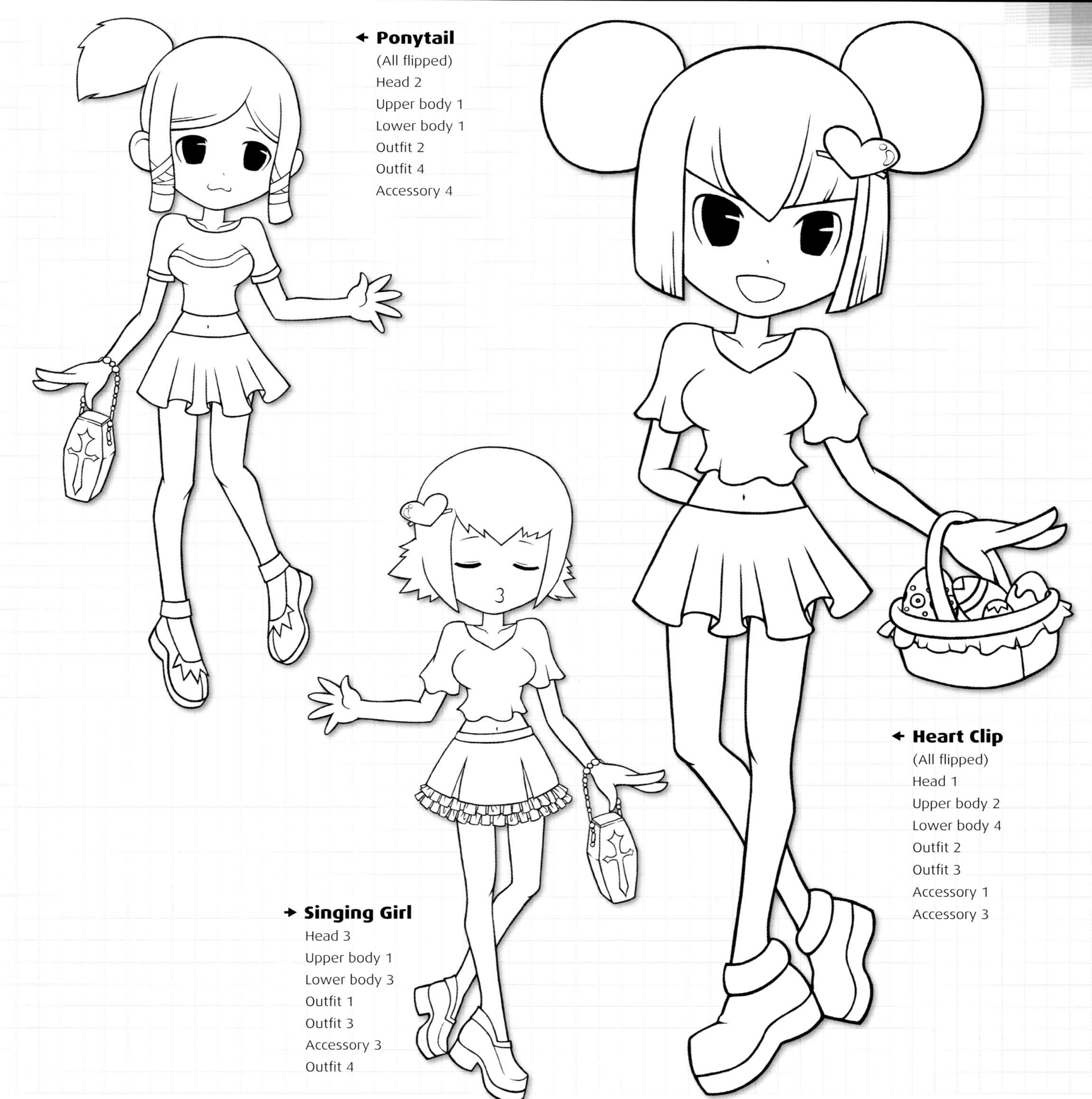
Ponytail
(All flipped)
Head 2
Upper body 1
Lower body 1
Outfit 2
Outfit 4
Accessory 4
Heart Clip
(All flipped)
Head 1
Upper body 2
Lower body 4
Outfit 2
Outfit 3
Accessory 1
Accessory 3
Singing Girl
Head 3
Upper body 1
Lower body 3
Outfit 1
Outfit 3
Accessory 3
Outfit 4

KAWAII 3

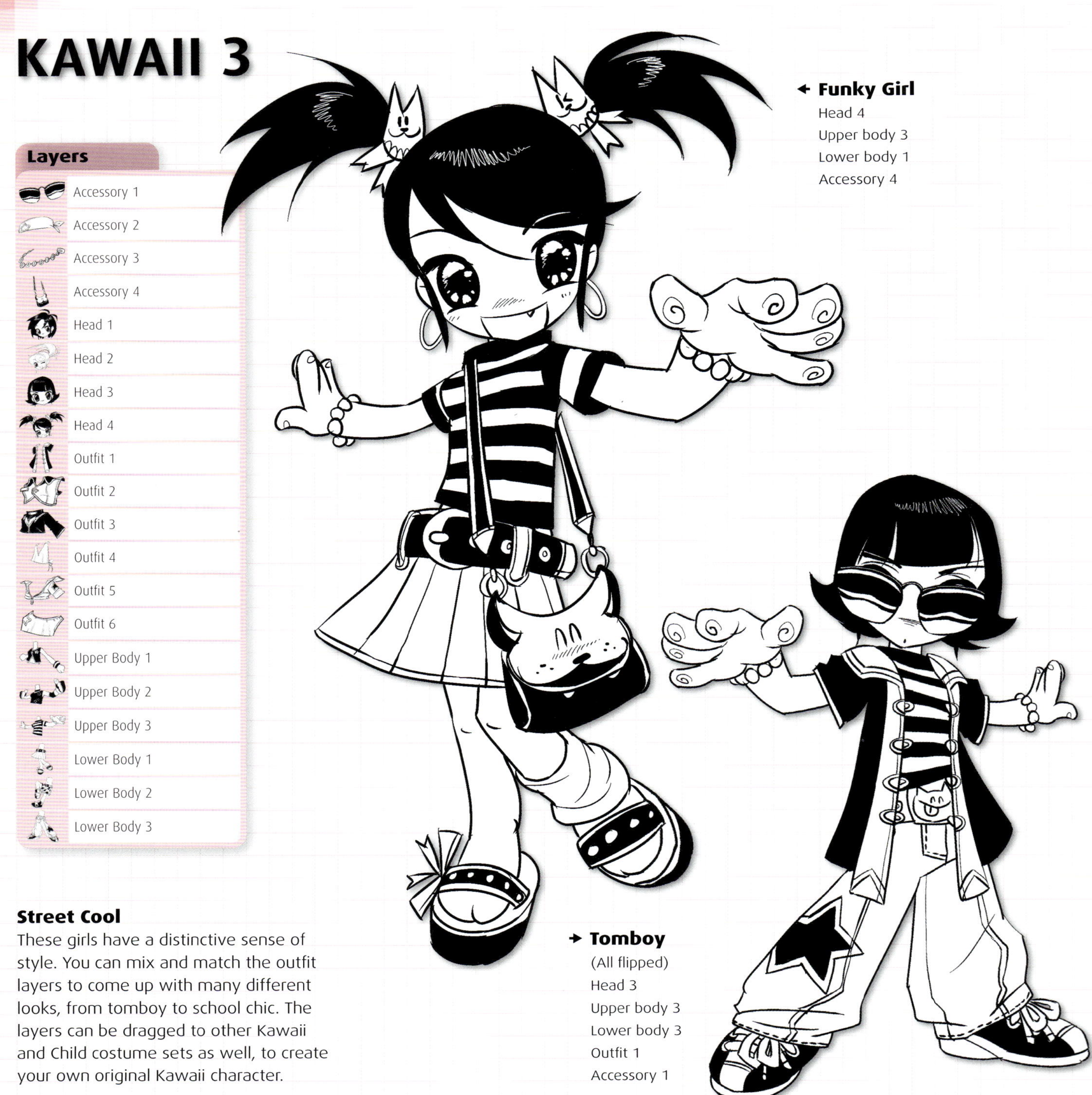

Layers

- Accessory 1
- Accessory 2
- Accessory 3
- Accessory 4
- Head 1
- Head 2
- Head 3
- Head 4
- Outfit 1
- Outfit 2
- Outfit 3
- Outfit 4
- Outfit 5
- Outfit 6
- Upper Body 1
- Upper Body 2
- Upper Body 3
- Lower Body 1
- Lower Body 2
- Lower Body 3

Funky Girl
Head 4
Upper body 3
Lower body 1
Accessory 4

Tomboy
(All flipped)
Head 3
Upper body 3
Lower body 3
Outfit 1
Accessory 1

Street Cool

These girls have a distinctive sense of style. You can mix and match the outfit layers to come up with many different looks, from tomboy to school chic. The layers can be dragged to other Kawaii and Child costume sets as well, to create your own original Kawaii character.

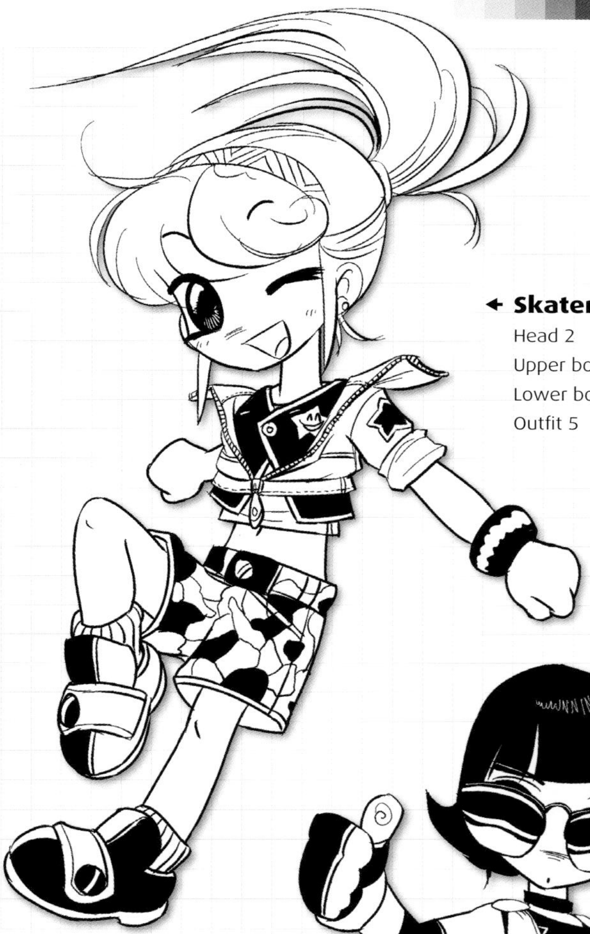

Skater Girl
Head 2
Upper body 1
Lower body 2
Outfit 5

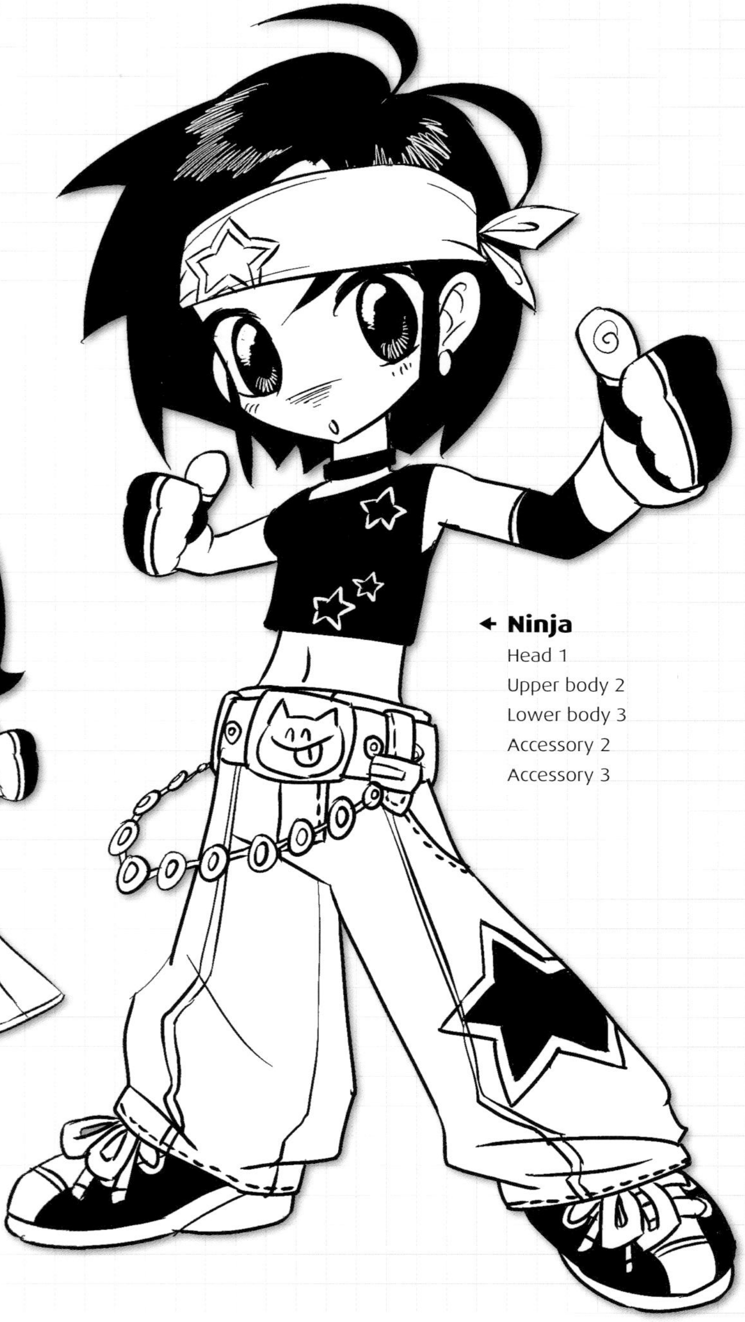

Ninja
Head 1
Upper body 2
Lower body 3
Accessory 2
Accessory 3

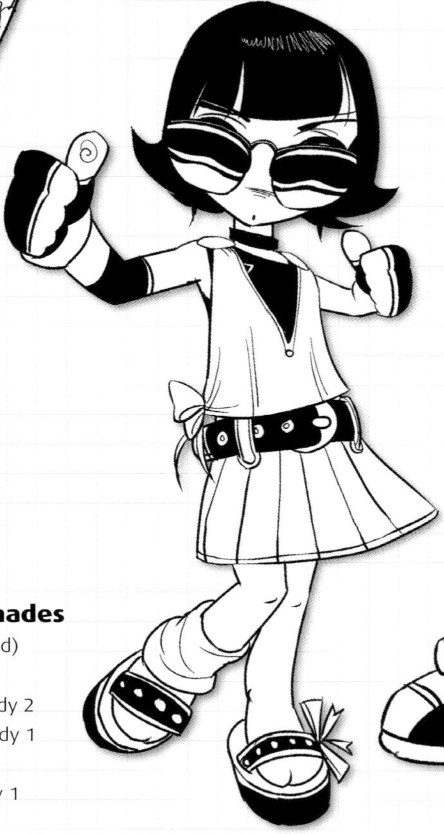

Cool Shades
(All flipped)
Head 3
Upper body 2
Lower body 1
Outfit 4
Accessory 1

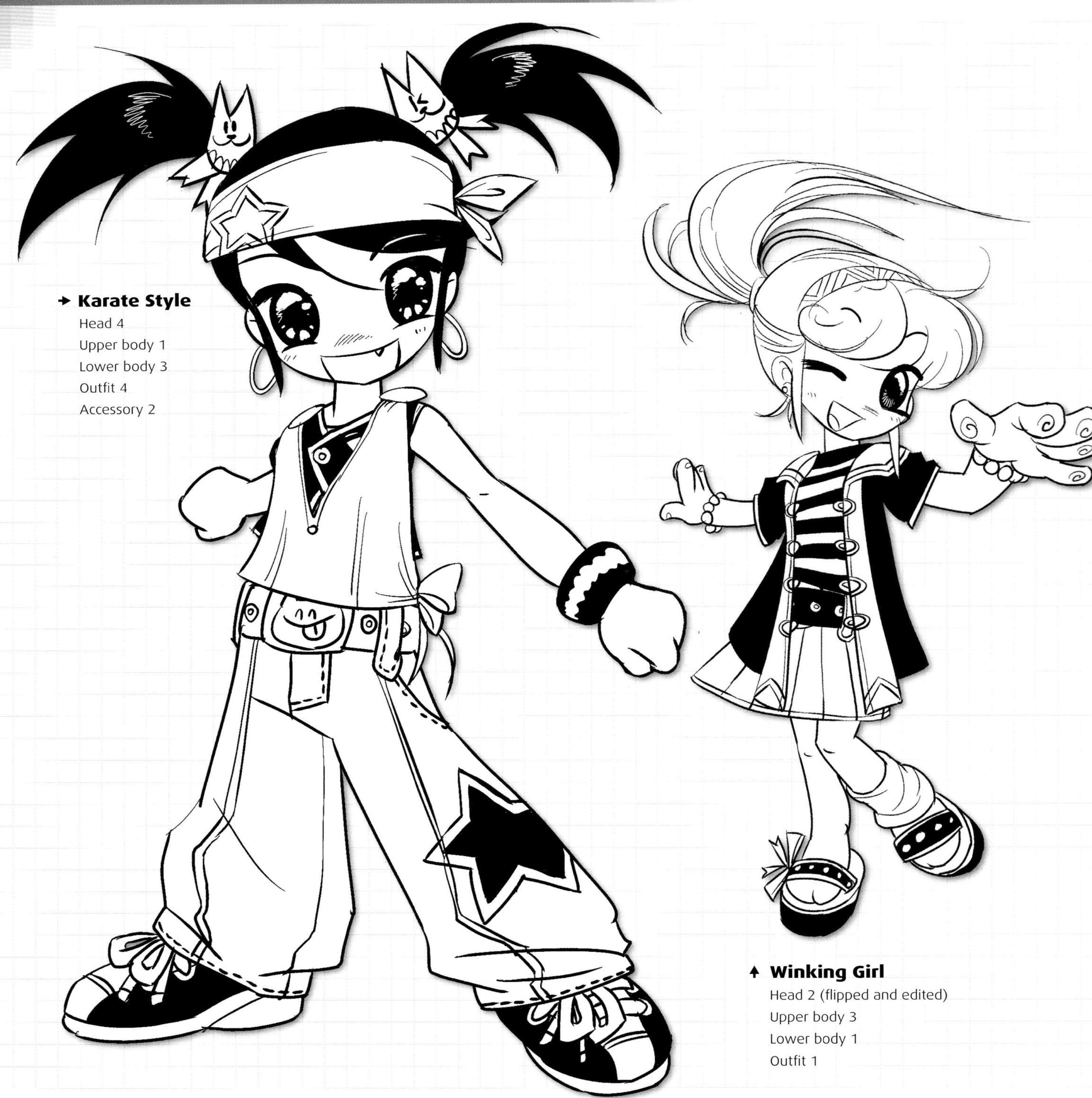

Karate Style
Head 4
Upper body 1
Lower body 3
Outfit 4
Accessory 2

Winking Girl
Head 2 (flipped and edited)
Upper body 3
Lower body 1
Outfit 1

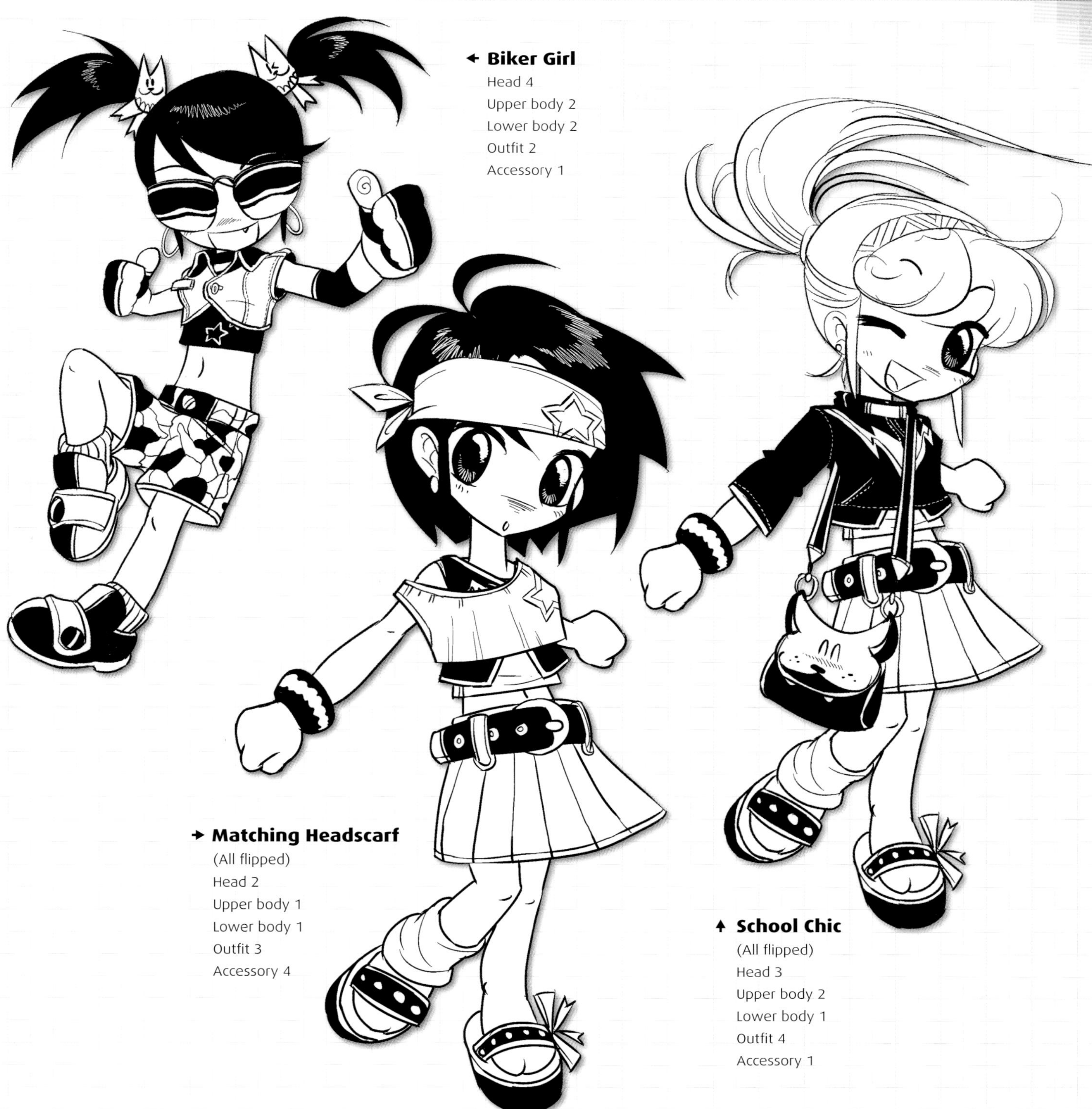

← **Biker Girl**
Head 4
Upper body 2
Lower body 2
Outfit 2
Accessory 1

→ **Matching Headscarf**
(All flipped)
Head 2
Upper body 1
Lower body 1
Outfit 3
Accessory 4

↑ **School Chic**
(All flipped)
Head 3
Upper body 2
Lower body 1
Outfit 4
Accessory 1

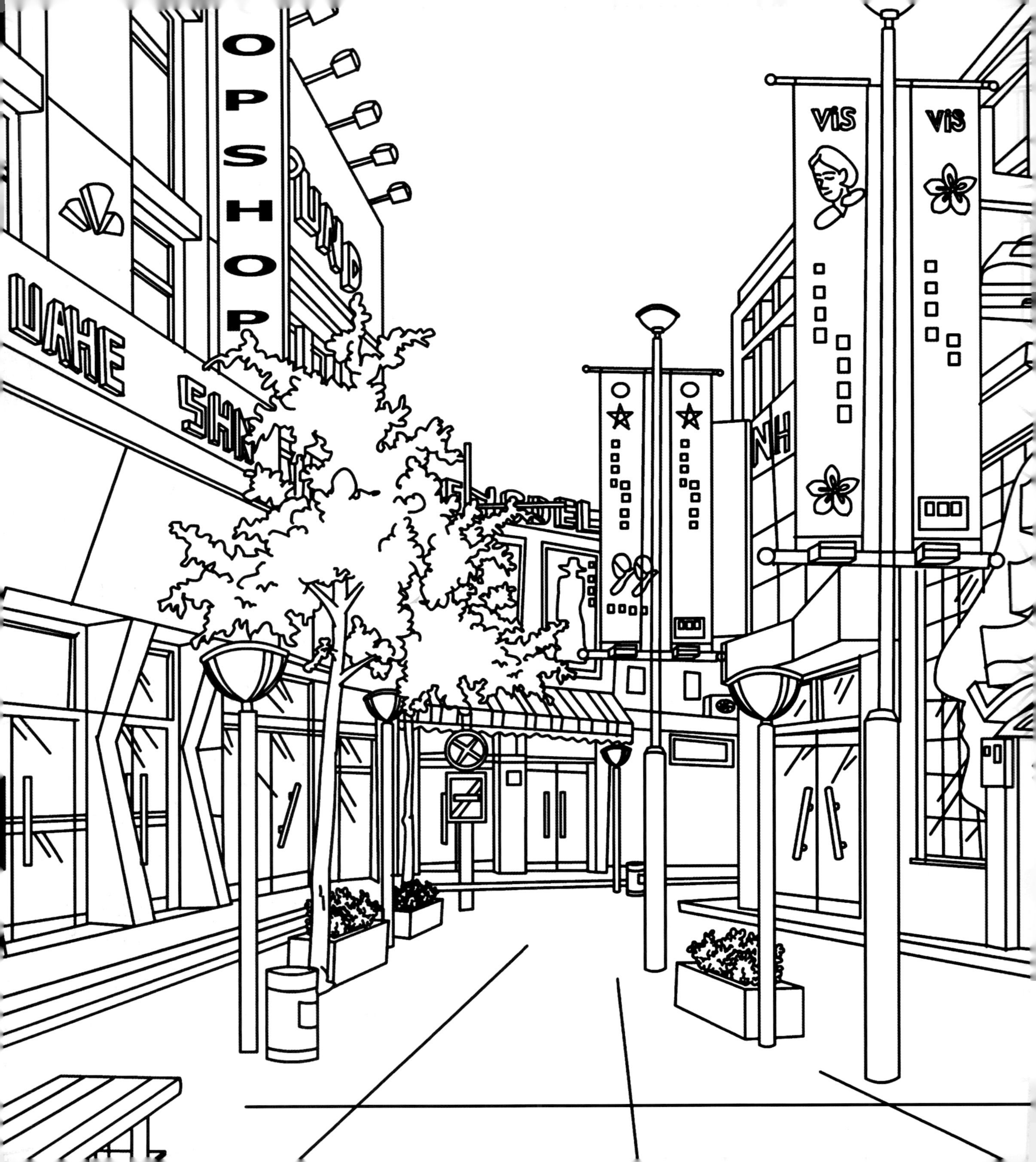
OPSHOP
UAHE
ViS
ViS
NH

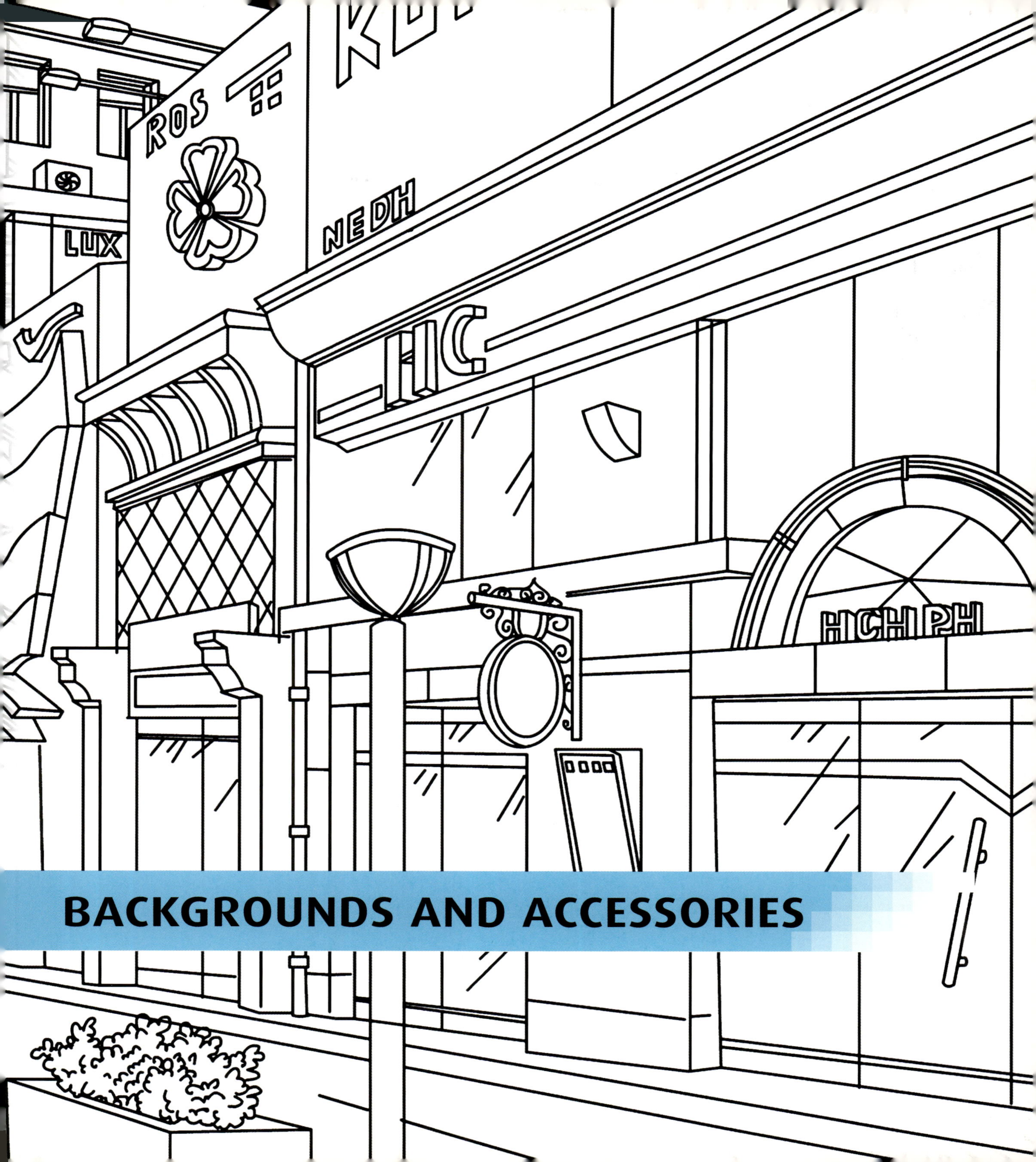

BACKGROUNDS AND ACCESSORIES

BACKGROUNDS

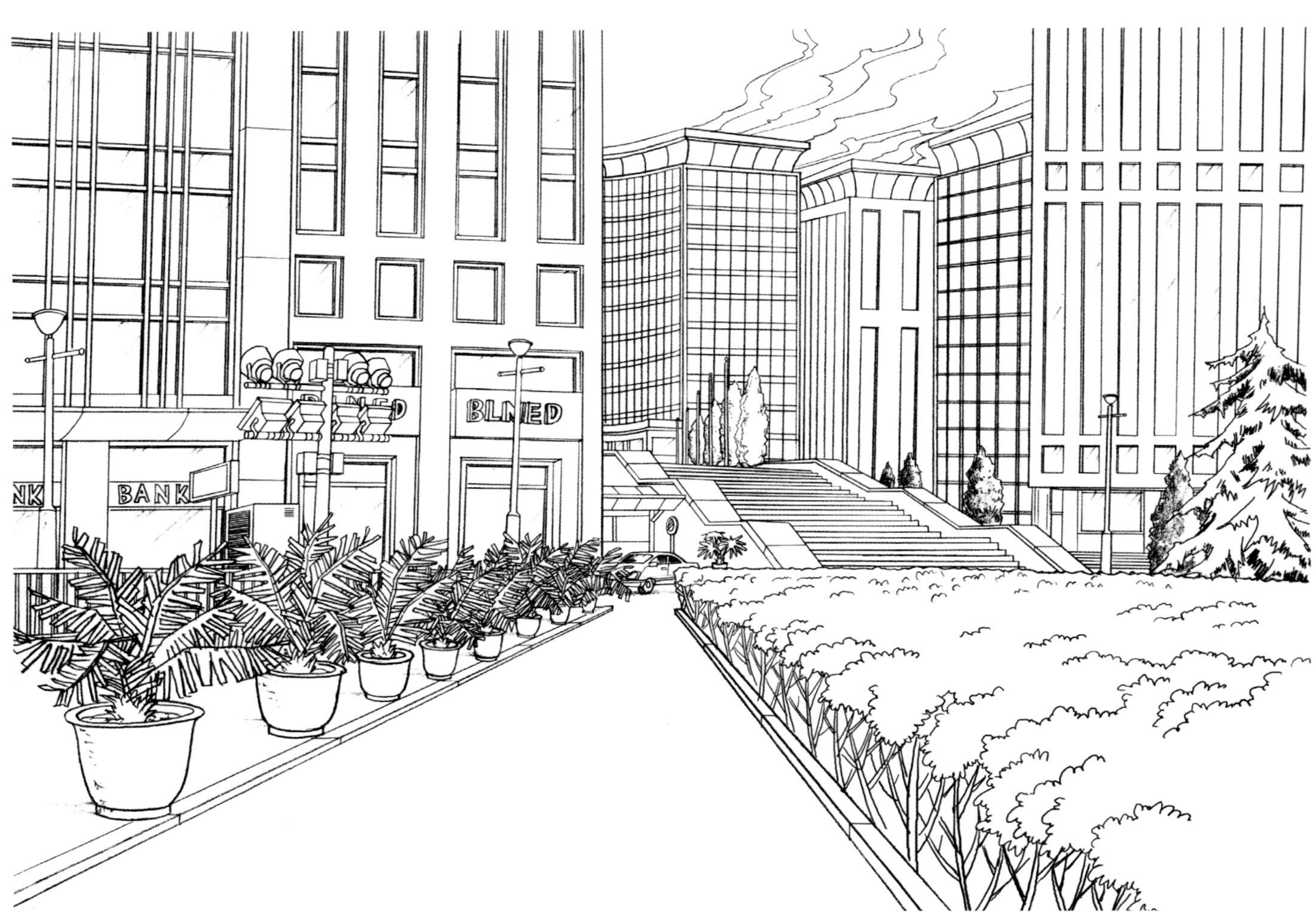

Background 1: In the City
This city scene could be used for any of the contemporary figures, or, depending on how you decide to color it in, it could be a futuristic setting.

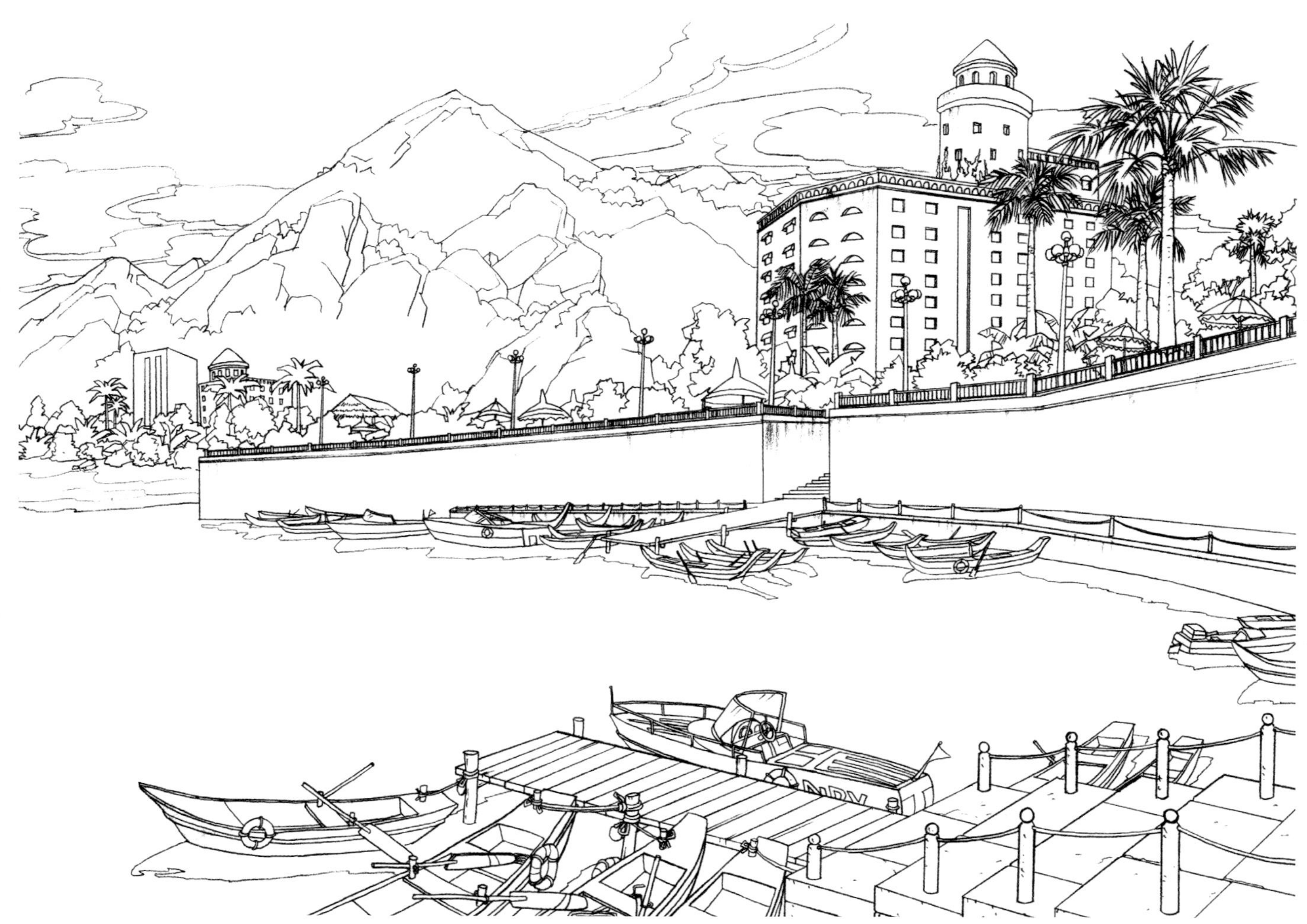

Background 2: Harbor

A historical harbor? A stylish pier in a holiday town? Or a landing site for sci-fi invaders? Your choice of characters and colors will decide.

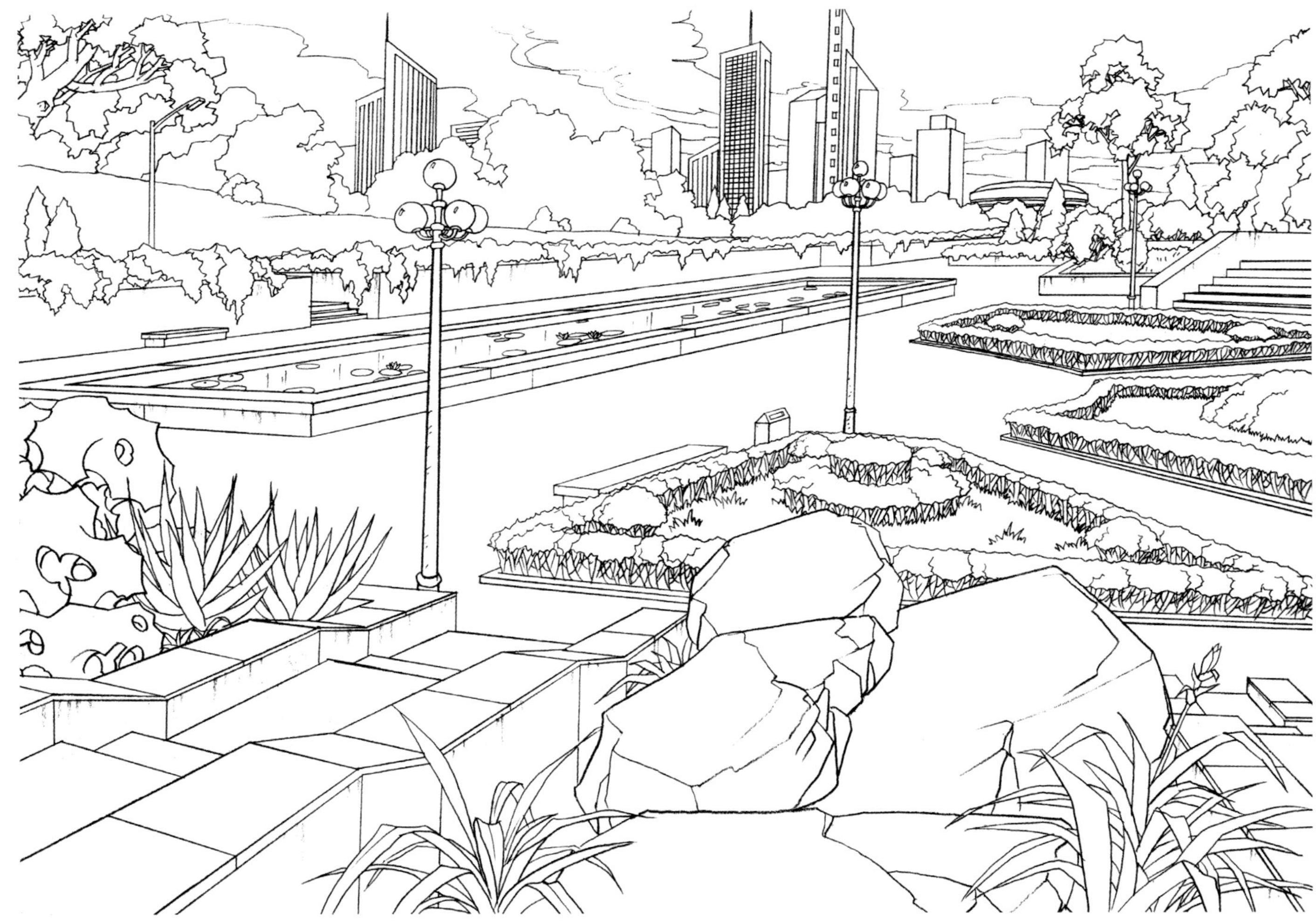

Background 3:
City Gardens

Ambiguous backgrounds like this one are great because you could make many variaions on it; be it night or daytime, sunny or rainy, present or future. Also, almost any character would fit in this setting.

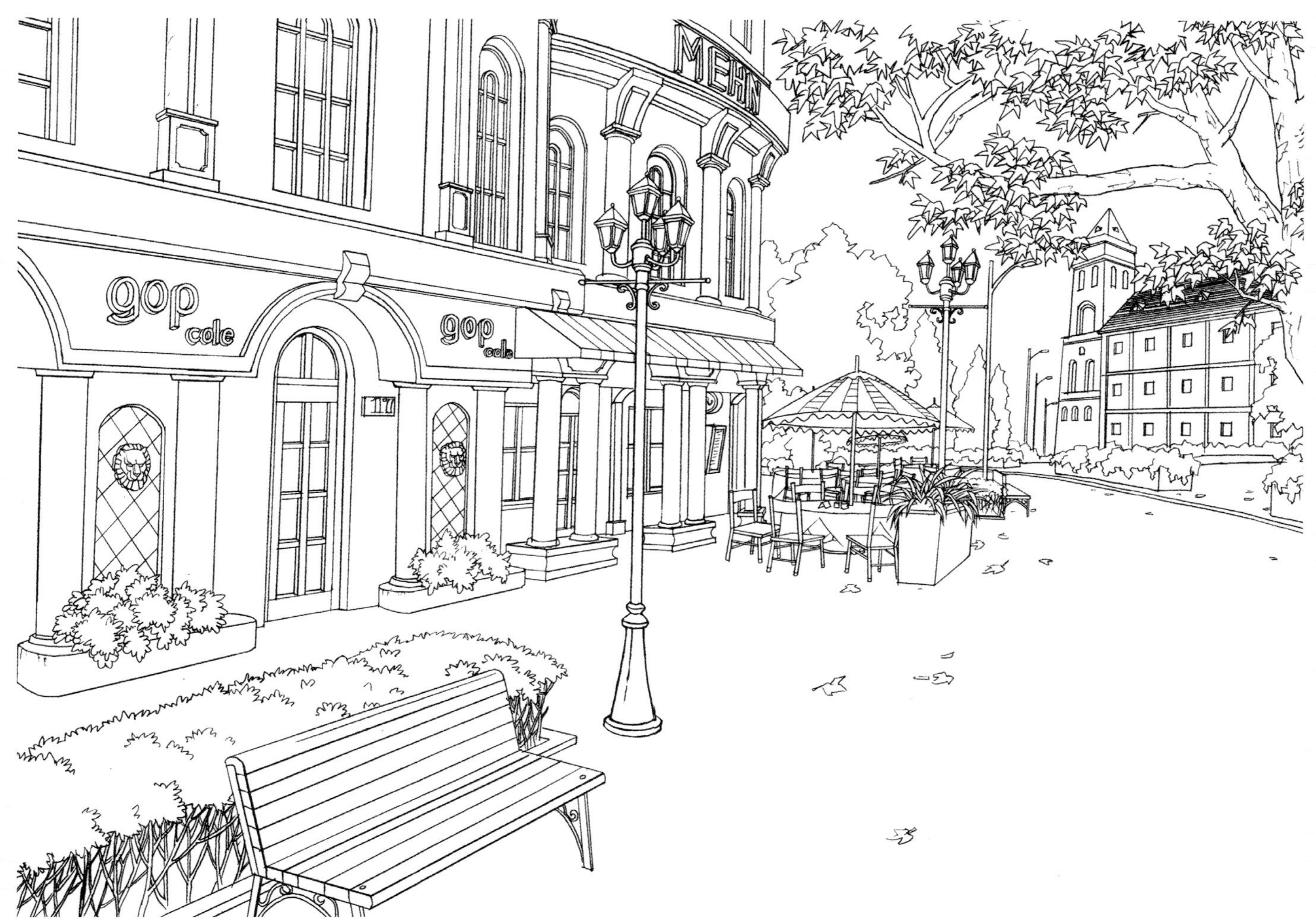

Background 4:
European Street Scene

The large empty space in the right corner is ideal for placing characters or accessories. As with the other backgrounds, depending on how you color the scene will affect the period and mood.

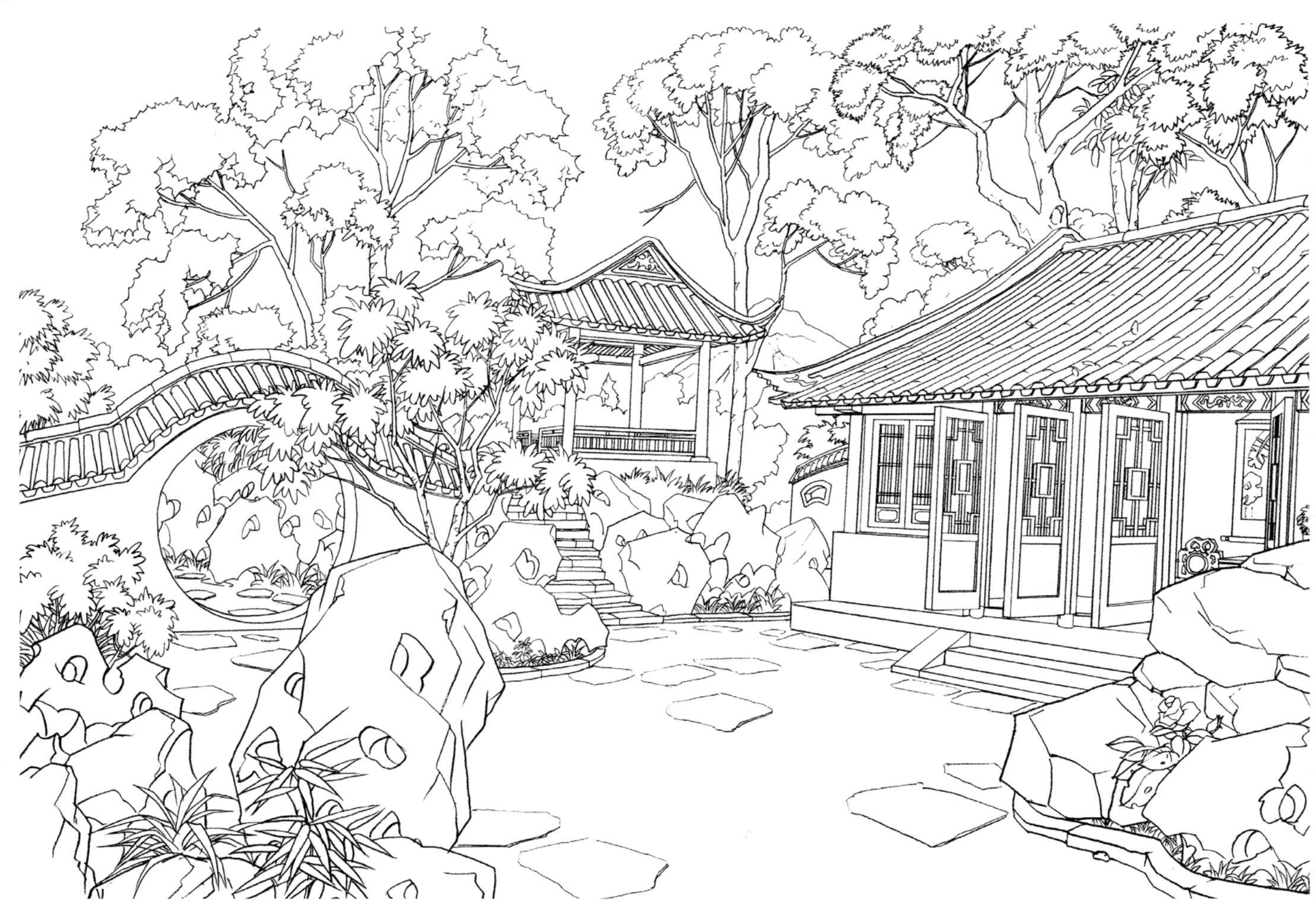

Background 5:
Traditional Japanese Garden

This is a classic traditional setting for the Asian characters to relax in. Or it could be a palace garden open to tourists and schoolchildren. If you want to place characters inside the pagoda or behind rocks, erase the bits that shouldn't be visible.

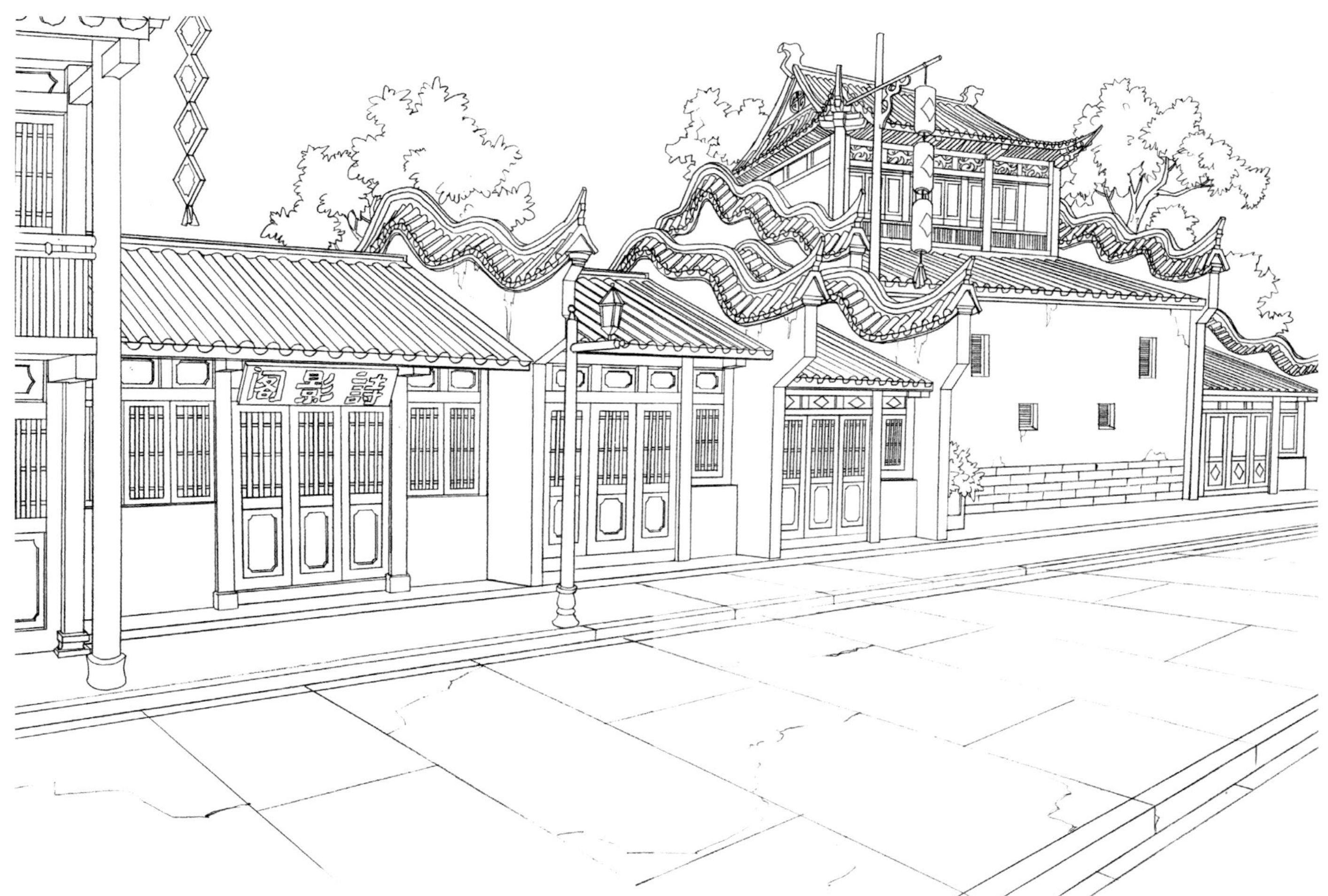

Background 6: Traditional Japanese Building

This building could be a school, a historical street scene, a temple, and so on. During the day, the hanging features could be street decorations, and at night they could be lanterns. Plain canvases like this background are as flexible as your imagination.

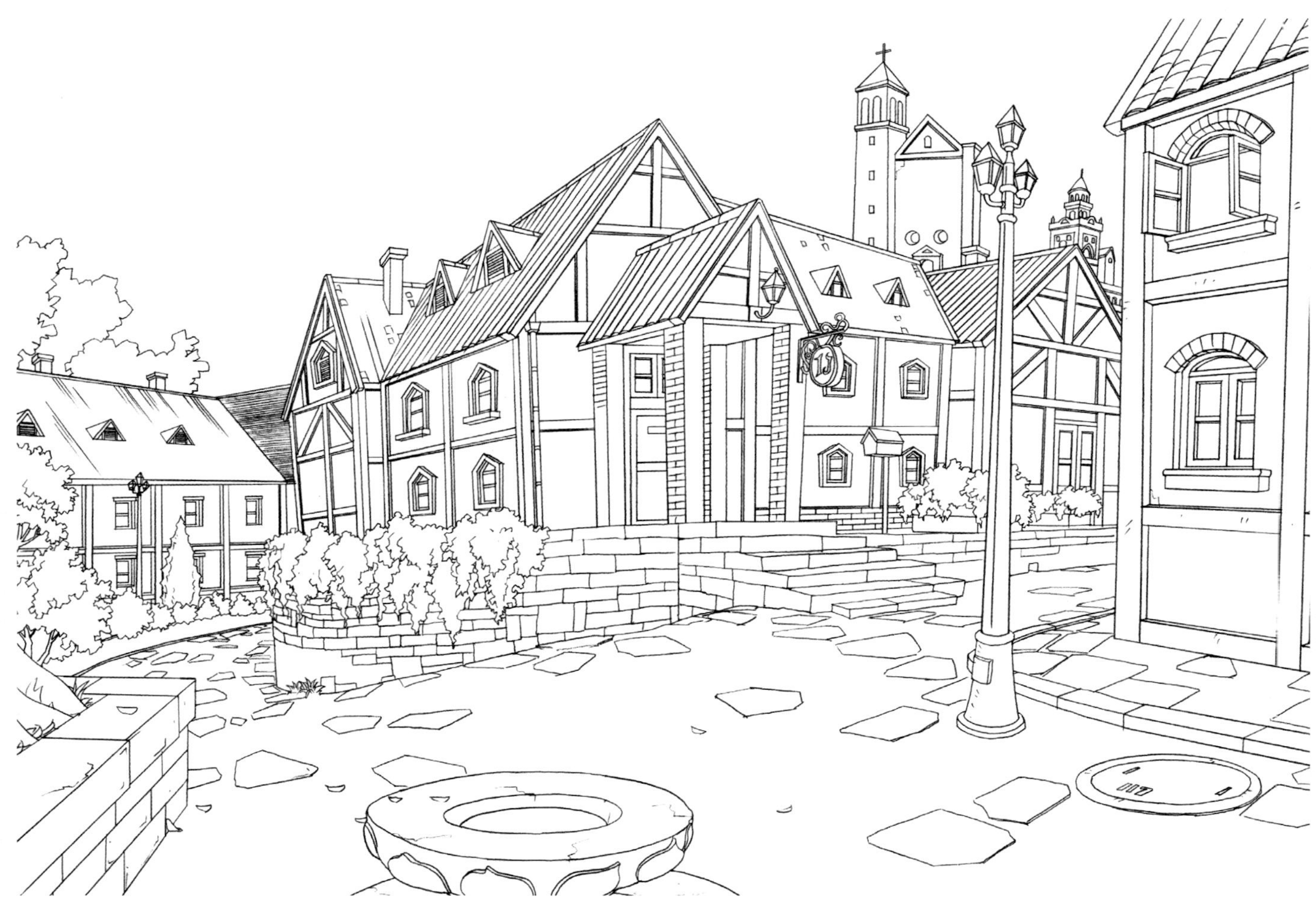

Background 7: Traditional European Town

Any of the historical characters would be at home in this idyllic town: Traditional European, Medieval Warriors, Femmes Fatales, and even the Mythical and Fantasy figures. It could be the scene of battle or a sleepy village gathering.

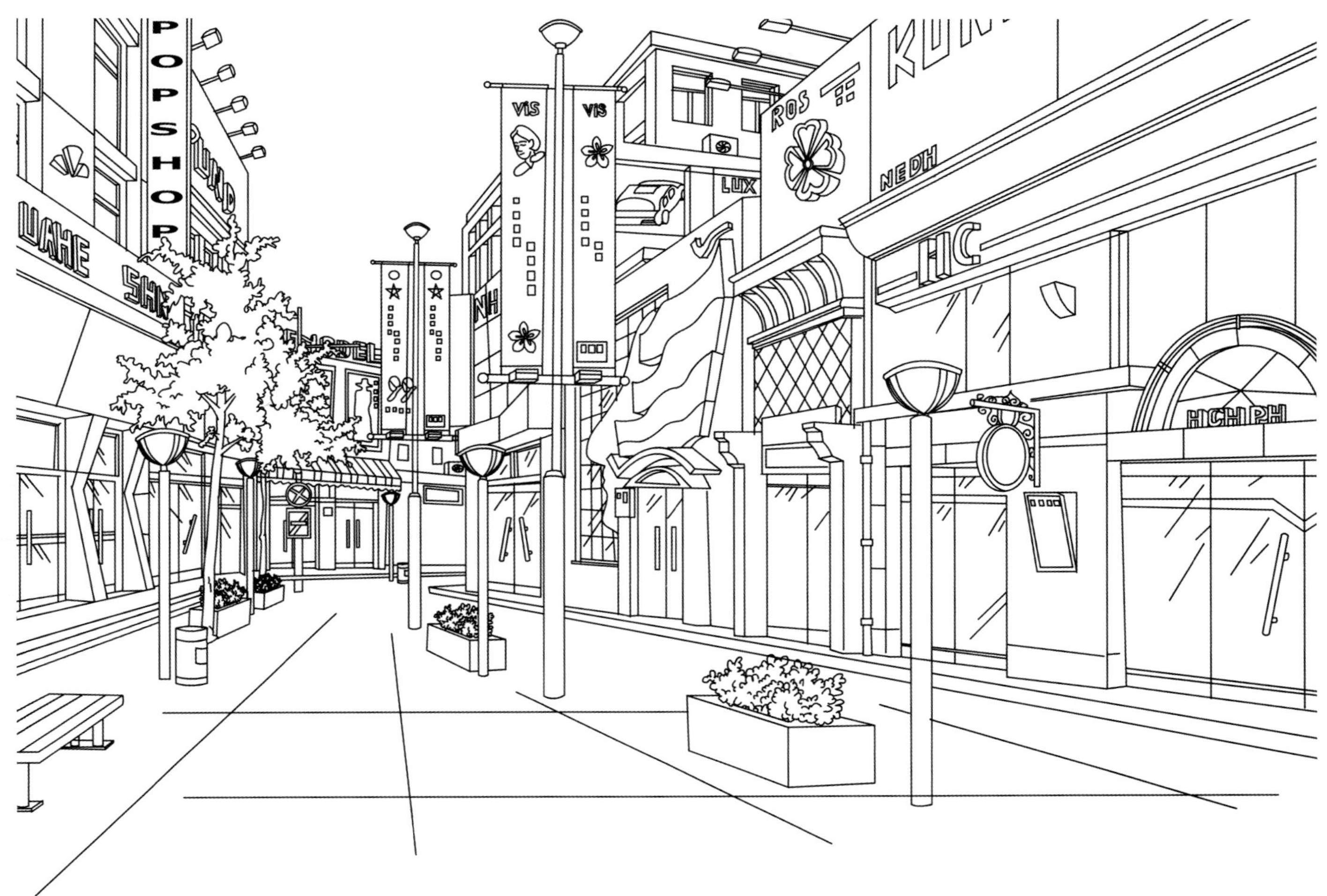

Background 8: City Shopping District

This is the ideal backdrop for fashionistas and contemporary shopping gals in need of some retail therapy. But, after dark, the same characters could be on the way to the cinema or the theater.

ACCESSORIES

To add an accessory to a character, simply open both files at the same time, and drag the accessory or the layer on to the figure. Alternatively, you could copy and paste the accessory. Using the techniques described on pages 22–24, you can adjust any object once it has been copied to the character file to place it where you like, and at what size you like.

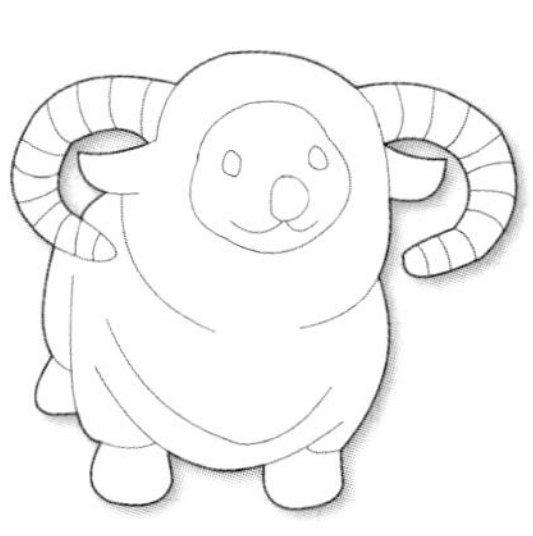

Ram

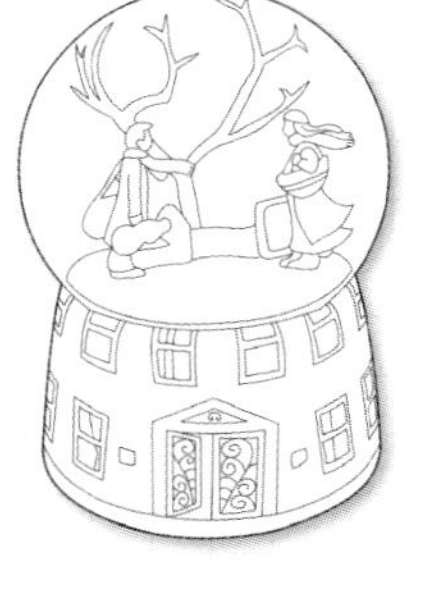

Snow Dome

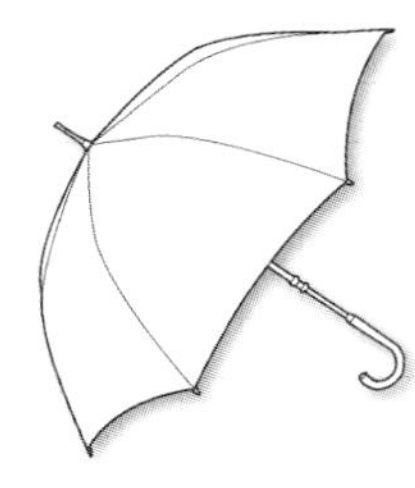

Umbrella

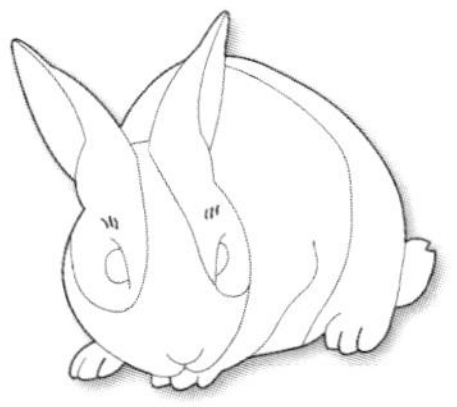

Bunny Rabbit

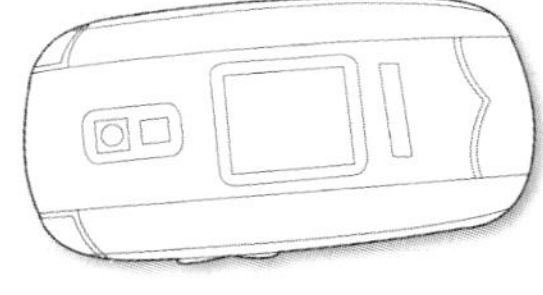

Mobile Phone

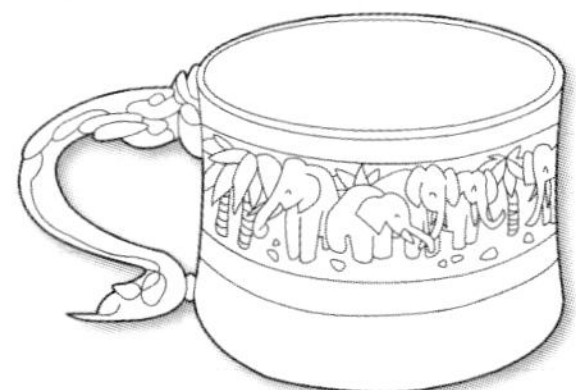

Elephant Mug

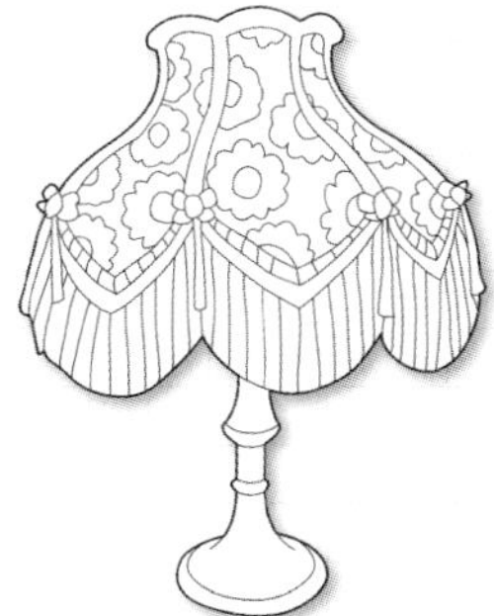

Lamp

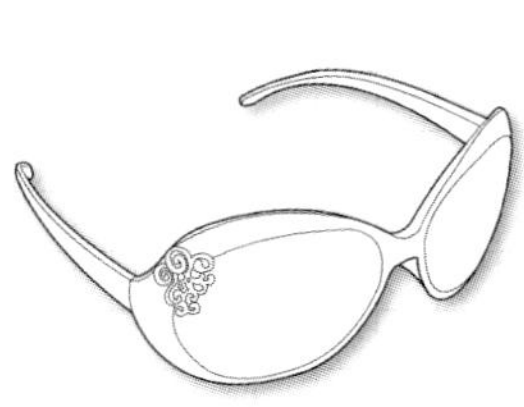

Sunglasses

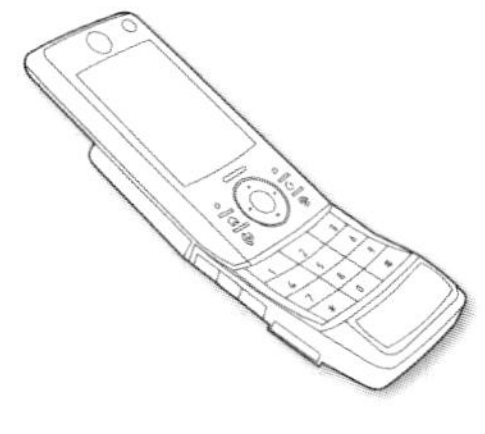

Mobile Phone 2

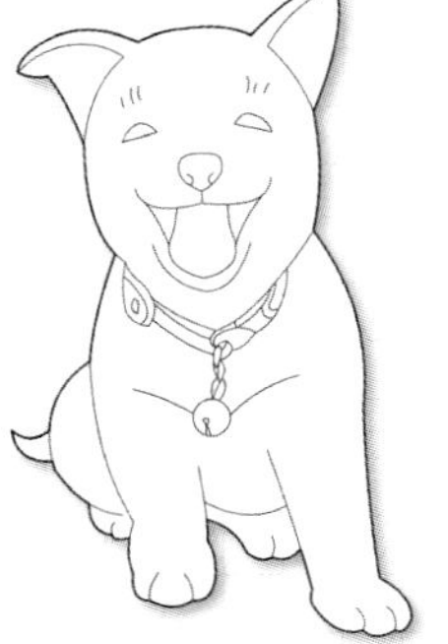

Pet Dog

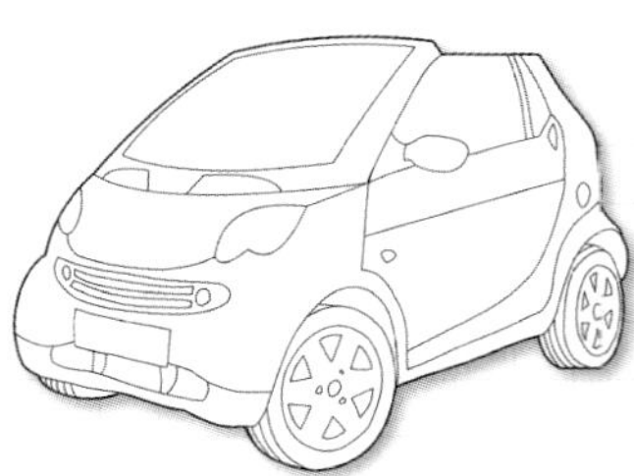

Car

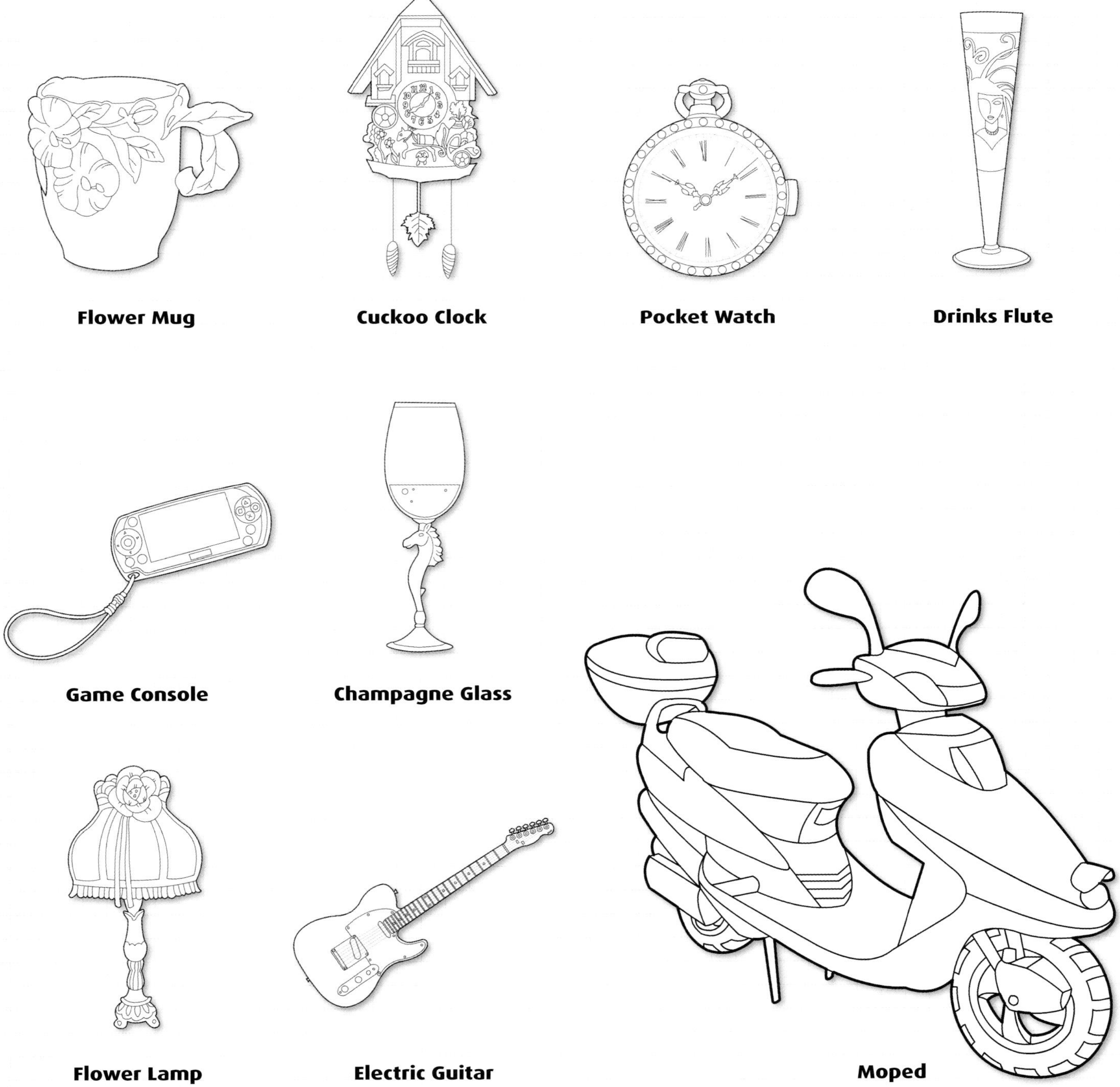

Flower Mug

Cuckoo Clock

Pocket Watch

Drinks Flute

Game Console

Champagne Glass

Flower Lamp

Electric Guitar

Moped

Accessories can add detail to both backgrounds and characters. Objects like the umbrella can be placed in the hands of many of the figures, while others such as the snowman can be used to create atmosphere in a scene.

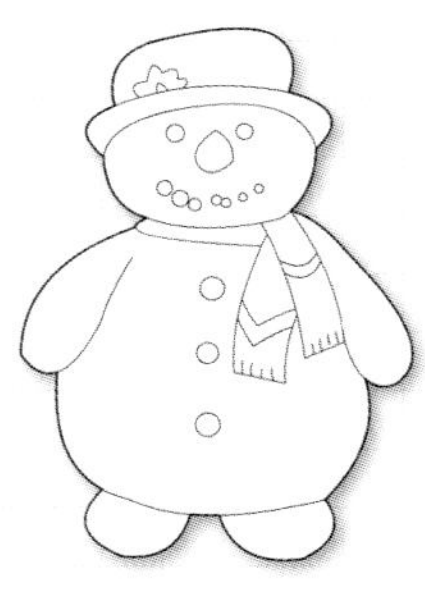

Snowman

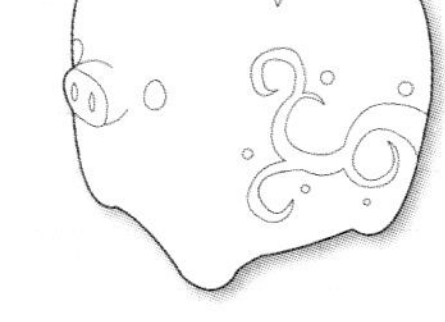

Pig Ornament

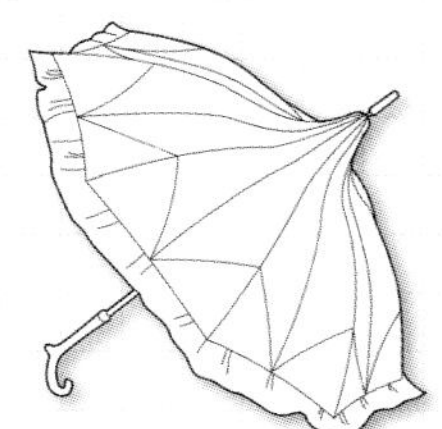

Parasol

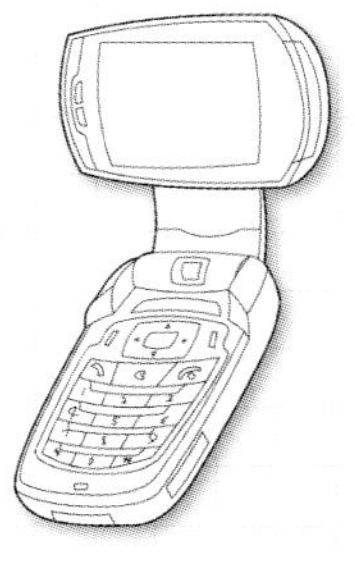

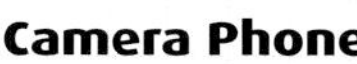

Camera Phone

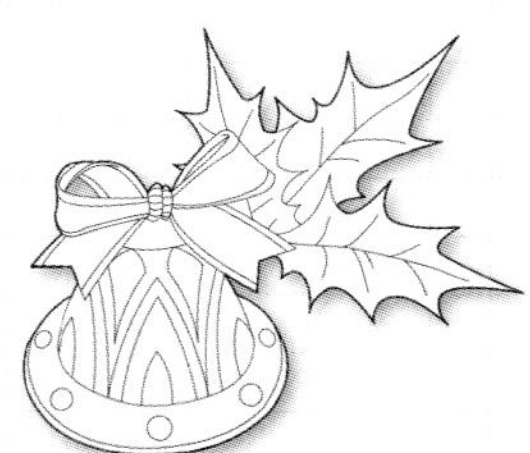

Bell

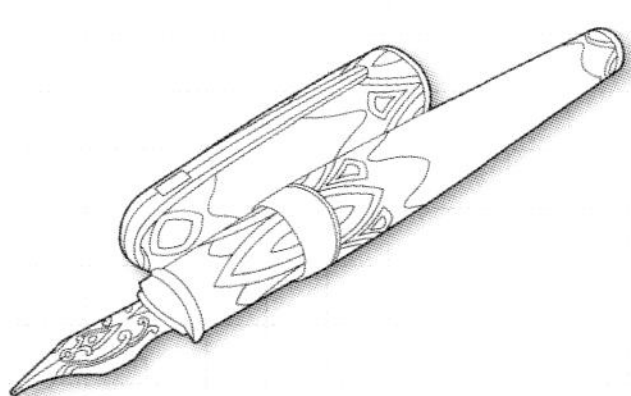

Fountain Pen

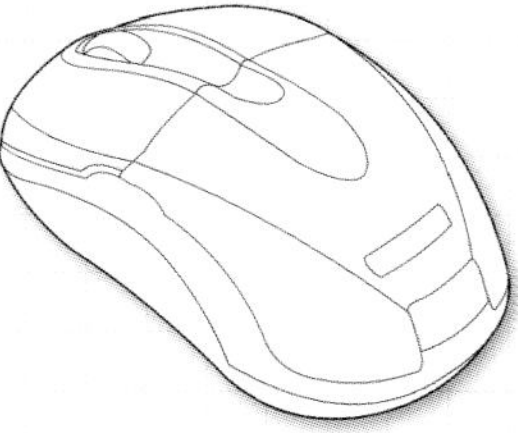

Mouse

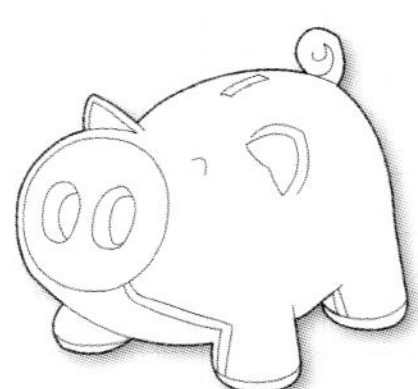

Piggy Bank

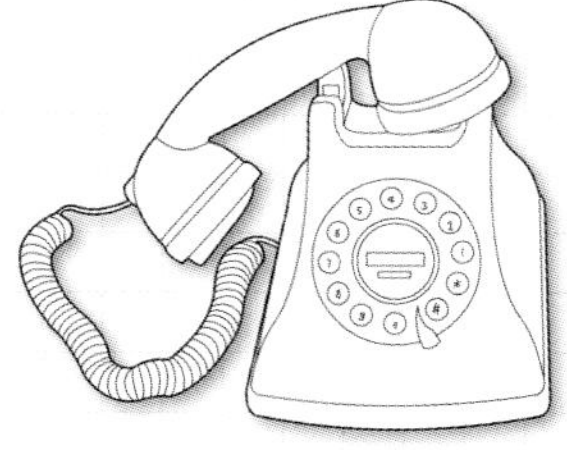

Retro Telephone

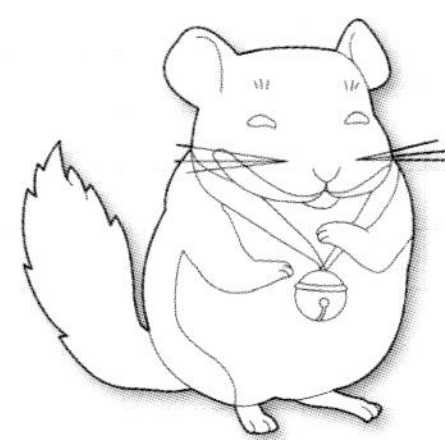

Squirrel

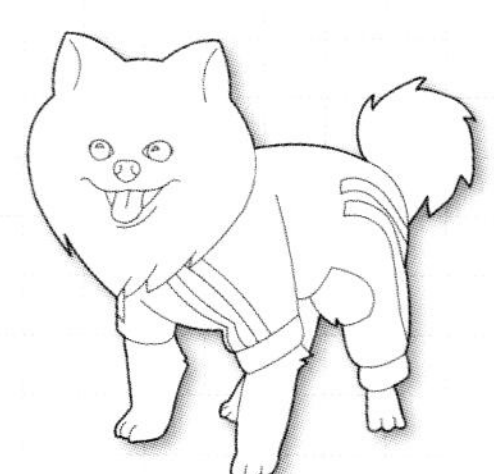

Pet Dog 2

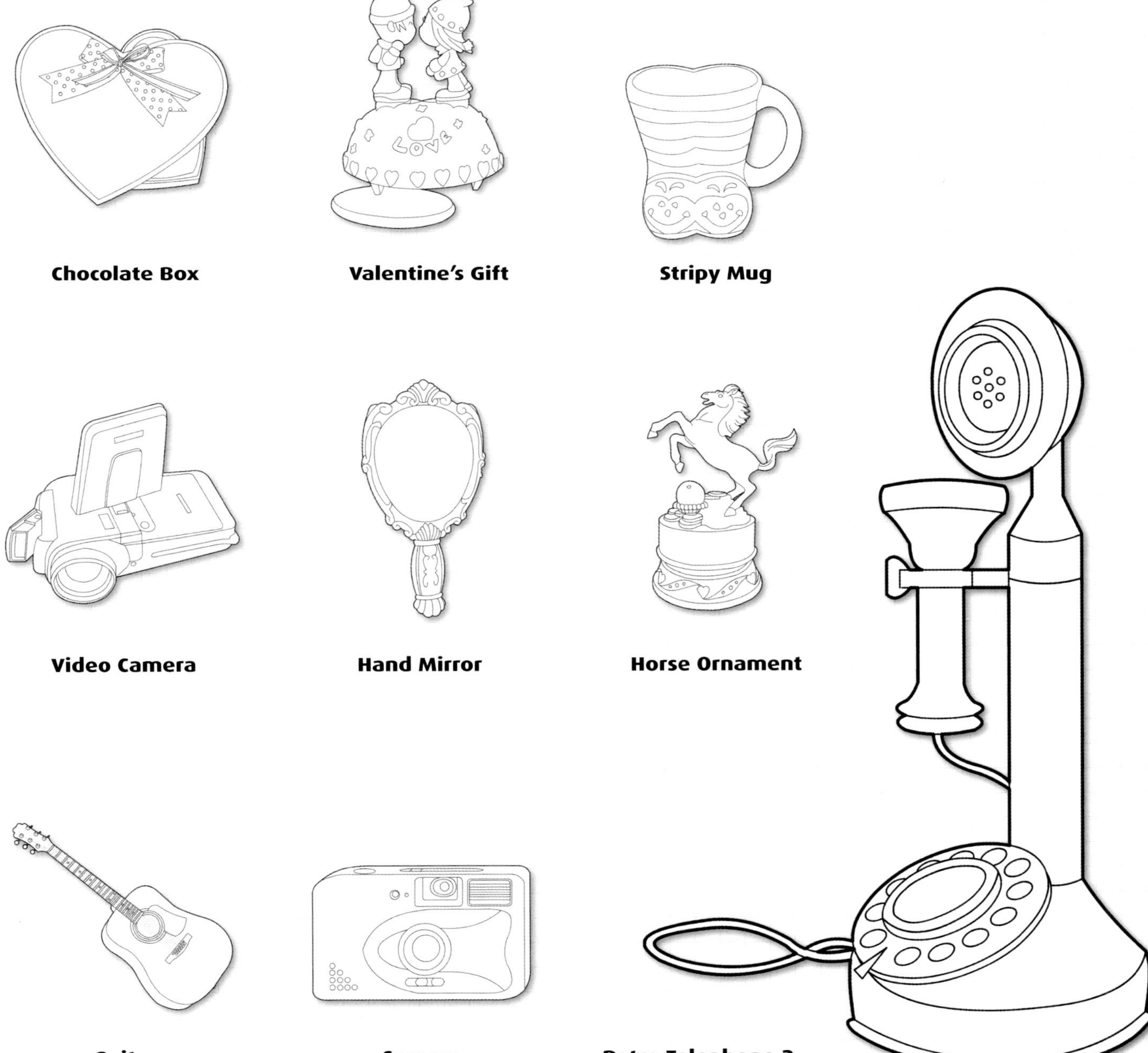

Chocolate Box

Valentine's Gift

Stripy Mug

Video Camera

Hand Mirror

Horse Ornament

Guitar

Camera

Retro Telephone 2

PUTTING IT ALL TOGETHER

As you begin to experiment with your characters, and build confidence in your skills as a budding mangaka, move on to putting it all together—mix costume sets, add accessories, and top it off with a background!

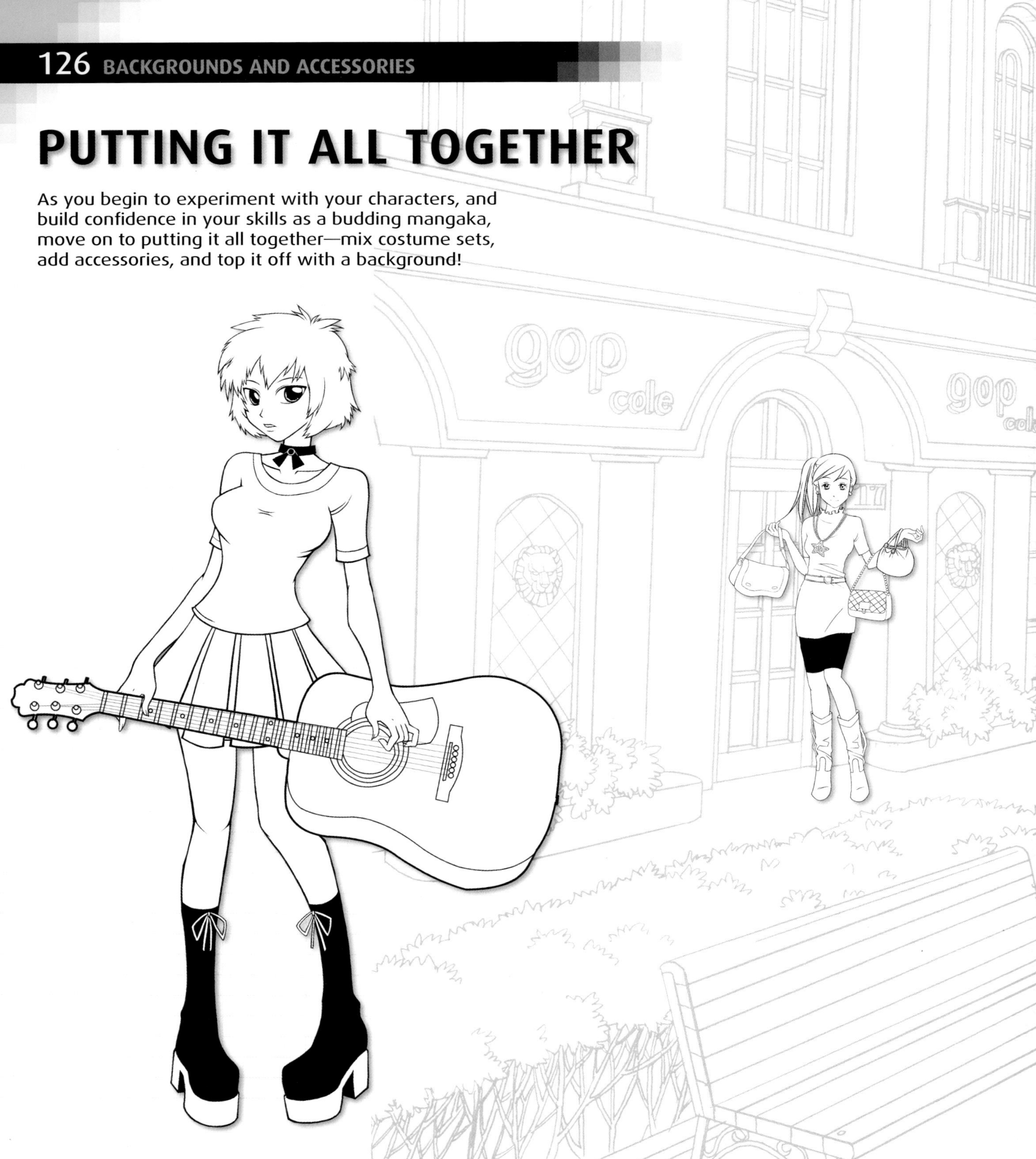

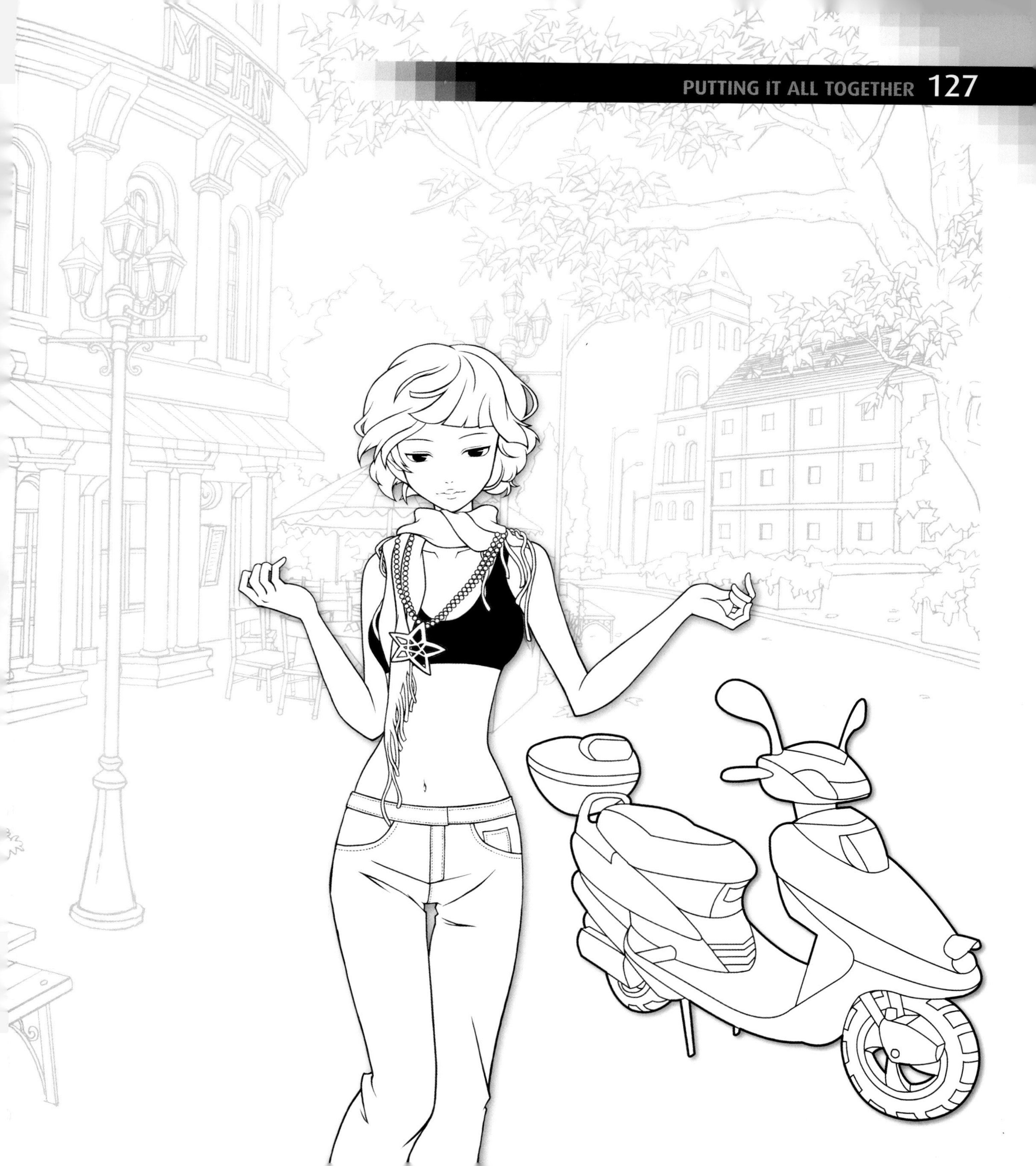
MEHN